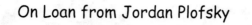

D0621950

The Driving FORCE

Extraordinary Results with Ordinary People

PETER W. SCHUTZ

Former CEO of Porsche AG

LEADERSHIP
PUBLISHING.com

A Division of Harris & Schutz, Inc.

Cover Design: Beth Hansen-Winter
Production and Composition: Rocks-DeHart Public Relations

LeadershipPublishing.com, a division of Harris & Schutz, Inc.
455 Palm Circle East
Naples, FL 34102
239-434-8186
www.LeadershipPublishing.com

ISBN-10: 0-9771289-0-3
ISBN-13: 978-0-9771289-0-7

Library of Congress Control Number: 2005931259

This publication is designed to provide accurate and authoritative information in regard to the subject matter covered. It is sold with the understanding that the publisher is not engaged in rendering legal, accounting or other
professional services. If legal advice or other expert assistance is required,
the services of a competent professional person should be sought.

Table of Contents

Alexander Hiam

AUTHOR AND BUSINESS CONSULTANT

Well, this is a lot stronger book than I expected, even after seeing much of the content earlier.

If I'd had the advantage of reading your book before writing mine, Making Horses Drink, *I could have simplified my advice in two words: "Ask Peter!"*

*I dedicate this book to my wife, Sheila,
who has made my life fun and
stands by me in my journey.*

Her wisdom, strength, and loyalty are still shaping my life today. Without her, there would be no book. At best, there would be an abbreviated story, a story hardly worth telling and inadequate energy and drive with which to tell it. Without Sheila, there would be no Peter W. Schutz to write this book.

Acknowledgments

A number of people deserve special mention:

My father, Dr. Leopold Schutz, has been my role model and inspiration. He was a central figure in my life until his passing in 1955, when I was just beginning to become a man. Even now, his commitment to family values and principles influence my thoughts and decisions.

My mother, Erna, without whose support our family might have disintegrated in the holocaust of World War II.

My first wife, Adrienne, who bore and raised our three wonderful children: Lori and twins Mitchel and Michael.

Adrienne's father, Sol Magram, one of the most truly caring people I have ever known; he was the first to teach me how much people matter. He did this by living the example. I did not fully understand his wisdom until years later.

My daughter Lori, who contributed to the clarity of this book.

My son Mitchel, who also helped to improve my efforts with his thoughtful editing and input.

My son Michael, whose management skill has confirmed much of what I have learned.

Richard E. O'Leary

CHAIRMAN, H. ENTERPRISES
INTERNATIONAL, INC.

*I*t has been my privilege to know Peter W. Schutz as a supplier, boss, client, friend, and neighbor for more than 20 years. During that period I have observed and shared Peter's transiting a full spectrum of commercial experience that ranged from excessive recognition of achievement to equally excessive criticism of results, largely imposed by generic economic cycles. Whatever the circumstances, Peter could call upon a leadership capability that was universally appreciated.

Peter has no peer in his ability to intellectualize the value-added potential of the most sophisticated electromechanical products in terms an engineer can understand and a customer can apply. Beyond that, he has few peers in assimilating a lifetime of experience-based lessons, rearticulating those lessons in the context of a current challenge, and enabling those challenged to constructively apply the lessons in formulating solutions for the problems at hand.

I might quibble with Peter's allusion that there is an element of excellence in business beyond making money, something that would hardly surprise him. Quibbles aside, The Driving Force should broaden the comprehension of business leaders who seek success while having fun doing business.

Introduction

I t was a Monday morning, always a good time to look ahead. I had just accepted the top executive job at Dr. Ing. h.c. F. Porsche AG and was contemplating what it would take to turn this company around and get it back on track. In the short time I'd been there, I had gotten the impression of a company that was idling in neutral, lacking the momentum needed to take advantage of its incredible potential and its loyal customer base.

There is a tradition at Porsche in which about 40 top managers have lunch together every Monday. Managers from all disciplines sit together. This particular Monday, I found myself seated at a table with a number of engineers and salespeople. The conversation ranged from the weather to the minutiae of the current work; it seemed, on the whole, to be fairly dull. There was not much excitement or animation in the dining room that day. During a break in the conversation, I found myself blurting out: "Tell me, what is happening at Porsche today that is so exciting that you can hardly wait to run and tell our customers and dealers about it?"

There was an uncomfortable silence.

Finally, several people began to stammer responses, but I had already learned what I needed to know. I decided to save them embarrassment. "Thank you," I replied, "I believe I understand."

I realized I had put my finger on a fundamental problem. Not a problem that would show up directly on a financial statement, but an opportunity that could hold the key to producing positive results in the future. Porsche needed an exciting challenge to power its turnaround. It lacked the driving force of motivated people working on something that truly energized them and had the power to excite customers as well. Without this driving force, a turnaround was not likely.

Subsequently, I had a conversation with Professor Porsche, the son of the founder and head of the family that owns Porsche, to formulate a revised strategy for the company. We spent a great deal of time discussing alternatives for products, tooling, and marketing. This became very complicated. At one point, as I was feeling overwhelmed with details, I remember asking: "Professor, say you were faced with the following two alternatives:

1. You could keep all of the products, facilities, and tooling in which Porsche has ever invested, but you had to replace all the Porsche people, or
2. You could keep all of the Porsche people, but had to replace all of the tooling, products, and facilities.

Which one would you choose?"

The professor's response was: "Of course, I would choose to keep the people. You see, Herr Schutz, that is exactly what happened here in Germany after World War II. All of the facilities, tooling, and products were destroyed in the war; only the people were left. We worked together to rebuild the company and that experience made the organization stronger."

"If that is true," I replied, "I plan to repeat the sequence of that process. I will first rebuild the company culture and its people by challenging them to re-energize and rebuild their company. After that, I will tackle the issues of product and facility strategies."

The Driving Force is my story. It is a story about a rather ordinary person who was able to accomplish some extraordinary things as a business manager. Looking back on my experiences, I have come to realize that business has its center of gravity in the management of people.

This book is also the story of people with whom I worked at Porsche and other companies during my career. I was dependent on the passionate efforts of hundreds and sometimes thousands of people. My management challenge was to get extraordinary results from a large number of people over long periods of time. It was *their* response to the challenges we faced together that made success possible.

"I love to manage, it's just people that I can't stand," is a frequent lament among some managers. I don't see it that way. I have learned that:

People Are *The Driving Force*

Yogi Berra, the hall of fame baseball catcher, once said: "Baseball is 50 percent hitting and fielding, the other 90 percent is pitching." I believe that 50 percent of management is products and selling, the other 90 percent is people. With energized, committed people, the driving force of that equation does add up to more than 100 percent and that makes extraordinary results possible.

I learned this firsthand when Porsche entered and won many of the top auto races by fielding racecars that were designed, built, and maintained to a high standard. These cars ran exceptionally well. A team of people implementing plans flawlessly was the key to winning consistently, even when we did not always have the fastest cars on the track.

I learned that people win the *real races* in the business world as well. The Porsche team made it possible for me to turn an ailing company around and return it to prosperity and success.

In my current work, I often see smaller or newer companies come from behind to grow faster than established competitors by virtue of their greater driving force.

As I look back on my varied management experiences, this has always been the formula for success: motivated, *passionately* motivated, people who know what to do and also what *not* to do in order to win.

The best team wins the most races consistently, even if at times they may not have the fastest car on the track. But how do they win these races? What happens to an apparently ordinary team of people that enables them to turn on that special something to produce extraordinary results?

There are many answers to this question. People need the right culture and values. They need something exciting to rally around. They need the right organization and sales strategy, they need an exciting focus for their work, etc. I'll share what I have learned about all of these issues with you later in the book. Most important is that they need a *leader* who makes it his or her job to nurture the driving force that separates ordinary, routine work from extraordinary effort and excellence.

When a Porsche racecar comes into a pit for service, the pit crew does whatever it takes to get it out on the road again, even if it means breaking all previous records for diagnosing a problem and making repairs. They pay little attention to rank or position—I sometimes found myself being ordered to go fetch a tool or spare tire if I happened to be on hand. They simply work together to get the job done as well as humanly possible, each person contributing to the best of his or her ability, or beyond. (Remember Yogi Berra's equation!) Imagine what might happen if a company could run that way.

I want to emphasize my belief that the principles of driving-force leadership and the experiences I share in this book are for managers of all companies. In my present capacity, I advise leaders from businesses of all sizes. I know managers of smaller businesses may not have the resources or culture to use many of the techniques and approaches suggested by management books which focus on larger companies. The concept of driving force is as applicable to a company with five or ten employees as it is to one with 500 or 50,000. It can even be applied by individuals who wish to energize their own work or career. Whatever your business, I hope you will find the approach I share here to be useful.

In this book, I want to share some insights that helped me strengthen the driving force at Porsche and can help other leaders take their businesses to the next level. The journey of a business is also the journey of its leader. The leader is in the driver's seat.

One of the important characteristics of many of the most popular Porsche models is that they are highly sensitive to the driver's touch. They perform like racecars, not typical street cars. Their high degree of maneuverability and sensitivity to any change combines with a lot of acceleration to make them exciting and *challenging* to drive.

I think many small businesses are more like a Porsche than an everyday car. The small business owner or entrepreneur has a small but potentially powerful vehicle to drive, one that is highly sensitive to the environment and the leader's touch. With skillful handling, these smaller businesses can give a more exciting and rewarding ride, but they lack the directional stability of the biggest companies and so require constant attention to the road.

Even though I have managed some rather large businesses, I am sensitive to the needs of my current clients. With their help, I have identified many experiences and techniques that apply especially well at *any* time in *any* business. I am not going to describe lengthy visioning exercises or strategic planning processes involving thousands of people, because such things are a luxury that can only be afforded by the managers of large, directionally-stable businesses.

Nashville *vs.* New York City

During my tenure as vice president of sales and service for Cummins Engine Company in the 1970s, we developed a country song entitled "Hummin' Cummins" as a way to promote an engine concept with truck drivers. We took our lyrics to a Nashville company called The Sound Shop to set them to music. The resulting song became very popular. It actually made it to the top ten country songs in 1976. Some people still remember it today.

In the process, I learned the difference between New York City music and Nashville music.

In New York City, a new song is created on paper. Notes and symbols are scripted. The song is played and revised, always recorded and upgraded on paper.

In Nashville, a group of talented musicians pick up their instruments and start playing. The song is developed in a series of "play-throughs" until it is just right. Any paper record of the song is created *after* the music has been created and polished. Often there is no paper record at all.

During my time at Porsche, many of the most effective innovations in our racing cars and our company as a whole, were created the Nashville way, not the New York City way. *In that context, this book is Nashville, not New York City.*

How This Book Came About

It has taken me a long time to get around to writing this book. The first thought of writing a book occurred to me shortly after I left the presidency of Porsche AG. The content was developed from my personal experiences which were sometimes bitter, but always interesting and educational. It was polished in over a thousand oral presentations to groups of managers and entrepreneurs, and then set into print.

My formal training is in engineering. This is therefore my bias. I take an engineering approach to solving problems and making the most of opportunities. For those readers who are not engineers, it may be important to point out that engineering is systematic and, unbeknownst to many, highly creative. Engineers must often *invent* solutions to their problems.

It has been my good fortune to manage several organizations, some of considerable size. These have included organizations engaged in engineering, sales, marketing, and corporate planning.

I realized many years ago that I am much more of a mechanic than a philosopher. I strive to avoid theorizing in this book. Instead, I have tried to restrict my comments to firsthand experiences.

I have had the good fortune to be associated with a number of people who contributed significantly to the science of management. At many stages of my management career, these people helped me extricate myself from difficult situations, most of my own making. If you think of these people as aircraft designers, then perhaps you can think of me as an airplane pilot who has tried to fly their aircraft, sometimes in very rough weather. I have had some wonderful flights and also crashed and burned a number of times.

The easiest way to share what I have learned from these experiences is a chronological history of a business career that moved through a number of stages. At each stage, I have tried to articulate lessons learned that made the succeeding stage possible. I have left out many details that might interest a historian but may not be relevant to help managers resolve management challenges they face today.

My purpose in writing this book is to help others achieve more than they consider possible and have fun doing it.

Shortly after I began the job of CEO at Porsche, a reporter came to interview me. Unlike most German CEOs, I ran a rather informal office. My desk was pushed up against a window. This put my side toward the door, which was virtually always open. If I was working at my desk, visitors knew that I was busy and would rather not be disturbed. Rather than communicating with visitors and co-workers across a large imposing desk, we would sit at a round table. It reduced barriers and facilitated communication. I frequently worked in shirtsleeves. It does get hot in Germany in the summer and back then, aircon-ditioning was not common in Central Europe.

This scene was not the norm in German industry in the 1980s; it was considered too informal by many. A visiting reporter wrote a story about "the new American Porsche CEO who came across more like an Idaho potato farmer than a business executive." It shocked some of our associates at the time and did not please the Porsche AG owners or the public relations department. I secretly suspect a potato farmer may be a better role model for a chief executive than a stereotypical corner-office control freak.

I have not invented anything new! I have benefited from the patient and wise efforts of a number of mentors who have been role models. I want to avoid giving the impression of taking credit for the genius of others. My poor memory for detail frequently results in my not remembering where, when, and from whom I learned something. What you will read here is the melding of the wisdom of others passed through my filters. I believe that learning from mentors is a key to success in any complex endeavor, especially business leadership.

If I was able to accomplish extraordinary deeds, <u>anybody</u> could, but not alone.

Here (in alphabetical order) is a list of some of the people who have been my mentors:

Ichak Adizes, a management consultant, whose genius provided true enlightenment.

Vaughn Beals, the man who turned Harley Davidson around and the most skillful manager I have known.

Franz Blank, chief union steward at Porsche AG. Franz taught me how to work with a labor union.

Jay W. Forrester, professor at M.I.T., taught me the power of thinking logically.

John Gilbert, vice president of Caterpillar Tractor Co., taught me about managing culture.

Jim Henderson, president of Cummins Engine Company, taught me to manage with heart.

Bert Jones, management consultant, made "people issues" come alive for me.

Dean Kamen, genius inventor. Dean exemplified the importance of having a clear focus on reality.

Don Krull, assistant chief engineer, Caterpillar Tractor Co., showed me how to stick with it until it is finished correctly.

Harvey McKay, CEO and author, shared his knowledge on *How to Swim with the Sharks* (bestselling book).

Dick O'Leary, attorney, taught me "just good business."

Professor Porsche, founder of Porsche AG. The professor urged me to "follow my dream."

Jack Rowan, sales executive, football coach, and soul mate. Jack shared his knowledge of how to inspire teamwork and true friendship.

Tony Sarandes, founder of Equiflor, an exemplary role model for a people manager.

Bob Snodgrass, automobile dealer and racecar driver. Bob taught me about friendship and loyalty in adversity.

John Weitz, bestselling author and clothing designer, showed me that it is important to have pride in heritage.

Larry Wilson, founder, Wilson Learning Corporation, taught me about selling and dealing with people.

Each of these people has shared their wisdom and insights with me, by both word and deed. Without such mentors, I would not have been a particularly apt pupil. Some of my readers may note that my mentors tend to be male. That is because, when I was coming up in management, women were not welcome in many of the key roles in business. This is happily no longer true today, and I encourage readers to seek a diversity of mentors. Often we can learn the most from those who are different from us and offer fresh viewpoints.

There's Nothing Like a Good Story

I use the technique of storytelling freely in this book to illustrate management principles. These are events as I remember them. They are presented in order to communicate principles rather than to record historical events. The objective in telling these stories is to help others benefit from my successes and failures as I recall them today.

I am convinced that one of the skills that characterizes successful leaders is that they are frequently good storytellers. A good story that illustrates a principle can be an effective, nonthreatening, nonjudgmental way to make a point. I will strive to live up to this ideal in the pages to come.

Lead-In Comments to the Book and Chapters

As I was writing this book, I contacted a number of people and asked them to write a few paragraphs about experiences we have shared. The group included people for whom I have worked, some who have worked for me, and others who were suppliers and customers. None of these people had read *The Driving Force*. My intent was to gather material that could be used as back-of-the-book-cover comments.

After completing the book it occurred to me that many of the comments I had received related to material covered in the 23 chapters I had written.

Consequently, a number of the comments appear as introductions to the book and most of the chapters in it.

Lester Bergsten

LT. COL. U.S. AIR FORCE. SR. STAFF ENGINEER CATERPILLAR TRACTOR CO. (RETIRED)

I have known Peter W. Schutz for over 30 years. My acquaintance has been both professional and social. As an engineer, he was very methodical and always challenged the envelope of technical limits. In addition to being a profound engineer, he developed as a very astute salesman on projects that became quite well accepted in the various professional avenues he undertook. He also exhibited outstanding leadership and executive qualities in his varied professional career.

He has always been a very gracious friend. No matter what level he attained in various professional fields, he always treated associates as equals. If a person needed a favor for a friend whom Peter had never met, he would step up and do that favor without question.

Of all my personal friends, I believe he is one of the most genuine and interesting persons I have had the pleasure of knowing.

1

Racing to Win at Porsche

New Year's Eve of 1980, was a turning point in my life. Not because I was going to start the chief executive officer of Porsche job the following week, but because on that New Year's Eve, Sheila and I got married in the Little Church of the West on the Las Vegas strip. We traveled to Germany together in January 1981, ready to tackle the Porsche challenge as a team.

The seven years that followed were like a fairy tale come true. There is simply no way that an engineer from the Midwestern United States could have written the script for the life Sheila and I led during those seven years. It turns out that Porsche is a cult, and if you are named the head of a cult, it makes you "king," and Sheila became "queen." Everywhere we traveled in the world, we were treated like royalty. (A good deal of acclaim came our way as a result of a philosophy Sheila practices: "If you treat ordinary people as though they were royalty, and royalty as though they were ordinary people, you can go a long way in this world!" Many people allow their egos to get in the way, abuse people they view as ordinary, and suck up to royalty, with the result being that they earn the contempt of all involved.)

When we arrived at Porsche in January 1981, I had never looked at the company balance sheet and profit and loss statement. It would have been a waste of time. Reading and interpreting a balance sheet or financial statement has never been my strong suit. I have always had people around me who knew how to do that well and could explain all I needed to know about financial matters. When I got to Porsche, I did not need any such help. I knew the meaning of those brackets around the numbers. Even I could interpret the meaning of those financial statements.

Porsche was in deep trouble. Morale was at a very low level. There was a lack of passion and excitement. There seemed to be no answer to my question, "What is new and exciting around here?" Instead of passion and excitement, a sense of malaise abounded. There was little or no fire.

Addressing this issue seemed to be the first order of business. I was searching for the key to getting the situation turned around when, during the second week of March, I attended my first sportscar race at Professor Porsche's suggestion. This was a 12-hour race in Sebring, Florida. For the first time, I saw a vehicle called a Porsche 935. I had never seen anything quite like it. The rear tires were about 20 inches wide and two big turbochargers hung on the back of the rear-mounted air-cooled engine. When that car was out on the track at full song and the driver shifted gears, flames would shoot two or three feet out of each exhaust pipe.

At 750 horsepower and 820 kilos, this was a rocket of an automobile! There were several 935s entered in that race; nothing else was really competitive. One of them ended up winning the race, and I returned to Germany higher than a kite. No one had told me about this part of the business!

Getting Started

I believe every business has a number of activities or issues that have the potential to be truly exciting. This is usually rather evident in a new venture, but if activities are allowed to become stale, life can drain out of any organization. A leader must identify exciting activities and become enthusiastic and passionate about them. I became excited about racing and decided to use racing to restore excitement and passion at Porsche to rebuild sagging morale.

Upon my return to Stuttgart, I could not think of anything better to do than go out to Weissach, the Porsche development facility, and convene a meeting. I announced, "Anyone who has anything to do with racing, in the cafeteria at ten o'clock!" A rather large group gathered. Some of them did not even work for Porsche; they were members of our supplier companies: Bosch, Bielstein, Siemens, and so forth. Many in that group had understandable misgivings about meeting me. Who was this American diesel engineer?

When they heard my version of what I had witnessed in Florida, it erased their uncertainty. They *knew* they had a problem.

I was excited and asked, "What is the most important race of the year?" They answered, "That is the 24-hour race in Le Mans, France. It will take place 62 days from today."

"Great," I responded. "What are we doing to get ready for that race?"

"We are preparing two cars," was the response. "They are called 924-turbos."

"What are our chances of winning this race?" I asked.

"Well, Herr Schutz, you really don't understand anything, do you? The cars we are preparing are production cars that we are modifying so they can run a 24-hour race. They will give a good account of themselves, perhaps even win in their class, but there is *no* chance of these cars winning the overall race when full-blown racing cars will confront us."

I thought about their response for about ten seconds and heard myself reply:

"Let me explain something. As long as I am in charge of this company, we will never go to any race without the objective of winning!"

If I had never realized it before, at that moment it suddenly became clear. If you are going to be an effective leader of any organization, one of the things you must learn to do is to articulate in the most concise and clear terms possible: **Why are we here?** What are we trying to be? What are we trying to do?

As a leader, I had faced the need to articulate such a vision a number of times before. This time I managed to get it right. From that moment on, there was a revived spirit of enthusiasm and determination for success in everything that we undertook at Porsche.

What made my statement so effective? What, in fact, had I told these people? Did I tell them to win every race, to be perfect?

As I thought about it later, I did not tell them *what* to do at all. I only told them what *not* to do. That is contrary to what we often think our job is as a leader. It turned out to be surprisingly effective.

Positive commandments can limit the organization's activity. Value statements, mostly in the form of prohibitions, can better define a culture within which members of the organization can be creative and take initiative.

I have learned that if you tell people what to do, you limit activity. I have come to know a number of successful people who have raised what I would call "boomerang kids." They throw them out and the kids keep coming back and some are 40 years old! Some parents complain: "These kids can't think for themselves. They do not accept responsibility. They don't know how to make a living!" Well, how could they? All of their lives you have told them what to do. You have made their decisions for them and given them more money than they could reasonably earn at their stage of life. Now, you are upset because they have never learned how to do these things on their own.

As a manager *or* a parent, it is advantageous to avoid making too many decisions for the organization or the family. Managers must define the culture; they must articulate values, and then *allow the organization to make as many decisions as possible*. That is the best way I have found to teach members of an organization to make decisions and take the initiative essential to achieving extraordinary results.

It is interesting how negative statements best define a culture. The Ten Commandments in the Bible, a foundation of our western culture, are not commandments for the most part. They also are not suggestions. (As a leader, you need to be firm about such things.) Only two of the ten Commandments are truly commandments: *Honor thy father and mother* and *Keep the Sabbath holy*. The other eight are *thou shalt nots*. They are *prohibitions*, not commandments.

Commandments can limit the organization's activity. Value statements, mostly negative, can define a culture within which members of the organization can be creative and take initiative.

The value statement I articulated at the Porsche racing meeting, "We will never go to any race without the objective of winning," has a commercial counterpart. After you have determined the company's objective, it might be, "We will not engage in any activity that is not focused on our commercial objective. Our resources are too limited. We cannot afford to squander them."

After that value statement, I went on to say something that turned out to be so brilliant that I could not believe I had said it. I was learning. I might have rolled up my sleeves and started trying to hammer out a plan for winning that race, but fortunately, I resisted this temptation. Instead, I went on to tell people in that meeting:

"Since I do not know how to do that, this meeting is now adjourned, and you will return at ten o'clock tomorrow morning and explain your intentions."

There was a deafening silence in the room.

It might appear that I had engaged in a few theatrics. Assembling *all* the people involved in racing instead of discussing the subject quietly with a few experts, then dismissing them precipitously, could leave the impression that I was trying to send an important message. Was I setting up a shared experience? Was I trying to introduce a new empowering management style? Was I trying to make the point that we were going to act instead of forming a committee? Was I trying to show I was serious about having them involved in making decisions instead of micromanaging the racing effort?

It was none of the above. I had no grand plan at this point. I was responding from my intuition and I was truly learning.

As it turned out, it had been a long time since this very competent group of people had been challenged in such a manner. They had been accustomed to hearing from their management, "Here is *what* you will do, here is *how* you will do it, this is *when* you will do it, here is your *budget*, here is your *schedule*, and if you fail, I will find some new people who are good enough to succeed." In contrast, I had just challenged them to solve their own problem(s), within the limitations of a value set by a leader.

The poor morale at Porsche was beginning to turn around by the time the racing group reconvened the following morning. In its place was some real electricity, not just in the racing department. The word had spread throughout the company like wildfire!

When I met with the racing group at ten the next morning, a spokesperson stepped up and said, "Herr Schutz, we have two cars in the museum, they are called 936s. They won this race a few years ago, but they are now obsolete. We have also built a racing engine with which we hoped to go racing at Indianapolis in the United States. Our management canceled that program. They said that we could not afford it, but we saved all the pieces! We propose to take those engines and change them over from alcohol to gasoline. No problem, Herr Schutz, we know how to do that. We can then pirate some old transmissions out of 917 racecars, put all of that together and we might just have something."

I had no clue about the soundness of that proposal, but was confident they had understood me clearly when I said that we would not go racing without the objective of winning. If they understood that, and this was their idea of how to achieve that objective, I knew I had to be as good as my word and not try to meddle with their solution. I decided to accept their proposal on the spot. I responded, "We have 61 days left; let's get to work and go racing."

A few days later, I got my next lesson in management. The telephone rang in my office in Stuttgart, and a man's voice said, in the most delightful Belgian French accent I had ever heard, "Mr. Schutz, you don't know me, my name is Jacky Ickx." He went on to say, "I am a retired racecar driver." (Yeah, right. Jacky was probably the most successful long distance sportscar driver of his entire era.) "If the rumors that I am hearing are true, I would like to once again drive a Porsche at Le Mans." Shortly thereafter, we received similar calls from Derek Bell, Jochen Mass, Al Holbert, Hurley Haywood, and Vern Schuppan. All the best drivers were calling and asking to drive a car that they had never even seen. Our newfound excitement at Porsche was already spreading!

Another point this story reminded me of is that if you want to attract the best people in a given profession, you do not usually accomplish that by offering the most money. Money is important and has to be adequate, but the real attraction for such people is to be part of a winner. They want to be a part of an organization that is striving for excellence and has a culture that makes it possible. *The best people tend to go to the company with the strongest driving force.*

Turning the Corner

Le Mans is a small town about 150 miles southwest of Paris. The 24-hour race had been held at that location annually for 48 years preceding the 1981 race. The location is a beautiful part of France, particularly in the late spring when it seems everything is blooming. Sheila and I found the drive from Stuttgart to Le Mans via Paris in the newest prototype Porsches to be a true delight every year.

Le Mans became a different race after 1981. Big changes came in the years that followed. In 1981, the various racing teams prepared the competition cars in a number of small villages near the track. From 1982 onward, the cars were assembled alongside the racetrack in tents erected for that purpose.

For a number of years prior to 1982, Porsche rented a small garage in the village of Teloché. This was a two-story barn-like structure that became a beehive of activity in the weeks preceding the big race. After the cars were assembled, they were driven about ten miles to the racetrack over public roads.

Sheila and I stayed in a wonderful old converted farmhouse bed-and-breakfast located in the idyllic little French village of La Fleche, about 15 miles from the racetrack. This location had served to house members of the Porsche family at race time for a number of years. Staying there contributed to a wonderful experience every year.

Le Mans is an eight-and a-half-mile track. The racecourse consists, in part, of county roads closed to the public during practice, qualifying, and the race. Special steel guard-rails are erected to offer some degree of safety for racecars, drivers, and spectators. The portion of the track that borders the racing pits and most of the grandstand area is dedicated exclusively to the race.

A major portion of the racecourse itself consisted of a three-and-a-half-mile stretch of track that ran west to the village of Mulsanne. This part of the track was virtually straight, a screaming high-speed stretch of racetrack called the Mulsanne-straight. At the west end of this straight stretch of racetrack was a right angle corner. It was the intersection of two county roads.

Because speeds on the Mulsanne-straight became dangerously fast and gave rise to a number of fatal and near fatal tire failures, two chicanes (the racing version of speed bumps) were inserted in 1988 to hold car speeds within manageable levels. A few years before that, the right-angle corner at the end of the Mulsanne-straight was changed to a gradual transition from the Mulsanne-straight to the intersecting road.

On the southern edge of the public road that made up the Mulsanne-straight is a romantic little French café. During the race, a steel guard-rail is erected to protect the café and its occupants from speeding racecars. From 1981, and through the years before the insertion of those speed limiting chicanes, Sheila and I would sit in this café in the middle of the night and drink hot chocolate with an elbow resting on the guardrail that was the only separation from the speeding cars. It was incredible to hear the roar of an approaching racecar at full throttle. The roar would rise to a crescendo as the car raced into view and literally flew past at over 220 miles per hour. The Doppler effect gradually dropping the engine sound frequency during this high-speed drive-by was sensational.

After collecting our fill of this excitement, it was customary to go to the corner at the western end of the Mulsanne-straight. It was possible to stand right at the corner, watching the cars as they came straight at you at full speed. After the corner was modified, spectators were no longer permitted to get that close to the track.

In the middle of the night, the first evidence of an approaching racecar would be the bouncing reflection of headlight beams against the higher treetops. Next came the distant sound of the straining engine, subdued to a murmur by the intervening distance. The car would appear over a small rise in the road as the engine sound rose to a throaty roar. About 150 meters (492 feet) before the corner, the engine would shut down and the brakes would begin the task of slowing the car from over 220 miles per hour to about 30 miles per hour to negotiate the right-angle corner. All four brakes would become fiery disks, glowing yellow-hot as they absorbed the immense energy of the speeding racecar. After negotiating the right-angle corner, the engine would once leap into action, emitting its captivating roar again in second gear. As the car pulled away at full throttle, the turbochargers on the rear-mounted Porsche engines would light up, glowing from a deep red to a brilliant yellow as the power built up. The naturally aspirated six-cylinder BMWs and 12-cylinder Ferraris emitted a roar that was truly music to the ear of any racing enthusiast.

This activity continued for what seemed like an endless 24-hour period. Nobody slept; we ran on pure adrenaline.

After the end of the race, furious activity was needed to pack up and prepare for the trip back to Stuttgart. The race ended at 4 P.M. Everything was packed and ready for the return trip by about seven. At eight o'clock, the entire racing contingent except the drivers, would convene in a little tavern-restaurant in Teloché around the corner from the team garage. A riotous victory celebration followed. Lots of good country food, lots of local beer and wine, and above all, good fellowship.

By the time the drivers made an appearance, usually about ten o'clock, the celebration would be at a fever pitch. Frequently, Sheila would be the only woman present on these occasions; she was 'one of the boys.' The glow of those victory celebrations will be with us forever.

Compared to those unforgettable experiences, racing is a great deal more sophisticated and orderly today. The cars are much more complicated, more expensive, and much faster. Yet, somehow, the memory of proximity, sound, and smell of those days remains an unrivaled joy. I also know that the basic elements of success are still the same. There has to be a commitment to winning. People need to be excited to be there and eager to make great things happen. The excitement of those races helped energize our company throughout the years as we worked to turn an economic corner that was perhaps as treacherous as the turn at the end of the Mulsanne-straight.

We went to that Le Mans race in June of 1981 and, of course, we won. If we had not won that race, it is unlikely that

I would be writing this book today! We played the race up as big as we could and I believe that it signaled a turnaround for Porsche in 1981. It signaled a return to being a winner.

Not only did we win that race, but I also believe Porsche redefined 24-hour racing. The winning car ran the entire 24 hours and *nobody laid a wrench on it*. All we did was add fuel and oil, and changed the tires and brake linings.

Standing on the winner's podium with Professor Porsche, Jacky Ickx, and Derek Bell, my spirits were soaring. With 450,000 people cheering, I knew we were on our way. We had made a start on the road back to the top.

After Porsche won Le Mans in 1981, the racing governing board initiated major changes in the racing rules for 1982. The Porsche 936 would never race again. Gone were welded steel tube frames with cosmetic fiberglass bodies and open cockpits. Instead, the new rules required an aluminum monocoque structure much like an airplane, with an enclosed cockpit for the driver. This was a new challenge for our team.

In the winter of 1981-82, Porsche developed a new racecar, the Porsche 956. The development schedule was so tight that Porsche went racing at Le Mans in 1982 with three new untried racecars. They were numbered 1, 2, and 3, and that is how they finished at Le Mans in 1982, one, two, three. They were so far ahead in the closing laps of that race that they drove the last few laps in an echelon formation to signal their total dominance.

After that race, some of the European press people cornered me and asked, "How do you explain this? Three brand new, untried cars, and such total dominance?"

I responded: "You are seeing this wrong. It is true that the cars are new, but the people are not. *Cars don't win races, people do!* This is the same team of people that won last year." Although I did not tell the press, it was the same team of people I was counting on to take the company to the next level and make it a winner again.

Porsche won Le Mans every year for seven years; each year, the winning car ran through clean. I will never know if we had the fastest cars or the best technology. I do know we had the best performing people. Anyone who stepped up against Porsche in a long race in that era knew that if they stumbled, they could not win. A new standard had been set. It was the flawless execution of the fundamentals by a totally committed team that won those races.

Much remained to be done before Porsche would once again become a profitable world leader in high performance sports cars, but the 1981 Le Mans victory was the event that signaled the beginning of the Porsche turnaround.

Shelly Williamson

STAFF ENGINEER, CATERPILLAR TRACTOR CO.
(RETIRED)

I first met Peter in the early 1950s when we started our careers in the Cat training program as mechanical engineers in the research department of Caterpillar Tractor Co. Peter was assigned to engine research, and I to applied mechanics. Peter was a quick study and made significant contributions to his projects. He was impressive in meetings reporting on his findings. He had an exceptional ability to see the big picture.

I followed Peter's career after he left Caterpillar with much interest. I was delighted to watch him become vice president of sales at Cummins and CEO of Porsche.

After Peter retired from Porsche I occasionally heard about him from mutual friends, people who had shared the training year in the 1950s. I was reunited with Peter at his friend Donald Krull's retirement party. I took him to see John Gilbert, one of his mentors, and was invited to visit him at his home in Naples, Florida.

Peter's leadership knowledge and insights are astounding. The friendship formed in our early days at Caterpillar is valued highly.

2

Hiring into the Tribe at Caterpillar

I graduated from the Illinois Institute of Technology in Chicago with a B.S. in mechanical engineering in June 1952. The next 16 years (except for two years in the U.S. Army) were spent working for Caterpillar Tractor Co. in Peoria, Illinois, designing and developing diesel engines and gas turbines. I was occupied with engineering duties that were very challenging and opportunities to operate as a manager were rather limited. *My years at Caterpillar were spent observing management from the vantage point of one being managed.*

In the 1950s, Caterpillar impressed me with the manner in which people were chosen and infused with the company's culture. It was called *Yellow Blood*. (The company's products were painted yellow.)

Yellow Blood, The Caterpillar Culture

Before college graduates went to work on the job for which they were hired, Caterpillar put them through a one-year orientation program. In the course of this year, they had the opportunity to work in most parts of the company and get to know the organization from the inside.

Every Friday, the entire group of about 85 new people would gather. On these occasions company executives would explain activities in the part of the company for which they were responsible.

This served the following purposes:

- It built a close camaraderie among the new hires. To this day, 50 years later, I still have contact with some of the people who shared that orientation experience with me.
- It purposefully created some hurdles to clear, so that only the truly committed ended up working at the company. About three quarters of those who started this year of orientation were still around to finish it. If you were not committed enough to tough this year out, you were not committed enough to be a *member of the tribe*.
- It familiarized new hires with important contacts in all parts of the company. This greatly facilitated the opportunity to explore innovative solutions to business challenges that involved disciplines other than those in a person's assigned area of work.
- It promoted loyalty in those who made it through. After leaving Caterpillar later in a career, many of these people remained loyal as customers or suppliers.
- It infused new hires with *Yellow Blood*. It instilled a *company culture*.

As a part of the program, trainees worked on numerous Caterpillar assembly lines. A trainee spent a half-shift at every position of such a line. The time I spent sharing the workday with hardworking union people never left me and it proved valuable time and again when I needed the support and enthusiasm of people later in my career.

I would like to share some events I experienced during the orientation program that were typical of the friendly human bond I discovered. They helped me understand the factors needed to elevate performance and create a driving force to bridge a gap that can exist between management and labor.

The Driving Force in Daily Work

I particularly recall working with one man on the D-8 tractor assembly line who told me he was "building cap screws" (cap screw assemblies). At that time, the Caterpillar D-8 was the largest and most powerful track-type tractor in the industry, a potentially exciting thing to build. But cap screws were not exciting.

How does one build cap screws? You take a cap screw out of one container, a lock washer out of another, slip the lock washer onto the cap screw, and place the assembly on a rail. Voila! Another cap screw has been built.

Building a cap screw constitutes a seemingly demeaning and senseless task. Nobody building them is going to energize a business or help it produce exceptional results.

I recall walking this man to the end of the D-8 tractor assembly line to show him how the cap screws he was building served to hold the final drive case onto the D–8 tractor transmission. I wanted to change his perception of the job.

He was not building cap screws; he was helping to build the biggest and most powerful track-type tractor in the industry.

At one point in my orientation, I was assigned to travel with an experienced Caterpillar service engineer to a construction site in Iowa, where Caterpillar equipment was being used. In the early 1950s, Caterpillar was experiencing a number of rather serious product problems.

A customer complained bitterly about such a problem and the associated out-of-service-time for some major pieces of equipment.

The service engineer announced, "The Caterpillar dealer organization is so strong and competent that we could build junk for ten years and still be in business."

The customer replied: "Well, buster, you have five years to go."

Such arrogance can do major damage to any business. I learned that the *tribe* has to take good care of its culture in order to stay healthy.

These experiences, both good and not so good, were the beginning of my education in managing people. The newly hired engineers, lawyers, accountants, and MBAs who shared such experiences enriched human relations at all levels of Caterpillar Tractor Co. in those years.

Preserving the Culture

I learned that it is not enough to have a culture and explicit values. Management must be ever vigilant to assure that the culture is not violated. The salesperson who boasted about the company's strength to an unhappy customer violated the culture and put the business at risk.

A willful violation of the culture must be dealt with promptly and firmly. Failure to do this will dilute and ultimately destroy the culture.

A personal experience during my time at Caterpillar drove this home to me.

I was a brilliant (I believed) young engineer. I thought I was much smarter than I actually turned out to be, but did manage to do some notable things. This served to confirm my high opinion of myself. My conduct relating to others in the organization was often rough and insensitive.

One day, I was summoned to the office of John Gilbert, a vice president and one of the top engineering managers at Caterpillar. I was certain I had been summoned to receive compliments about some recent engineering accomplishment. Instead Gilbert, a large and powerful presence, shouted at me, "Schutz, just exactly who the f___ do you think you are? You may think you are hot stuff; I don't care how smart you are. Let me spell it out for you: If you do not change the way you conduct yourself and the manner in which you relate to others in this organization, Caterpillar will have no further use for you!"

Man, oh, man, did I ever get the message! That incident changed my life forever. I will be eternally grateful that Gilbert cared enough to help me.

What he did was preserve the Caterpillar culture. He taught me that one cannot behave the way I had and still be a member of the Caterpillar family. He spelled out the clear consequence of violating the company's values and principles.

Committed people like Gilbert, people who will do what is necessary to preserve the culture, are indispensable to any outstanding company. Without such champions, even an outstanding culture will not survive.

With what I have learned in subsequent years, I believe the wonderful camaraderie that prevailed in the early 1950s between all operating elements at Caterpillar might have been more enduring if elements of company values and culture had been documented explicitly at that time. The perpetuation of values and principles by future generations of management is greatly facilitated by documentation.

Documentation is a responsibility of the leader. Failing to do it can result in the loss of important things that make an organization strong. This is particularly true with the short tenure all too common in today's management ranks.

Before and After

I returned to Caterpillar after two years of military service in June of 1956 and found the company changed in a number of significant ways. Trainees in the orientation program no longer worked on the assembly and machining lines in close contact with union people. The entire program had been scaled back in both time and content.

It is likely that the somewhat adversarial climate that has characterized union relations with management at Caterpillar in the past few decades had its roots in changes that occurred during the mid-1950s. Something may have been lost in an effort to save time and money in the orientation program for new hires.

Could the traditional *tribal* approach to establishing a corporate culture be viable in today's highly competitive and exacting business climate?

In all likelihood, the answer would be no—but we need to achieve the same ends to produce exceptional results. By the time I was in a position to establish such a program as CEO of Porsche in the 1980s, the world had changed, so my efforts to strengthen Porsche's culture had to be different.

The world has changed in a number of ways:

People have become more impatient. *I want it all, I want it now, and I am not prepared to invest the time and effort to do things in the old ways.* This is an increasingly common attitude today, especially among young gifted people.

The increasingly competitive operating climate could make such a one-year program much too expensive. This is particularly true for publicly held companies that need this sort of operating culture the most.

(It is interesting to note that the military services continue to train officer candidates in this manner).

The need for bringing new people into the tribe is greater than ever, but tried and proven programs to fill this need are frequently no longer viable. As in many other aspects of management, updated activities are in order.

In subsequent years, at both Cummins Engine Company and Porsche AG, I was able to get satisfactory results with the following:

- Significantly shorter and more finely tuned orientation programs that lasted weeks or months instead of a year.
- Apprentice programs. At Porsche, we benefited from a very effective apprentice program funded jointly by schools, the government, and industry. Each class consisted of about 125 apprentices. Approximately half of

these apprentices ended up as Porsche employees at the end of the three-year program.

- The most important task is hiring people compatible with the organization's culture. Hire people for *who they are, not just for what they know and the skills they have mastered.*

Hire character, teach skills. Never the reverse.

Choosing People

Culture is a critical component in business. Culture must be accepted and practiced by all members of the business family. A respected colleague, Ed Ryan, articulated the following observation:

> *People are often hired for what they know, and let go (fired) for who they are.*

In the 1950s, Caterpillar Tractor Co. avoided hiring people who grew up more than a few hundred miles from Peoria, Illinois. History indicated that people drawn from areas outside this perimeter did not stay with the company long enough. (I recall hearing that the company name was not Cat, but Kat: Kentucky, Alabama, and Tennessee, the home states for many Caterpillar people.)

If there is something a person does not know or a skill is lacking, training or practice can overcome the difficulty. If someone is not prepared to accept and share the values and principles that define the culture of an organization, it is not likely it can be corrected by remedial training.

Ed Ryan goes on to teach: *Hire slow and fire fast.*

Many organizations and managers get that backwards. They hire fast and then drag the sometimes inevitable separation out to the detriment of all involved. (Some people deal with marriage in the same flawed manner.)

Managers can be well-served by implementing a structured, slower hiring practice. This is easy to say, but it takes discipline to put into practice.

*It is important to hire the **right** people.*

The question is, How do we recognize the *right* people? What is it that makes someone *right* for the business?

I submit that *right* most often means an individual who is prepared to share the values and principles that comprise the culture of the organization. They must be prepared to become members of the tribe.

If those values and principles are not explicit (documented in writing), how will we recognize the right person when we encounter him? In order to hire the right people, the organization is well-advised to have a documented set of values and principles. (This was mentioned previously as an important factor in preserving the company culture.)

Here is one way to use that documentation effectively:

In hiring, priority might be placed on the compatibility of the organization's culture and values with those of the candidate rather than the knowledge and skills that are documented in a typical resumé.

Let me track through a typical hiring interview and recommend an alternate approach:

- The candidate submits a resumé of education, skills, and experience.
- The candidate meets with a company representative.
- The interviewer proceeds to ask a number of questions.
- A hiring decision might then be made based on the information gathered and the impression the applicant makes.

Hiring is based primarily upon knowledge, experience, skill, and a general impression.

An alternate approach that puts emphasis on culture rather than just knowledge, skill, experience, and general impressions might be structured as follows:

Instead of reviewing an applicant's resumé, the hiring party presents a documentation of values and principles to which the hiring organization and its people have made a commitment. The applicant is asked to review and study these values and principles. "Take all the time necessary, study them overnight if that is desired. Ask any and all questions that arise and we will strive to answer them." The objective is to test the applicant's understanding and willingness to commit to the company culture.

If the applicant is not prepared to become a member of this business family, it does not matter how knowledgeable and skilled he is, he will not help the business advance. He will not fit. If a commitment to the organization's culture on the part of the applicant is not forthcoming, the hiring process can stop right there. Unless the cultural elements are shared, it is not likely a fit can be achieved that will endure and flourish in the daily pressures of business.

If the applicant is prepared to become a member of the organization and commit to share its culture, the hiring process can proceed. Now it is time to study the resumé of skill, knowledge, and experience, and a hiring decision can be made.

Questioning Questions

My brother, Rudy, who is also a manager, once shared the following observation with me: "Stop asking so many questions. People are very good at answering questions. Beyond that, a question can be perceived as threatening; a question can intimidate. Instead, use statements to elicit information. For example, 'I can imagine there are a number of things you are wondering about as you apply for this position.' "

Notice a statement, not a question, opens the door to the candidate's reply. A statement does not *require* a reply, whereas a question does. You now have an opportunity to see what a candidate chooses to do in this situation.

The reply, if offered, can be enlightening. If a reply is not forthcoming, it also tells the interviewer something about the applicant.

25

Or, have the applicant ask the questions. A great deal more can be learned from questions asked than from practiced answers to standard questions put to a candidate.

I have found this technique to be equally effective when I do "managing by walking around." Instead of challenging employees with questions that might be perceived as threatening, make statements that elicit a voluntary reply.

When People Behave in an Unacceptable Manner

On occasion, I am asked by clients, "How do I deal with someone who is dishonest, cheats, mistreats others, or is guilty of other activity that does not fit into our organization's culture?"

My answer is, "In business, we, as managers, do not have time or skill to deal with changing a person's character. The best way to deal with such problems is to avoid them. Do not hire such people, and if they are already working for the organization, let them go!"

> *Avoid hiring people who are not prepared to commit to the established culture of the business.*

If you already have some mismatched people, don't feel bad about easing them out through standard procedures. They probably are not enjoying their work any more than you are if they do not fit the organization's culture.

Dealing with Poor Performers

Every organization will have a number of poor performing people who do not respond to efforts to train them or are simply contrary. I believe it is a mistake to spend an inordinate amount of time with such people. In most cases, they comprise a small percentage of the total workforce. Some managers spend valuable time with this 10 percent or so and ignore people who are doing their best.

Giving attention to poor performers can perpetuate dysfunctional activity. Try to ignore poor performers and give management attention to the good performers instead. This can serve to motivate poor performers and sometimes the good performers will weed the poor ones out without overt action by managers.

Seeking a Work Ethic

I do not recall ever having been disappointed by hiring someone who grew up on a farm. Most people who grow up on a farm learn a work ethic I value. They become accountable for a number of chores as young children, some rather unpleasant. They are trained to do what is necessary.

When I worked in Germany, I learned the following German saying: "The apple never falls very far from the tree."

My views on company culture and hiring are to this day strongly influenced by those early experiences at Caterpillar Tractor Co. The time that is invested in finding and hiring the right people, people who are prepared to become members of the tribe, will pay significant dividends.

Discovering the Customer

After some 13 years in a number of diverse engineering tasks, I was privileged to participate in a project that was new for Caterpillar. Ford Motor Company needed a diesel engine for their line of medium-duty trucks to compete with General Motors and International Harvester Corporation. Both competitors had converted gasoline engines to operate as diesels.

Ford inquired if Caterpillar could convert Ford's Super Duty gasoline engine to diesel operation. An analysis disclosed that this was not practical. Cylinder pressures for diesel engine operation exceeded the capability of available gasoline engines.

Subsequently, Ford hired Caterpillar to design, develop, and build a suitable diesel engine for Ford medium-duty trucks. The resulting engine was very successful; it stayed in production for 31 years as the Cat 3208 diesel engine.

A major challenge as we designed this engine was to determine just how tough it had to be. Weight was critical, and the then-normal diesel design philosophy would have resulted in an excessively heavy engine. Although lighter, gasoline engine design would result in a diesel machine inadequate for the demands projected for these trucks.

I was assigned to clarify the engine specifications. To accomplish this, I instrumented a number of trucks operating at the Glendale Dairy, in Glendale, Arizona. I rode in these trucks as they carried out their normal mission of collecting milk from a number of dairies and gathered data to define the engine operating duty cycle. We then derived engine specifications from the resulting information.

Today, this method of developing specifications for a large variety of equipment has been raised to a level that makes my efforts in the 1960s seem amateurish. But in its day, it was a significant step forward. We had gone further than others to determine what the customer needed to succeed, a fundamental element of success in business.

The opportunity to work directly with equipment operators literally changed my life. I enjoyed interacting with customers. I discovered that much of the excitement and energy of the business could be found out in the field. Our products and services were used to solve real problems for real people who were grateful for our solutions. *I learned that the driving force of the business was not those engines I had been designing, but the sum total of what our organization could do to help customers achieve their objectives.*

I did not want to return to my former engineering duties after the 3208 engine job was completed. I wanted to continue working with customers and aspired to become a professional in customer service and selling. I sought a transfer to the Caterpillar sales department and was told it was not possible. Caterpillar insisted I stay with engineering, but I felt I could be effective in other roles.

Sometimes it is difficult for the leaders to believe in their people and take a risk by giving them new opportunities to grow. I have tried to avoid that mistake in my management activities. In any event, I had run into a roadblock in my own journey.

So, I left Caterpillar Tractor Co. after 16 years.

Hugh Rose

CUMMINS DISTRIBUTOR (RETIRED)

*N*o one views this world as does Peter, whether a problem involves engineering, management, or human behavior. He sees it differently than others involved, and a clear solution emerges where no one else believed it existed. It then makes complete sense and works, and no one saw it before Peter's analysis.

Peter is a steadfast friend who stands to be counted when others are afraid to do so.

3

"Loving an Engine" at Cummins

I ended the previous chapter with my realization that a company's driving force was not only in its products, but in the attitudes of the people who sold them and the customers who used them. That was the beginning of a journey for me, a journey that brought me to another engine maker where I learned more about the power of customer attitudes and feelings and the ways they can be harnessed to sustain a company's driving force. Much of what I was able to accomplish at Porsche and beyond was built on my experiences at Cummins Engine Company.

A number of my Caterpillar contemporaries had gone to work for Cummins Engine Company in Columbus, Indiana. I was recruited by Vaughn Beals, then Vice President of Engineering at Cummins. (Later in his stellar career, Beals returned Harley Davidson, the motorcycle company, to growth and profitability.)

Beals hired me into Cummins Engine Company in 1967 as director of product planning. In 1972, I was appointed vice president of sales and service for Cummins diesel truck engines in the United States and Canada. This was an important development in my career. Many people who are more capable than I do not get an opportunity to advance. At some point, most people need an angel to help them get a crack at the brass ring. Beals was my angel.

I quickly discovered that the sale and service of truck engines was about people, not just engines.

Trial by Fire

Shortly after I started my sales and service job at Cummins, I was faced with a major engine service problem in the fleet of a big customer. The problem had existed for a number of months. It was a big deal. I was inexperienced and scared.

I made my way to the fleet's headquarters in Oakland, California. Upon entering their offices, I was greeted by an extremely angry and agitated fleet president who was accompanied by two lawyers. In a rude and threatening tone, he stated that **my** engines, Peter Schutz's Cummins engines, were defective. He threatened to take the matter to court to recover the perceived loss of business and profit resulting from failure of **my** Cummins engines to perform.

I was at a total loss. The only thing I wanted was to get away. I explained I understood the concerns and asked if I might think about the situation and return at 8:30 the following morning to continue the discussion.

Upon retreating to my hotel room, I tried to organize my thoughts. Two truck manufacturing executives had become my mentors—Ken Self, president and founder of the Freightliner Corporation, and Murray Aitken, president of Kenworth. These wise men were legends in the trucking industry and generous with their time and wisdom to help a neophyte like me learn the ropes and survive in a tough industry.

Since Freightliner had built the trucks of the fleet in question, I decided to turn to Ken Self for counsel in my time of need.

His Portland, Oregon, office informed me that he was in San Francisco (only a half hour from where I was) on Freightliner business. I got in touch with him at his hotel. We met for a drink and I related my problems to him.

Self responded by telling me a story about his son. When his boy graduated from college, he decided to make him a present of a new Buick. His son took his girlfriend with him to the dealer and picked the new car up. From there, they set off to a big graduation party. The new car broke down on the way. They were stuck until the dealer could send help to get them going again.

After their late arrival at the party, Self pulled his son aside and asked him and his girlfriend to do themselves a favor. "Do not mention the breakdown of the new car," he said. His son took the advice, but the girlfriend did not. To the enjoyment of all present at the party, she told a funny (to her) story about how they got stuck with the new car.

The car was never satisfactory after that incident. Months later, Self's son called from college to inform his father that he had sold the Buick and bought an old M.G. sports car. The old M.G. had many problems, but that was OK. It was his baby, his car. He loved it with all of its faults and it worked for him.

I was dumbfounded. What did this series of events have to do with my problem?

Self went on to tell me about the early years of Consolidated Freightways fleet operations.

Consolidated Freightways was the founding company of Freightliner Truck Company and operated trucks powered by Buda diesel engines. These engines were not adequate for the task and had numerous breakdowns. Cylinder heads cracked and failed on a regular basis. Only the dedicated effort by Consolidated Freightways people kept the fleet on the road in a marginally acceptable fashion.

Then, one day, they bought a truck powered by a Cummins diesel engine. This engine turned out to be far superior to the

Buda engines and soon the fleet was equipped with additional Cummins-powered trucks.

From that day on, the Buda engines were totally inadequate. They never hauled freight again.

What did this story have to do with my problem? I thought about it that night in my hotel room while I tried to figure out what I would say to my angry customer in the morning. Finally I got it. *An engine that is not loved will not perform!*

That is what Ken Self, a legend in the trucking industry, taught me that evening in a San Francisco hotel bar over a friendly drink.

When I went into my meeting at 8:30 the next morning, an angry customer and his lawyers pounced on me once again. This time I was ready. Before the fleet president could get up a good head of steam, I suggested that we, just the two of us, withdraw into his private office. I closed the door and made my pitch.

"You have been telling me that **my** engines are defective. Let me clarify something. *They are not **my** engines, they are **your** engines; **you** bought them.* If your engines turn out to be defective, you can call them mine and sue me and the company I represent to recover perceived damages. You might even win such a lawsuit. But I am going to tell you something else. By the time such a lawsuit is settled after several years in court, your company may be out of business and *you* will be out of a job long before that."

His eyes were bulging and I thought I could see steam streaming from his ears, but I pushed on: "Your problem is not Cummins Engine Company or the engines. *Your problem is hauling freight with these engines, the only engines you have, be they yours or mine.* Unless you find a way to do that, you are out of business. You must learn to love your engines, because engines that are not loved will not function. All of your organization must learn to love these engines and you must lead the way."

He was still sitting down, barely. At least he didn't have his hands around my neck.

Encouraged, I continued.

"Now, if you are willing to do that, I will commit myself, along with all the resources of the company I represent, to help you haul your freight, save your job, and save your company."

Now I was sure I could see the steam come out of his ears. He was so angry I thought he would blow his top.

Then suddenly, he seemed to get it. Taking a deep breath, he sat back in his chair and said, "OK. How do we proceed?"

That very morning, we designed a program that included his best maintenance person and my best service engineer. We scheduled briefings at every terminal of the fleet. We explained the merits of the engines and what it would take to allow the engines to operate satisfactorily. Above all, we tried to teach drivers and mechanics to love those engines, if for no other reason than that they were the *only engines they had* and without them, there would be no jobs for any of them.

Within weeks, the engines were hauling freight well enough to complete the normal truck leasing cycle. My customer survived the crisis, and the fleet was eventually re-equipped with new trucks, powered by more adequate Cummins Diesel engines. *We did not lose the customer.*

I will be eternally grateful to Ken Self and his seemingly silly stories about loving an engine. I have found that the concept can apply to everything including family members, friends, and enemies, as well as any business undertaking I have participated in. Love and commitment can make many things work.

A Second Incident

In 1976, Cummins Engine Company experienced major engine failures in trucks operated by a major western truck fleet. Evidence suggested the probability of abuse on the part of the truck drivers.

Continued monitoring of this customer's fleet operations indicated that most of the failures occurred shortly after the vehicles left the company's home terminal. In fact, to our surprise, *failures occurred within less than 100 miles after drivers left on a scheduled trip.*

It simply did not make sense. Trucks don't break down more frequently at the beginning of a trip than at other times unless the drivers are behaving differently. But why would drivers abuse the trucks at the outset of a scheduled trip? We decided to investigate and learn more about these drivers and their work.

When drivers reported for work, each received a trip ticket with detailed instructions. Professional dispatchers composed the trip tickets. The dispatchers worked in front of a large scheduling board in a dispatch room. The drivers waited for their trip ticket at the opposite side of this rather large room.

Separating the dispatchers from the driver waiting area was *a large glass pane*, stretching from the top of a table all the way to the ceiling. Drivers would wait and watch from the other side of the pane as the dispatchers compiled their trip ticket.

This often proved to be a frustrating wait. Drivers were anxious to get going and the dispatchers seemed to go about their business in a rather relaxed manner.

The drivers would finally receive their trip ticket through a small hole in the glass pane that separated them from the dispatchers. By the time this took place, many drivers were fed up and angry with this endless process at the mercy of the seemingly uncaring and all-powerful dispatchers. The impression was that the dispatchers actually *enjoyed* the driver's frustration and impatience.

The drivers would storm out of the dispatch room with their trip ticket and vent their frustrations on the truck. The dispatcher was safe behind the glass pane, but the truck was not. Just put the truck into low gear and stand on the accelerator. Smash it into the next gear and with a little extra effort significant damage could be accomplished.

We removed the glass pane in the dispatch room.

The culture of the dispatch process was totally changed. Face to face, it resulted in a significantly improved relationship between drivers and dispatchers. The dispatchers and drivers chatted in a friendly manner. They got to know one another personally and began to appreciate the work involved in each other's roles. The truck abuse abated and the engine problems were solved.

The perceived indifference and abuse of power on the part of the dispatchers had been the root cause of the engine failures. *A glass pane had gotten in the way.* I learned to look for glass panes or their equivalent in many later cases throughout my career as a business leader. Often invisible barriers between people are the root cause of performance problems in business. The driving force is stifled.

Ed Friel

Vice President, Cummins Mid-States Power, Inc.

*T*he life lesson I learned from Peter was the power of true empowerment...not only empowering employees, but empowering ourselves to be the best we can be.

Peter truly believed in empowering the people in our organization at Cummins. We were encouraged to make customer decisions quickly and do the right thing for the customer with an eye to the future. Peter supported us totally; we were never second-guessed when we took genuine care of the customer.

Peter taught us the importance of understanding our business from the customer's perspective, to walk in the customer's shoes. We were continually urged to think about how the customer would feel, of how much value the customer would place on building a relationship with us. Peter urged us to be "partners" and consultants with our customers long before the current popularity of the concept.

Peter taught us the importance of preparation...of knowing not only our product, but learning and anticipating the customer's real needs.

Peter's use of humor, his openness, and his honesty in just being himself was an example for us in building our own relationships. His humility and his ability to poke fun at himself endeared him to his customers and to those that worked for him.

4

A Crash Course
in Selling

I started this book with the story of how we first turned the corner at Porsche by taking advantage of the driving force of a group of people dedicated to achieving extraordinary results. I will share more of that story in later chapters. But right now, I want to tell you a bit more about my early lessons in sales. You see, I was fortunate enough to get some practical experience in selling. By the time I got to Porsche, I had already learned that a company's driving force cannot stop at the front door. It has to spread from the leaders and people of the company all the way to the customers. If customers aren't as excited about what you are doing as you are, you have not mobilized the driving force needed to optimize the business.

I had gone to work for Cummins Engine Company in order to become active in selling and relating to customers. When I was named vice president of sales and service at Cummins, I was suddenly in the position of having to start my sales career at the top.

I had never sold anything professionally. This did not bother me. I had spent most of my professional career in design and development of diesel engines, largely for application in trucks. In my mind, I thought no one knew more about truck engines than I, particularly not the salespeople who were competing against me. I planned to simply focus on proving to potential customers that our engines were superior to all the competition. It couldn't be that hard to sell a superior product, could it?

But first, I had to collect some data to prepare my case. I began to study our product performance in detail.

After diligent examination, I discovered, to my horror, that the Cummins engine I was preparing to sell did *not* have the best fuel efficiency in the industry. It did not have the lowest weight, nor was it the least expensive. No matter how I tried, I could not establish a convincing case that it was the most reliable or easiest to repair, or could haul freight at a lower cost per mile than competitive engines.

This left me terribly distraught. I was prepared to go to Cummins top management and explain what a noncompetitive product I was being asked to sell.

In the quiet of my office, I saw myself making this presentation, explaining our product's shortcomings. I then tried to imagine the response I was likely to receive. I could hear, "Peter, do you think you are telling us things we have not known for a long time? We know all of that. If we wanted the engines analyzed and fixed, we would have named you chief engineer, not vice president of sales. We don't expect you to fix these engines or improve them. We just want you to *sell* them!"

WHOA! I was not ready for that. I knew I would not make that presentation.

But what was I going to do?

I thought back to some of the lessons I had already learned. I reminded myself that to the customer, *it is not about engines!*

My job, and my company's job, was not to build and sell engines; it was to add value for customers and exceed their expectations. *That* is what it's all about.

If I was going to do that, I had to begin by identifying my customer.

In Search of the Real Customer

I realized that if I simply thought of my customer the same way my competitors did, I might not do so well. After all, I couldn't expect to win at their game if I didn't have a better product. So, I realized I needed insight. I needed to see customers more clearly than the competition did. Otherwise, how would I know how to give them extra value and exceed their current expectations?

The fastest growing group of truck customers in the early 1970s was the truck leasing industry. Ryder, Leaseway, and Saunders were some of the leasing companies that were redefining the trucking business. Instead of buying heavy trucks, many companies that operated trucks were leasing them from those companies. This was a fundamental change in the industry, so it naturally attracted my attention. I realized, that to make any major headway in sales, I would have to recognize that the leasing company was my customer.

Only after the customer is identified *clearly* can we begin to define customer expectations. If I had decided that my customer was anyone who bought truck engines, my view of their expectations would have taken us back to where we started: to the problem of offering them a better-performing engine, something I could not do at the time. By focusing more narrowly, I found I could explore new and better answers to the question of what my customers needed.

I asked myself, *What is a leasing company really trying to do?*

Later in my career, I would find this simple form of question could also be applied to other types of customers. To boost sales of Porsche sports cars, it was necessary to understand what the dealers and customers really wanted and to make sure we helped them find it.

Like any other business, a leasing company is trying to make money. What was the key to being competitive and making money in truck leasing, or leasing in general? I was not sure, I had never run a leasing business. We had to do our homework. *We had to really understand our customer's business.*

One key to making money in a leasing business turns out to be *residual value*, the price the company can command for equipment after completing a leasing cycle. The capital a leasing company has to tie up in its equipment is affected as much by the residual value of the equipment as it is by the initial purchase price. If the residual value of objects a company is leasing is higher than that of the competition, a lower lease rate can be charged. The company must recover enough residual value to replace the equipment at the completion of the lease cycle.

Most of the truck leasing companies operated under similar conditions. They had similar operating criteria and expectations. This was encouraging to us, because if we came up with a better strategy or approach, we could probably offer such a program to all the major leasing companies and make significant sales.

A group of customers with similar expectations makes up a market niche.

If the defining expectations of a market niche are only price and quality and nothing more, it often signifies that we may have defined the market niche too broadly.

A well-defined market niche will allow us to see opportunities to exceed the expectations of the customer beyond the obvious ones of lower price and higher quality. One of the keys is to find the customer for whom it is possible to develop a value-adding solution, the kind of customer who contributes to a company's driving force.

In the early 1970s, when heavy truck leasing was in its infancy, many leasing companies offered low lease rates in a very competitive market by purchasing barely adequate trucks with barely adequate engines. They provided inexpensive equipment in order to offer low-priced lease rates. At the expiration of a typical three-year lease, these trucks had a rather low residual value; few people wanted to buy them. Leasing companies would sell them back to a truck dealer, who then sold them off to someplace like South America or a third world country.

We wondered if we could introduce a different business model to the industry.

We took our idea to a truck leasing company in Alabama, suggesting that they purchase premium trucks with higher horsepower engines in order to ensure a better residual value for their fleet.

We were told, "Leasing customers do not want premium trucks; they do not want higher horsepower engines. They will not pay a premium for such things." That was true, but we had a solution. We could *cut the engine power* by adjusting the fuel pumps, so that the engine performed like others in the leasing fleet. We pointed out that it was not necessary to charge a premium for the lease. When such a truck came off its three-year lease, Cummins would examine the engine, fix any deficiencies, set the power back to the original level, and cover the engine with a new engine warranty.

Who would want a three-year-old premium truck with a high horsepower engine and a new engine warranty? The answer was many owner-operators who drove as independent contractors.

A used premium truck brought a premium price in the owner-operator market niche, particularly if it included a custom paint job to the new owner's specification. Owner-operators like to personalize their trucks.

Again, we had an idea we thought might add some value. We recruited students from the University of Alabama's industrial design department to sit with prospective owner-operator customers to design and redesign five-color custom paint concepts. For a minor cost, we could offer a significantly better-looking product to the owner-operator.

It turned out that such a used truck commanded a premium price. The high residual value facilitated a very competitive

45

lease rate. In some instances, the profit of the used truck activity could *exceed* the profit the truck earned from the three-year lease. We had a new way to sell our engines. We helped a leasing company make more money!

More Innovations for the Customer

Leasing companies liked the fact that we were trying to help them make money instead of just trying to sell them engines. So we looked for more ways to help them achieve their business goals.

Engine competitors were slow to respond with similar activity because we were doing things that were not normally a part of the business model in our industry.

Once we found these new ways to exceed truck leasing company expectations, the various engine shortcomings did not seem to matter so much. Our customers were not interested in buying truck engines; they just wanted to make money. By helping them do that, with the engine now only a component of the total offering, Cummins captured a large share of the truck engine business in that market niche.

Some of the other market niches that we identified at Cummins Engine Company included:

- Private local fleets.
- National accounts: Common carriers and leasing companies with nationwide operations, customers that could not be serviced effectively by any single regional Cummins distributor.

One of the important elements in realizing such a market niche strategy is to have access to people who are experts in the *customer's business*, not only the product or service that is being offered. I think it is interesting how seldom businesses do this. Many businesses are very expert at what they sell but do not have an intimate knowledge of their customers' businesses or lives.

In hindsight, I am glad I did not have a superior engine to sell. If I had, I might not have felt the need to strive for excellence in selling, which meant finding creative solutions to exceed the customer's expectations. In our efforts to find other ways to succeed in sales, I was forced to learn how to refocus the business away from selling like our competitors did, and toward unique ways of adding value.

I was learning how to avoid a serious problem that causes trouble for many businesses. I was learning about the pitfalls of competing in a commodity business. I define a commodity business as one that offers a product or service available from a number of competing sources, with comparable value added. I discovered that Cummins could not succeed in a commodity business. It was not possible to compete on product features or price alone. Cummins needed to move beyond a commodity business. In my experience, many businesses fail to take advantage of this opportunity.

Beyond the Commodity Business

When Sheila and I returned from Germany to settle in Naples, Florida, we soon became active in our own business enterprise, Harris and Schutz Inc., consisting of just the two of us. We have operated our speaking and consulting business out of our home.

We did business with a wonderful little office products company in Naples. This business had been active for a long time. It was a wonderful neighborhood store. The people there were knowledgeable and courteous. For example, if I needed paper for my copy machine, they could explain exactly which would be best suited for the job I was doing at the time. If we needed something they did not have in stock, they ordered it.

Then, one day, Office Depot moved into Naples.

After that, the company did not last long. It seemed there was no way they could compete with Office Depot prices for copy machine paper, or most anything else. To the average customer, this business seemed to be nothing but a smaller, higher-priced competitor to Office Depot. The subtle differences provided by their superior knowledge and helpful service were not enough to differentiate them from Office Depot. Cheap prices and wider selection won the day. They were competing against a giant in a commodity business. In that scenario, Goliath is always going to win.

One day, the printer for my trusty computer quit and was not repairable. "No problem," I was told. "Just go to Office Depot and you can buy a new printer for less than $200." This proved to be true; Office Depot had a printer for sale for about $125. They also had one for $250, another for $300, and several more for as much as $800. I finally tracked an elusive employee down and asked, "What is the difference between all of these printers?" "Well," I was told, "this one is $250, that one is $400, and we have them all the way up to $800."

I went to see the store manager and asked if there was anyone in the store who could explain the differences between the various printers to me. He replied: "If there were such a person, they would not be working here. We cannot afford to pay what it would take to employ such a person."

How did Office Depot put a knowledgeable local store out of business?

They did so by spreading overhead and management expenses over a large number of retail outlet locations that shared operating expenses. That is what it takes to operate successfully in a commodity business today. This is not new, but it has been raised to a whole new level of scale and efficiency by modern technology.

To compete in a commodity business by selling something that customers view as equal to what your competitors sell, it is necessary to have a large, centralized operation. Like McDonald's, Office Depot, or Wal-Mart, it is necessary to be bigger and more efficient than competitors. Not many businesses can manage to do that. Most need to come up with solutions more like those I was learning about at Cummins. They need to find ways to engage customers that go beyond the short-term appeal of a lower price.

We could never have turned Porsche around by cutting prices. In fact, if we had tried that strategy, I am sure the company would be out of business today.

Success Stories

It often seems impossible to get out of a commodity business and gain full control over one's fate. Most breakthroughs in business involve doing just that. Whenever I feel stuck in a competitive situation, I look back to stories that help me reset my thinking and start focusing on building driving force, instead of worrying about what my competitors are doing.

The history of Cummins Engine Company is one of my favorite examples.

Irwin Miller was a banker in Columbus, Indiana, in the early 1920s. The Miller family employed a chauffeur by the name of Clessie Cummins to drive and maintain a number of their vehicles. Clessie was a tinkerer. He built a diesel engine in the Miller garage and installed it in an automobile; a revolutionary concept at that time. Diesel engines were big and heavy and better suited to a railroad locomotive or seagoing ship.

He drove this diesel-powered car to the big New York City Automobile Show in the summer of 1932. The car achieved unbelievable fuel economy on this long trip. Without formal sponsorship by a major automobile manufacturer, Clessie's diesel car was refused admission to the big show. Undaunted, he displayed it at the curb in front of the show entrance. The enthusiastic public response encouraged Clessie Cummins. Upon the completion of his uneventful return trip to Columbus, Indiana, he decided his Cummins diesel would be an ideal engine for a long-haul truck.

At the time, White Motor Company, based in Cleveland, Ohio, was the leading manufacturer of such trucks. So, Clessie took his diesel-powered truck proposal to Cleveland and offered to supply Cummins diesel engines to be installed in White trucks.

He was resoundingly rebuffed. "White Motor Company builds gasoline-powered trucks," he was told. "There is no demand for a more expensive and heavier diesel truck engine. If such a demand should ever materialize, White Motor Company would build a proprietary diesel engine, a White Motor Company truck diesel engine for White diesel trucks."

Clessie returned to Columbus after that rejection, but was still convinced that his diesel engine made economic sense for a long-haul truck. The outstanding fuel efficiency achieved by his diesel car on its round-trip to New York City was solid confirmation of his engineering calculations. He took his engine to a local truck repair shop near Columbus, Indiana. There, he located a truck owner whose gasoline-powered truck was in the shop for a major engine overhaul. He offered the truck owner a deal he could not refuse: "Do not rebuild the gasoline engine; install this Cummins diesel instead. Do not pay for the diesel engine and installation. Pay me the difference of the fuel cost that the diesel engine will save over the gasoline engine. The engine and installation will be paid off in two to three years."

Thus, the first Cummins diesel engine was installed in a White truck.

No one had asked for a diesel-powered truck. This fact established Clessie's approach as a marketing rather than selling activity. As opposed to selling, marketing is not the result of reaction to a customer need. Instead, it is *proactive*.

The word spread quickly among truck operators. The Cummins diesel engine was redefining long-haul trucking. Several other truck owners went to the truck repair shop clamoring for a Cummins Diesel engine to repower their gasoline-powered White trucks.

Soon thereafter, truck customers approached the local White truck dealer asking to buy a new White truck powered by a Cummins diesel engine. When the White truck dealer tried to order these from the Cleveland White Motor Company factory, the response was, "Such a truck is not available; order a gasoline-engine-powered truck instead." The dealer inquired: "Can you ship a new White truck without an engine?" "That is not possible," was the reply.

So, White truck dealers ordered gasoline-powered trucks for their customers, who then drove the new trucks to the repair shop, removed the gasoline engine, and had a Cummins Diesel engine installed in its place.

Eventually, White Motor Company could no longer ignore this activity. "If this gets to be a big business," they decided, "White Motor Company will build its own truck diesel engine. In the short term, the Cummins Diesel engine will become a factory (Original Equipment Manufacturer, O.E.M.) option for a White truck."

Clessie Cummins, a tinkerer in a garage, had redefined the truck industry.

Several aspects are significant:

- No one had asked for a diesel-powered truck.
- The differentiated product, a truck diesel engine, was first recognized at the truck operator level. In other words, the end consumer "got it" first, when the major players in the industry were sure it would not work.
- The truck dealer put pressure on the truck manufacturer to supply a Cummins Diesel engine.
- Major deliveries and engine sales subsequently took place at the truck manufacturer level.

The truck repair shop, and others like it, grew into the Cummins distributor network. This network is a significant part of Cummins Engine Company operations to this day. It has prospered through parts and service business and is a major differentiating element in Cummins customer support activity.

Unrelenting innovation to differentiate the total Cummins offering in both technical performance and customer support has taken and kept Cummins Engine Company operating beyond a commodity business.

It takes persistent, diligent, effort to stay ahead of the competition to accomplish this. Any lapse of innovation and effort will allow the organization to sink into a commodity business once again.

White Motor Company never succeeded in building their own truck diesel engine. They were striving for a commodity business. Cummins Engine Company had moved beyond it.

During my tenure at Cummins, customers were addressed with a view of achieving a differentiated posture at every level, so that the Cummins truck engine would not become a commodity.

For instance:

- When turbocharged diesel engines were introduced, Cummins researched and redefined engine cooling specifications for this new technology. Although several truck manufacturers were active in this field, many lacked the engine expertise to deal with this technical development.
- Cummins introduced the concept of flexible engine production schedules. This redefined the engine inventory that a truck manufacturer had to keep on hand. It was an early form of just-in-time inventory management. In its time, it had a significant impact on truck manufacturers' inventory expenses.
- I have already described efforts to transform the truck fleet operators' view of their business based on our realization that a leasing company's profits are tied to residual value. We side-stepped commodity-oriented selling when we persuaded these companies to specify premium trucks with premium features which redefined their business. This is reflected today in the sort of automobiles a rental company specifies. Most of the cars are fully equipped with premium features, even though the automobile rental business is brutally competitive. Operators of automobile

rental and leasing businesses now know that they are basically in the used-car business. The role that salvage value plays in such a business is old hat today, but in the early seventies, it redefined the leasing business and helped keep Cummins Engine Company out of the commodity business.

- Beyond that, it was determined that a major challenge, or annoyance, was the warranty repair activity at a typical truck leasing company. When a truck engine experienced a failure during the warranty period, the truck had to go back to an authorized truck dealer for warranty repairs. This was often complicated by the fact that the truck lessee operated in a location remote from the truck dealer that delivered the truck originally. Engine warranty business is not usually profitable for a truck dealer. There are often delays in such warranty repairs; the normal and more profitable business takes precedence. Most of the truck leasing companies operate repair and maintenance facilities of their own. We, Cummins, asked them, "Would you like to perform warranty repairs on Cummins engines in your own shops?" The reply was, "That would be great; can we do that?" Cummin's reply was, "Of course not, but if you would send some of your key maintenance people to the Cummins plant in Columbus, Indiana, we could train them to be Cummins warranty administrators and your repair station could be certified as a Cummins warranty facility. Warranty repairs could then be performed in that facility."

The competition found it difficult to replicate this activity promptly. It was too unorthodox.

The Driving Force of Drivers

The above examples helped us keep Cummins from having to compete on price alone. They were important to business success, but it turned out that the truck driver offered even greater opportunities for differentiation.

For as long as anyone could remember, truck drivers and truck fleet operators had been at what can best be described as war. Drivers wanted more engine power; fleet operators wanted low operating cost. Common knowledge was that this was not a compatible combination. The accepted solution was to limit the available power in the truck so drivers had no choice but to drive slowly.

Beyond that, the trucks could only be described as thunder boxes with limited sound insulation, no air conditioners, no radios, and virtually no provision for driver comfort. Drivers hated the trucks, hated the trucking company, and hated the trucking company management.

Drivers often took this hatred out on the equipment. Trucks and engines were abused as a matter of routine.

We at Cummins attempted to persuade truck fleet operators to equip vehicles with more powerful engines that would be more pleasant to drive. We suggested noise insulation, air conditioners, and high-fidelity sound systems.

"Impossible," we were told, "You clearly do not understand this business. Trucking is very competitive; such hardware is simply not affordable."

The prevailing opinion among managers was that truck drivers cannot be counted on to cooperate. Instead of tearing up inexpensive trucks, they would tear up expensive equipment.

Then came fuel price escalation and shortages. It appeared it would be a difficult time for us to promote increased engine power, sound insulation, and hi-fi sound systems for those trucks. This was the circumstance in which Cummins developed the country song, "Hummin' Cummins," that I mentioned in the introduction. This song, written in contemporary trucker's language, the CB radio lingo of the time, told a story of engine *Reserve Power* and resulting fuel savings. It was not just a song. It was also a message addressing the image and pride of the truck driver, the economic concerns of truck fleet operators, and the national concerns of fuel conservation.

Branding played a significant role in this activity. *Reserve Power* and *Formula Engine* were Cummins branding elements in this effort. The song "Hummin' Cummins" became popular and supported driver recognition.

Many truck fleet operators opted for the higher horsepower Cummins Formula Engines. The total *formula* also included more comfort for the truck driver, a move to more sound insulation, hi-fi sound systems, and air-conditioning. This was accomplished without any significant technical engine differentiation or investment in engine technology.

Perhaps the most important element in achieving the differentiation that allows a business to go beyond the commodity business is the need to truly understand the customer's business. Knowledge of the product or service is also important, without that, there can be no advance to differentiation.

Detailed knowledge of the customer's business is a key to differentiation.

If a business is successful in becoming a differentiated leader in serving a specific market niche, it can become the market leader in that niche. It no longer has to compete head-to-head on the basis of price.

Two key advantages accrue to the leader of a market niche:

1. *It is easier to retain market leadership than it is to achieve it.* Once market leadership is achieved, never let up. As Satchel Paige, the baseball pitcher, used to say as he was aging, "Never look back; someone might be gaining on you." In business, there is always someone gaining on you.

2. *The market leader* sets prices *in a market niche*. If you aren't able to set your own prices, then you know you aren't a market leader yet. Keep working at it! The market leader can raise prices to improve profits, or lower prices to control the ability of competitors to gain ground.

When I was selling truck diesel engines to Ford Motor Company, I recall a visit in which the Ford people were very excited about a new automobile that was ready for introduction. My Ford colleagues took me into their inner sanctum to show me their new car. It was beautiful. I remember asking, "At what price will this car be offered to a customer?" The answer was, "As soon as Chevrolet announces a price for their new Impala model, we will know how to price this car: 5 percent below the Chevrolet Impala."

Chevrolet was the clear market niche leader at that time. They were setting prices for their own products and Ford had to follow along. This is the same syndrome that drove my favorite neighborhood office supply store out of business. I wish they had seen the writing on the wall early enough to redefine their business and get out of the shadow of Office Depot. Maybe they could have switched to leasing office and computer equipment to businesses like mine. I just want to have good equipment that I can rely on, I do not want to have to become an expert in buying and maintaining it. There must have been some way to turn the superior expertise and customer service into a differentiated offering had they only realized they could never survive as a commodity business.

I do not want to leave this chapter without sharing something I learned about selling that is often missed. It gets at the heart of the problem of creating and maintaining your "driving force" out there in a competitive marketplace. This was told to me as a true story many years ago and I have always remembered it.

Little Tommy was ten years old, in the fifth grade in Detroit. His daddy was employed by General Motors, and was sent to the Soviet Union in the 1970s to help the Soviets design and build an automobile assembly plant. The project was successful and the father returned to Detroit with a wonderful set of color slides that depicted the development of the project.

Tommy's fifth grade teacher asked students' parents to come to school and explain how they earned their living.

Little Tommy beamed as his daddy blew the kids away with his incredible color slide show. His father went back to the office feeling confident that he had made his son proud.

However, that evening Tommy came home from school with a long, sad face. "What is the matter, Tommy?" asked his dad "I thought it went very well at school today."

"Daddy," Tommy replied, "sometimes I wish you had an *interesting* job like Mr. Murphy. Mr. Murphy drives a fire truck; he brought it to school and gave us all a ride around the block!"

If you really want to sell something, you must bring the fire truck to school.

William G. Hanley

CEO Cummins Great Plains Distributor

I *was one of the fortunate ones to have been associated with you for a little over ten years on both a personal and business basis during the late 1960s and early 1970s. It was a true pleasure, and I still have fond memories of those days.*

In reflecting on our times together, I will never forget the time you took your management team to Minneapolis for three or four days of soul searching. We read the book I'm OK, You're OK *and had breakout sessions learning about ourselves. I still remember the quote: "It is not who you think you are but how others perceive you to be." That basic viewpoint and understanding has been very important to me personally through the years.*

I also remember how you developed the low-rpm-engine concept and had an internal contest to name the engine for marketing purposes. We had a lot of fun with this project and it built a strong team commitment when the engine was released for production and sale. By the way, as you know, this is one of the most successful products Cummins Engine Company ever produced.

Another rewarding experience that we enjoyed was working with the Cummins Distributor Network, which involved both personal and business relationships. These relationships had a great deal to do with my "becoming one of them." As you know, you were personally very helpful to me in fulfilling my career objectives and I will never forget it.

Thank you, Peter, for allowing me to be part of your team back then. Good luck with your book The Driving Force.

5

Identifying Our Driving Values

Values and the right culture can guide a manager through challenging situations, even if the future is not clear. Often, in our turnaround at Porsche, we had to trust our values and believe that if we were true to them, we would eventually find solutions to our problems.

Value orientation is something I learned from a number of my earlier experiences. I want to tell you about three experiences, each of which reflects a core value I find important in the creation of driving force.

Maintaining Momentum in Hard Times

Early in my career, I learned that driving force has to be nurtured with additional care during difficult times, when the temptation is to focus on cutting back and protecting the company to the exclusion of trying to move it forward. I believe it is *especially* important to move ahead in tough times. How a team responds when the car is having problems in an auto race frequently determines the outcome. These become the critical moments of the race that separate the winners from the losers. The same is true in business.

In 1975, the North American trucking industry underwent a significant slow-down. *Cummins lost 85 percent of its truck engine order backlog within a ten-day period* in January 1975. This was a dramatic business deterioration. How might a business respond in such circumstances?

An immediate response might be to quickly cut as many expenses as possible. The principle is simple: to minimize operating losses and make sure the company has the cash flow to make it through the difficult times.

Henry Schacht, Cummins' chief executive officer, convened an all-employee meeting and explained the seriousness of the situation. A number of factors were addressed openly: The need to limit purchase of outside materials and services, the need to reduce inventories, and the need to adjust wages and salaries.

There were some necessary layoffs and salaried people agreed to a temporary 5 percent salary reduction. These cost reduction activities were more or less effective, but beyond this inwardly directed effort, some aggressive outwardly directed activities were initiated. Without an outward orientation, a business risks losing its driving force during a recession or other business challenges.

We initiated a series of customer calls on organizations with whom Cummins had never done business. These were customers who were not in the market to buy engines at the time; we knew it, they knew it, and they knew we knew it. Normally, they would not have been worth calling on, but these were not normal times, and we were determined to build for the future in spite of the current recession.

We made presentations to explain our company culture and advances in technology to initiate thinking about the potential of joint business activity in the future. None of us were under any pressure to sell or buy; there was little going on. Instead, we built relationships that might result in future business.

As a part of this activity, I made a trip to Pontiac, Michigan, and called on a gentleman by the name of Bob Stelter, a General Motors vice president in charge of the GMC Truck Division. Up to that time, GMC had never offered a Cummins diesel engine in any of its truck models. I also knew that GMC had few, if any, orders on their books for new trucks.

We had put a truck engine package together at Cummins. It was a standard basic engine with some relatively minor adjustments in the manner in which the engine turbo-charger was matched. The objective was improved driveability and fuel consumption. We had branded this engine a Formula Engine. It was an engine that in conjunction with a revised truck rear axle ratio and other minor innovations, would constitute a new *formula* for improved truck performance. I explained our work in this area without any expectation of making a sale. The entire pitch was an "I just thought you would like to know" kind of presentation.

At the conclusion of my speech, Stelter asked that I accompany him into his private office and closed the door. "Peter," he said, "that presentation you just made is probably the most timely you have ever made in your career. GMC Truck Division has zero orders for new trucks in the months of March and April, zip, nothing. We have decided to build 340 new over-the-road tractors with an innovative new spoiler mounted on the cab roof to reduce air resistance and improve fuel economy. These vehicles will be called Dragfoilers. Since we have no orders for these trucks, we plan to invite about 300 of our GMC truck dealers to Pontiac, Michigan, in April to pick these vehicles up and drive them back to their dealerships all over the United States. It will be a huge promotion to pump up some interest and new business. After your presentation about your new Formula Engine, I have decided that all 340 new Dragfoiler trucks should be powered by this engine."

"Bob," I said, "that decision is probably the most timely that you have ever made in your career."

"Oh," Stelter added, "just one more thing. In order to make this happen, it will be necessary to get a $400 discount on each engine." I walked over to his telephone, called Henry Schacht, the Cummins CEO, and asked for approval of this deal. Unhesitatingly, I got the green light. I turned to Stelter and said, "You have a deal!"

He was speechless. "I have never experienced anything like the teamwork that Cummins has just exhibited."

There is no substitute for an organization that knows what it is trying to do and therefore empowers its members to perform *promptly*. This proved to be particularly true in tough times. When an opportunity arises, there is no substitute for prompt and decisive action. Yet, it is easy to become paralyzed by a problem such as a recession or the loss of a major customer and fail to act decisively when opportunities arise. I admired Henry Schacht's willingness to support me at this critical moment and go along with the proposed discount. That kind of support is part of the formula for sustained momentum.

I was in my hotel room the night before the big dealer drive-away. It was about 3 A.M., and I was going through the anticipated events of the next day.

The 300 General Motors GMC truck dealers were starting all 340 trucks and were preparing to drive them to their respective dealerships all over the U.S. and Canada. Suddenly, it hit me: 340 trucks on a cold March morning in Detroit. How many might fail to start? How many might stop running before they really got on their way? If things were even 99% perfect, there would be four trucks left behind.

So, at three o'clock in the morning, I called our Cummins Distributor in Detroit, Von Boll, at home. I explained my concerns and Von responded in typical Cummins style. By 7 A.M., his service trucks and people were on the scene. Sure enough, about seven vehicles needed some help to get started. Beyond that, Von had positioned radio-equipped service vehicles at every major artery leaving the area to assist any vehicles that encountered problems after they got under way.

This was another example of Cummins teamwork in action; an organization of largely ordinary people performing at an extraordinary level with outstanding leadership.

The subsequent dealer drive-away was a huge success. It was the beginning of a most fruitful cooperation between Cummins and GMC, two units that had never done business together before. Cummins' share of GMC heavy-duty tractors rose to over 60 percent.

Turning up the heat during a recession had paid off big-time. Market share is very difficult to increase in good times. A recession is most often the best opportunity to increase market share, particularly in a mature industry. Companies that maintain their driving force in tough times have a significant advantage over those that don't. The commitment to driving force keeps a business proactive and helps it persist even in the face of serious challenges. This became a core business value for me.

Choosing the Right Customers

When you are trying to grow, it often seems like there is no such thing as a bad customer. A sale is a sale. If their money is good, what can be wrong about selling to them? Some of the smaller businesses I advise in my current work are not very selective about with whom they do business. I have found that success depends not only on finding customers to buy your goods, but on finding the *right* customers. It is vital for the leader to be clear on who the right customer is and with whom they do *not* want to do business.

My first awareness of this occurred when I was working at a Standard Oil filling station on the south side of Chicago during my high school years. When I was 15 years old, Fred Stern, the owner of Stern and Stern Standard Super Service Station, taught me something I have never forgotten. "Peter," he said, "there is no future in doing business with people who don't have money."

Very simple, and yet, how true!

My next lesson on this subject came when I was at Cummins in the 1970s. We were selling diesel engines for heavy trucks. As is true of any mechanical product, these engines were not perfect. Shortcomings manifested themselves in a number of ways. Fuel consumption was not always up to a customer's desires and engine reliability and service life might fall short of expectations.

In pursuing fixes for such shortcomings, we would attempt to work with a trucking customer to identify the magnitude of the perceived problem and implement solutions.

A frustrating situation would develop with customers that could not capture the information necessary to quantify the problem(s). In such cases, we might hear, "It is costing too much money per mile to haul freight with these Cummins engines." We might respond, "What is it costing; what would constitute a reasonable cost?" "We do not know, but it is too much, and the Cummins engines are the problem."

In such a circumstance, it is frequently impossible to take corrective action and satisfy the customer.

Of all the customers we served in my time at Cummins, it was most rewarding to work with leasing companies and the more knowledgeable fleet operators. These customers knew what was happening in their business and could quantify shortcomings. Focused corrective action was then possible. It was not necessary to deal with situations in which a customer was striving for results that had little to do with the operation of the Cummins engines or the trucks.

And so we decided that…

> …*we will not do business with customers who are not managing an orderly business.*

Putting the product or service into the hands of a customer who does not share the quality standards of your business can undermine the reputation of your business.

At Cummins, we determined that the majority, about 70 percent, of major engine failures had their origin in cooling system deficiencies or malfunctions. Some truck manufacturers were installing inadequate radiators and related cooling system components.

In general, these manufacturers were combining our engines with inadequate cooling systems due to a lack of experience and understanding of the operation of turbocharged truck diesel engines. Unlike their naturally aspirated counterparts, these turbocharged engines did not lose power at higher altitudes. The reduced cooling power of the thin air at high altitudes was compensated by the engine power loss of the naturally aspirated engines. The new turbocharged engines could produce high power at higher altitudes and seriously overload the cooling systems. The result was a rash of engine failures due to inadequate cooling.

Many of the truck manufacturers dealt with this situation and redesigned truck cooling systems, but some did not.

Cummins' reputation was at stake with truck operators and drivers, to say nothing of the expense incurred in repairing engines that failed, some within the warranty period.

We made a pivotal decision. A detailed engineering analysis was performed to define acceptable engine cooling and installations. This included cooling as well as intake air filtration, lubricating oil cooling, and filtration. We decided that until such time as a truck manufacturer provided for an engine installation that could satisfy these specifications, Cummins Engine Company would no longer accept an engine order from that manufacturer.

It was in Cummins Engine Company's best interest to forego an engine order rather than endanger its reputation by inadequate engine installations.

The expense incurred in repairing failed engines was not the primary motivation; *it was about reputation, which is priceless.*

In order to verify the adequacy of an engine installation, Cummins built and operated a test facility at the Engineering

Center in Columbus, Indiana. If a truck manufacturer requested it, Cummins was prepared to perform the engineering work that assured proper engine installation in order to qualify the customer to order engines.

It was true that some truck manufacturers felt Cummins was getting involved in issues that did not concern a supplier to an original equipment manufacturer (OEM). Cummins expended considerable money in order to carry out this policy. It is also true that this policy returned significant dividends. How much? To this day, I am not sure. I do not know that I could justify the approach on the basis of a traditional financial model focused on the short term. We did it because it was consistent with a basic value and I was confident that we would do better by being true to that value.

It is often impossible to quantify the direct consequences of actions designed to ensure that you sell to the *right* customers. The strategy can manifest itself in increased market share, outstanding reputation, and increased profitability in the longer term.

In the 1990s, I was engaged as an advisor to a computer software company founded by a group of bright young people. Business was good, but a problem had developed. A customer would hire them with specific requests for a computer software system. Upon completion of the job, they would be informed that the system was not what was really wanted, and they were expected to re-do the system to meet revised specifications at no charge. This had become a major operating issue.

It became clear that it was necessary to qualify a customer before accepting an order for a computer software system. I shared the insight I had learned at Cummins and urged them to avoid doing business with customers who are not prepared to meet defined quality standards. Learning how to qualify a customer went a long way toward solving the problem.

It is difficult for the quality of any business to rise above the quality of its customers.

Doing Business with an Open Hand

One of the most important values, and a value often difficult to implement, is:

It is necessary to give before we take.

In the short term, businesses can often profit by taking as much as they can in their relationships with suppliers, their people, customers, or communities. The temptation is to play a competitive game to grab as much as you can, with little regard for how others are faring. In order to create and sustain driving force in a business, it is necessary to engage the energy and enthusiasm of others.

In a number of instances, I found a very adversarial operating climate between the management of a trucking company and the people who drove and maintained the trucks. In extreme cases, management was at war with its people and labor unions.

Some of this antagonism had its foundation in the perceived lack of horsepower of the truck engines of that era. Drivers complained that they were given inadequate equipment to drive, while the managers of the trucking companies complained that drivers abused equipment and could not be trusted. These fleet operators actually "de-rated" engines. They purposefully reduced the available power of the engines in efforts to control driver abuse of the trucks.

The resistance of drivers to this situation was so great in one western U.S. truck fleet that drivers would bring a bowling bag containing their own modified engine fuel pump along on their trips. As soon as they were out of town, they would pull into a truck rest area, remove the company fuel pump, and replace it with their own pump. This neutralized the company effort to control the driver by reducing fuel pressure and thus reducing engine power. The drivers could now drive the truck the way they felt it ought to be driven, without the handicap of reduced horsepower. As they approached their destination, they would once again pull off the road and reinstall the company pump so nobody would be the wiser.

Some drivers would insert objects such as soft drink bottle tops, aspirin bottle caps, and similar debris into the fuel return line of the truck engine. This blocked the fuel return flow to the fuel tank; it would raise the fuel pressure in the system and increase engine power.

When I learned about these practices, I saw them as a natural expression of the drivers' need to have some control over their work and the way they performed it. It was clear to me that these drivers felt a strong need for more engine power. The war for control of the engine between the managers and the drivers was a good example of trying to lead by taking rather than giving. I could not believe that a fleet operated by drivers at war with their managers could be fully productive and efficient. What if these companies took a more open-handed approach and began to trust their drivers with better equipment? This offered the possibility of creating positive attitudes and boosting performance.

Happily, I was in the business of selling engines, the more powerful, the better. So, I began to encourage fleet operators to offer higher power equipment to their drivers. I tried to alleviate the long-running war between management and labor.

Not all truck fleet management teams saw the situation the way I did. I recall a presentation of this concept to the CEO of a successful major common carrier truck fleet who walked out of the meeting with the comment, "I can't believe I am listening to this sh—." The approach was clearly not applicable to all companies.

We won some converts, including Yellow Freight Lines, a major common carrier. The management agreed to re-equip Yellow's fleet with higher power Cummins engines. The results were decidedly positive for both the company and the drivers. The drivers were overjoyed to have more powerful trucks to drive, and operating costs were reduced.

Some of the Yellow Freight drivers made up a sign consisting entirely of debris removed from doctored fuel pumps and presented it to me in a humorously exaggerated ceremony. The sign simply stated, "Thanks, Peter." I proudly display this token of recognition; it hangs in my hobby workshop.

This program was very successful. We helped bridge a gap between management and unions, improved the operating climate, and increased operating profits for our customers. Cummins sold many high-margin truck engines and market share rose to record heights.

Still, all was not well in paradise.

As the leader of this revolutionary development, I was invited to address the 1977 Teamsters Union annual convention in Washington, D.C. I was honored by the invitation, but some of my colleagues and customers were horrified. As highly visible advocates of innovations to improve the lot of the typical truck driver, we were seen as the enemy by a number of fleet operators.

In their view, I had crossed the line and was fraternizing with the enemy.

I ran into conflict, in part, because the strategy had worked beyond our expectations. The Cummins engine had become so differentiated in the eyes of the truck drivers and their union, that there was no substitute. They demanded Cummins engines to drive. Fleet owners felt they had been forced into a position of paying a premium for the Cummins engine and some of them blamed me. I was faced with increasing pressure to change my sales strategy and was ordered to not give the keynote address to the Teamsters Union annual convention.

My values had gotten me in trouble, and now I faced a difficult choice. I could back down and walk away from my sales strategy, which is something everyone should be prepared to do, if a strategy is not working. I felt my strategy *was* working. Sales were up, my company was profiting, and all my customers, from company management to the truck drivers who used our engines, were in a position to benefit. I was being ordered to walk away from a successful strategy for one and only one reason that I could see. It clashed with some traditional management values.

It was time to close the Cummins chapter and seek the next challenge that life might offer.

Reverend Arthur Holt

Sr. Minister (Retired)
Unity Church of Naples

*P*eter, your life story is exciting and inspirational, proof that any good man can make it to the top and beyond. I feel extremely privileged to be counted among your personal friends. Your wisdom expressed in our conversations, and your letters of counsel were most helpful in guiding me through a major transition as I succeeded the reverend founding minister of our church. Your recounting the achievements you made possible at Porsche was not only fascinating, but inspiring because the message was clear; the potential for my own success was mirrored in their metaphors.

6

Managing from Values

When the invitation to speak to the Teamsters Union brought the conflict over my selling strategy to the boiling point, I again faced a situation in which my personal values were not compatible with the corporate culture of the company for which I was working. At Caterpillar, I had forgotten the importance of teamwork and was overly impressed by my youthful accomplishments. I was clearly wrong. This time, it was harder for me to accept that I was wrong. I puzzled over my attachment to a strategy and realized that backing down would constitute disloyalty to an important cause.

It felt right to pursue a strategy that reached out to drivers as well as owners. This was consistent with my personal values and principles. Being ordered to depart from this and focus on OEMs (original equipment manufacturers), made for a serious crisis in my mind. I began to think more deeply about the basic values at stake and how I felt about them.

Give and Take in Business

I believe *giving before taking* is an essential orientation for business and business leaders. It extends into personal life as well.

This became clear when making customer calls in a recession with no intent to press for engine orders.

The saying is "give and take," *not* "take and give." In a civilized society, it is necessary to *first give, and then take.* To grow as a person, it is necessary to first give, pay our dues, and delay the gratification of taking. The approach to life that says: "I want it all, I want it now, and I am not prepared to do what it takes to earn it," hinders growing as a person. The hardships we surmount in *giving* teach us to appreciate what we can later *take*. I found this fundamental in building character and defining personal leadership values.

An example of this is evident in how the United States develops character in military officers. When an individual is admitted to West Point, Annapolis, or the Air Force Academy, the first year's experience is characterized by a great deal of hazing—contrived obstacles placed in the way of progress. Perhaps this makes no sense in the eyes of some, but it is clear to me that the purpose is to force an officer candidate to *give* respect before they can expect to *take* respect from others.

I experienced this in basic training as a draftee in the U.S. Army. Someone who has not had the opportunity to *first learn how to* give *respect to authority* may not learn to *appreciate it. They may never learn how to* take *and use authority effectively without abusing others.* Perhaps worse than that, they might never learn to delay gratification, work for the long term, and learn to help others along the way, even if it means having less for oneself in the short term.

I feel this very deeply because, in my personal case, delay of gratification was the key to my survival and the survival of my family.

Escape

My father, Leopold Schutz, was born into a large Jewish family in Hindenburg, Germany. He had three brothers, four half-brothers, and two half-sisters.

He studied medicine and before the outbreak of World War I, went to sea as a ship's doctor with the North German Lloyd Steamship Line. It came to pass that his ship was docked in Japan when war broke out. Since Japan fought on the side of the Allies in World War I, the ship and its crew, including my father, were interned in Japan for what was to be the duration of the war.

I remember my father telling me the story of how he escaped from the detention camp and made his way to San Francisco. Since the United States did not enter the war until several years later, he succeeded in making his way to New York, boarded a German blockade-runner, and made his way back to Germany. He was subsequently sent to the Russian front as a lieutenant in the Army Medical Corps.

After the end of the war, my father set up a pediatrics practice in Berlin. He married my mother, a Christian woman, and they raised my younger brother, Rudy, and me.

During the 1930s, Adolph Hitler came to power in Germany. This had a major impact on our family. I remember *"Kristallnacht"* (the night of shattered glass) in November 1938 as though it were yesterday. I remember the burning of my school and the defacing of my father's office sign with "JUDE" (Jew) written across it with red paint. I watched as innocent people were brutally beaten by Nazi stormtroopers.

Even before the outbreak of World War II, there was severe rationing of butter, milk, and meat for Jews. Many stores were off limits. An ironic experience was that my birthday, April 20th, is the same as Adolph Hitler's. Germans celebrate birthdays in a big way. After Hitler came to power, there was a big parade for his birthday. (The Nazis found many reasons to have parades.) I thought it was my birthday every time there was a parade.

I shall never forget one experience that took place in October 1938. My father had secured exit visas for himself, my mother, my brother, and me to go to Shanghai, China. It was a desperate measure, but it was getting late in the game; Jews had to find a safe haven somewhere. It was not easy. Most countries were not willing to take on German Jewish refugees. America had a strict quota system and the wait for a number was counted in years.

My father taught at the University in Berlin. The Nazis had imprisoned a number of young Jewish men, among them three of his students. One of the sporting activities the Gestapo carried on at that time was to release such people without money or papers and give them 48 hours to leave the country. Since leaving Germany in these circumstances was virtually impossible, these people were hunted down like animals and most frequently killed or tortured after capture. I remember these three students knocking at our door seeking my father; they had nowhere else to turn. It was the first time that I, at eight years of age, had ever seen a grown man cry. They were absolutely desperate. My father never hesitated. He gave those men three of our exit visas and enough money to get out of the country. We never heard from them again.

It put our family back to square one as far as getting out of Germany was concerned. It was an incredible example of putting the needs of others ahead of one's own! My mother was on the verge of hysteria after my father did that.

Later, my father succeeded in securing five exit visas to Cuba. The fifth visa was intended for my father's brother, Mac, who was managing the family business in Hindenburg. My father contacted Mac and convinced him that time was short. "Come to Cuba with us," he said. Mac came to Berlin and he and my father set off to Hamburg to try to book passage for all of us on a ship to Cuba. For 55 years, I believed a story I was told: My father bribed government officials to secure those Cuban visas.

Mac was a bachelor and had a faithful housekeeper, a lady who had been in his employ for a number of years. Shortly after my father and Mac left for Hamburg, my mother received a telephone call from Mac's panic-stricken housekeeper. The Gestapo had come to Mac's house to arrest him. She told my mother that she was very sorry, but she had told the Gestapo that Mac had gone to visit his brother, my father, in Berlin. She was afraid to withhold that information; she feared for her personal safety.

Within 12 hours, the Gestapo was at our house in Berlin looking for not just Mac, but my father as well. My mother informed them that both men had set off to Hamburg. She did not know exactly where they were going or where they planned to stay.

My mother had no way of getting in touch with my father. By the time the Gestapo got to Hamburg, my father had left for Bremerhafen since he had no luck getting passage in Hamburg.

In Bremerhafen, my father was able to secure passage to Havana, Cuba, on a Norwegian freighter, the Trafalgar. Mac and my father returned to Berlin without knowing that the Gestapo was in hot pursuit.

Upon hearing that the Gestapo was on his trail, my father never hesitated: "We are leaving tonight, not tomorrow, but right now with whatever we can carry easily." We made our way to Stettin, in Upper Silesia, and boarded a Swedish ferry to Oslo, where we would catch up with the Trafalgar. We took a train out of Berlin; it was too dangerous to fly. There were many trains for the Gestapo to watch and only a few airplanes.

The train arrived at the Stettin ferry dock late in the afternoon of March 21, 1939. Trains normally drove right onto the ferryboat, a rather large ship. Once aboard the Swedish ferry, we would be safe, beyond the reach of Hitler's Gestapo. However, our train stopped short of freedom. (To an eight year old, it seemed we were stopped forever; actually, it was probably about an hour.) We noticed people were being taken off the train and were standing on the adjacent track with all of their baggage. Gradually, the detraining activity was closing in on our car. My mother was very upset, and my father was putting what few valuables we had with us in my brother's pockets and mine. Suddenly, a huge (to me) S.S. officer entered our train compartment and confiscated all passports and visas. My parents and uncle Mac were barely able to conceal their panic. It could all end here, so close to freedom.

After what seemed like another interminable period, the S.S. officer returned and threw our papers and passports on a seat in our compartment. Almost immediately the train began to move and we were OUT! In my entire life since then, I cannot recall such a huge feeling of relief. We had made it.

I remember it as though it were yesterday. The ferry was leaving the harbor. The weather was cold and blustery and it was getting dark. My father took me with him as he climbed up to the ship's bridge. Upon my father's request, a very understanding captain took us to the radio room, where my father sent a telegram back to Berlin to let our friends know that we had escaped to freedom successfully.

After Hitler invaded Poland on September 1, 1939, an escape such as ours became nearly impossible.

What Goes Around Comes Around

It was not until many (about 55) years later that I found out how our family actually got those lifesaving exit visas to Cuba.

Hugo, one of my father's brothers, was an attorney practicing in Breslau before World War II. Hugo and his eldest daughter Lori (who now lives in Florida) got out to Havana, Cuba, and joined our little troop a few months after our arrival there. Hugo's wife, my aunt Erna, and their younger daughter Marianne, stayed behind in Breslau. Erna's mother was very ill and she did not want to leave her.

After Erna's mother passed away in the winter of 1941, she and Marianne rode the Siberian Railway to the eastern Russian city of Vladivostoc in Siberia. (Hitler did not invade Russia until June of 1941.) From there, they made their way to the United States. They beat the rest of us there by almost a year. Aunt Erna settled in New York where her husband later joined her. They have both since passed away. Marianne married Steve Wachsner, has two grown children, and lives in Los Angeles. We see one another during my occasional west coast trips.

Marianne has become the Schutz family historian. It was she who explained to me how my father had acquired those exit visas that allowed my family to leave Germany. It had nothing to do with bribery. It had to do with the value of giving, a value I now realize I learned from my father.

Before World War I, a number of the freighters of the North German Lloyd Steamship Line carried 10 to 16 passengers. Passengers ate their meals at the captain's table. There were many valuable items on board, including ornate solid silver tableware and coffee and tea service. After the ship was interned in Japan, the captain had been taken off the ship and my father, as ship's doctor, was in command. He commandeered a group of sailors, took all the silver off the ship, and buried it ashore.

Upon his return to Germany, my father informed the steamship line of what he had done. In 1920, after the end of the war, the steamship line sent a contingent to Japan to retrieve the buried silver and other valuables. They found everything in good condition, exactly where my father had buried it some five years before.

My father was contacted in Berlin after that event and told, "We (the steamship line) are very grateful for what you did for us: *If you should ever need a favor…*"

The steamship line procured the precious exit visas that were our salvation. It took 19 years for my father's action in Japan to be rewarded, proving once again that delayed gratification pays, big time!

Another incident in this difficult period left a deep impression on me when I was old enough to appreciate it. My father was Jewish, my mother was not. Although my mother had converted to Judaism, this did not matter in Hitler's Nazi Germany. If the mother of the children was not Jewish, the children were not Jewish.

As the persecution of Jews heated up in Germany, my mother's family prevailed upon my mother to: "Leave the Jew, this is his problem not yours and your children's. Come live with us, and let the Jew look out for himself."

My mother never hesitated; it was never an issue. *Her place was with my father, come what may.* It was a commitment, a question of loyalty.

The captain of the diesel freighter Trafalgar that took us to Cuba was a veteran skipper who had been torpedoed by a German submarine in World War I. His ship was sunk, and the German submarine crew machine-gunned survivors in the water, killing or wounding many of them, including our captain. Consequently, he hated the Germans so fiercely, that although he could speak German, he simply would not do it until he met my mother. My mother was a very beautiful woman; he decided to speak German to her. We became good friends during the voyage of almost six weeks on the stormy north Atlantic Ocean.

After we disembarked in Cuba, the Trafalgar returned to Norway just as World War II was starting. The Trafalgar continued to sail under the British flag after Norway fell to Germany, and eventually returned to Cuba. We enjoyed a great reunion with our captain and once again shared a dinner at the captain's table on the good ship.

The Trafalgar never completed her next trip. Torpedoed on the return trip to Norway, she went down with all hands, including our friend, the captain.

Life in Cuba was not easy, but at least we were free and safe from deadly persecution. We were poor as church-mice. We had nothing but our health and each other.

In Cuba, my father was not allowed to hold a job. The Cuban government did not issue work permits to European

immigrants for fear of putting the jobs of local citizens in jeop-
ardy. We survived because my father sought out an immigrant
with money who had purchased a shop that sold trinkets to
American tourists. My father managed this shop to earn a mea-
ger living. It was quite a change from being a successful doctor
in Berlin, but we survived.

Watching my parents deal with this situation left me with a
serene confidence in the future, a never-give-up approach to
whatever might come my way.

The following year we were reminded of the fate we had
escaped when the steamship St. Louis arrived in Havana harbor
loaded with European Jewish immigrants. The Cuban government would not allow the hapless passengers to disembark. I
remember my father renting a small boat and sailing out to the
anchored St. Louis with me. We could shout greetings to some
of our friends, but ultimately they and the ship had to leave
Havana harbor.

Denied access to any U.S. port, the ship and its human
cargo returned to Holland, where most of the passengers were
transported to *"Konzentrationslager"* (concentration camps).
Many, including our friends, perished in the Holocaust. (This
incident was later made into a movie entitled *The Voyage of the
Damned.*)

A Journey Completed

After two years in Cuba, we fulfilled our dreams; we acquired
visas to enter the United States of America. It took only two
years, because many quota numbers ahead of ours were voided,
since the holders of the prized lower numbers were trapped in
war-torn Europe. They were not in a position to make use of
their great fortune. In March of 1941, we finally arrived in the
Promised Land: The United States of America.

A Jewish relief agency shipped our family out of New York
City to Toledo, Ohio. The objective was to get refugees out of
New York City; they were piling up there in alarming numbers.

There is no question about it, Toledo was the low point of our odyssey. We had no money. Folding towels in a Chinese laundry was the only job my father could land. In Cuba, there was always the dream of tomorrow. All of a sudden, our tomorrow was here and now, and it was bittersweet!

In the United States at that time, it was not possible for a medical doctor to take a state medical exam and practice medicine without being a U.S. citizen, which took five years.

Our family's sponsor, Mr. Kleinert, a distant cousin in New York City, determined that the state of Illinois was an exception. With his help my father served a required one-year internship at the Jackson Park Hospital on the south side of Chicago and then passed his Illinois State medical exam.

My father resumed his medical practice on the south side of Chicago in 1943. Our family established a normal existence in America.

Shortly thereafter, we went to the movies to see *Yankee Doodle Dandy* starring James Cagney. The film moved us deeply; we were all in tears. Upon our return home, my father sat us down and said, "We are now Americans. There will be no further German spoken in this house." We had finally arrived; we were proud to be Americans.

Making Choices

Another incident reconnected me with my family's German past. My father died in 1955. In 1957, my brother and mother made a pilgrimage back to Berlin. My mother's two brothers had perished in the war, but two of her older sisters had survived and she was eager to visit them.

Upon being reunited with her surviving sisters, 19 years after their separation in 1939, the first words out of my mother's oldest sister's mouth were, "Now that the Jew is dead, there is no reason for you to go back to the United States; you can stay here with us." They had never made the step from taking to giving, and they could not understand the values upon which my parents made their choices. My mother chose to return to America.

I found myself reliving these many adventures as I considered my options in the face of mounting opposition to my sales strategy at Cummins. I had to be true to my values. I realized I really had no choice.

With all of the wonderful teamwork and success that I shared with my Cummins colleagues, whatever motivated me to leave the company?

Focus on the truck driver as my sales philosophy gave rise to some fallout, collateral damage if you will. As mentioned earlier, innovations to improve the lot of the typical truck driver were seen as unacceptable by a number of fleet operators. When I was invited to address the 1977 Teamsters Union annual convention in Washington, D.C., the response was dramatic. A number of fleet operators thought I had crossed the line. I was called on the carpet by Cummins top management, and instructed in no uncertain terms: *"You will not address the Teamsters annual convention in Washington, D.C."*

I felt so deeply committed to the truck driver-focused sales strategy and the related Cummins distributor organization, that it was not emotionally possible for me to abandon or tone down the concept and focus on original equipment manufacturers (OEMs) instead. I did not feel this was about ego. What I could not bring myself to do was to walk away from something that I had come to see as a commitment. It was a question of loyalty, a loyalty to the people driving the trucks, people I had come to view as a band of brothers, *my brothers.*

Twenty-five years later, I was retained as a management advisor to a major truck fleet in Calgary, Canada. I was extended the opportunity to drive a contemporary over-the-road tractor. It was a new Freightliner, powered by a Detroit Diesel engine. I was incredibly moved by what had evolved in the trucking industry in the intervening years. This truck was as luxurious as a top-of-the-line automobile. The engine was superbly powerful, and the noise insulation was outstanding; the air conditioning and hi-fi systems were equal to any luxury car installation. I could not hold the tears back as I drove this truck. It was more than I had ever dreamed possible. The incredible life and reliability of this machine was undoubtedly due in large measure to vastly improved technology: engines, transmissions, fuels, and lubricants. *There is no doubt in my mind that the professionalism such a machine inspires in truck drivers plays a significant role in achieving outstanding results.*

These experiences helped me realize that a generosity of giving is needed to awaken the spirit of driving force in others and get them to commit wholeheartedly to an endeavor.

During the winter of 1977–78, I received an offer to manage the Deutz Diesel and Gas Turbine Division of Klöckner Humboldt Deutz (KHD) in Cologne, West Germany. It was an opportunity to lead an entire business.

So, somewhat like my family in 1939, I left Cummins Engine Company after 11 years and headed (back) to Germany and the unknown.

Franz Blank

CHIEF UNION STEWARD OF PORSCHE AG
(RETIRED)

*T*he book title, The Driving Force, *brings to mind the passion of our common activities at Porsche. I am gratified that the friendship that we developed transcends our business success.*

I wish you success for your new book. It documents the principles of leadership that I learned to love and admire during the time we worked together.

7

Reaching Out
at KHD

The move to Germany and a new company was a traumatic event for me. The new culture and language were
almost overwhelming. Starting at a top management
position made a challenging situation all the more difficult.
Peter Graf zu Dohna, the young assistant to the company CEO,
became my savior during those trying first months in Cologne.
The terminology "Graf zu" is of considerable significance. It
indicates a social position (Count) that once ranked directly
under the Kaiser in German royalty. Before World War II,
Peter's family owned a large castle in East Prussia, a part of
Germany later occupied by Russia. Peter exemplified in all
facets what one thinks of when they hear the title of Count. His
impeccable manners and perfect high German were light years
from mine.

Peter took on the task of getting my German language skills
to an acceptable level and taught me the rudiments of German
etiquette as they applied to business and social situations. The

contrast of these factors with what I had known in the United States up to this point in my career was considerable. Beyond becoming reacquainted with the German language after 40 years, I had to upgrade from the vocabulary of an eight-year-old to contemporary German technical and business language.

One of the cultural elements that had to become second nature was table manners, a seemingly small thing, but fraught with peril. In Germany, it is customary to eat with both arms resting on top of the table and silverware in both hands. The American custom of holding the left arm under the table is not acceptable in German culture. Coffee must not be drunk during a meal, only after eating. Under no circumstances is it acceptable to take a drink from one's glass until the host makes the first formal toast. Learning these practices, among many others, was part of my indoctrination.

Many elements of general conduct also took some getting used to. For instance, there is a great deal of handshaking in Germany. Upon introduction to a couple it is considered *extremely* rude to shake hands with the man first. *Always* shake hands with the woman first. (I still have a problem when upon being introduced to a couple and a man extends his hand to shake while the woman avoids extending hers.)

In the U.S., people address each other as *you* or the equivalent. In Germany, there are two distinct levels of familiarity. It is either *"Sie"* or *"Du."* Upon meeting someone for the first time, the formal term *"Sie" must* be used to address one another. After the pair is acquainted (this often takes several years), the older, or more highly placed individual *may* initiate the use of *"Du."* This is considered an indication of a more intimate relationship that has significance in German society. To be *"per-Du"* with a well-known or highly placed individual is a cherished privilege.

I spent a lot of time and effort trying to avoid embarrassments arising from such rules of conduct. It is all too easy to appear rude or even to insult someone by accident when you do not know the rules. I learned to rely heavily on Peter Graf zu

Dohna, who was a master of etiquette and able to keep me out of serious trouble most of the time.

There were many other things I had to learn as well. As I began my tenure at KHD, I had a solid grounding in the product and customer aspects of the engine business, but was only somewhat familiar with the manufacturing dimension.

Labor unions are very strong in Germany. These organizations play a significant role in the hiring, structure, and accountability of a company's management team.

Corporate Structure in Germany: "*Mitbestimmung*"

The structure of a corporation in Germany differs significantly from its U.S. counterpart. The differences have a pronounced impact on operations. This is particularly evident in the choosing and appointing of top managers and in their accountability. The German system is called "*Mitbestimmung*" (a participative decision process).

The Supervisory Board: The "Aufsichtrat"

A German "*Aktiengesellschaft*," or AG, is a company that has issued and sold stock. By law, an AG has a supervisory board, or an "*Aufsichtrat*." In a business that employs more than 2,000 people, the supervisory board always consists of an even number of members. This can be as few as 12 or as many as 20, depending upon the number of employees. At very large companies such as Volkswagen or Daimler-Benz, there would be 20 members, the maximum. At Porsche, there were 12.

The shareholders, the owners of the company, elect half of the members of the supervisory board. Employees, including members of the union, if there is one, elect the other half, minus one, a "*Leitende Angestelte,*" who is elected by salaried people, such as engineers.

The chair of the supervisory board is selected from the owner-elected members. The vice-chair is elected from the employee-elected members. In the event of a tie vote, the acting chair of the supervisory board can cast the tie-breaking vote on the third ballot.

The duties and responsibilities of a German supervisory board differ significantly from those of a U.S. board of directors. The supervisory board is responsible for the following:

- Hiring and firing financial auditors. (If five-year-olds could hire their teachers, they would all get A's.)
- Signing off capital budgets.
- Approving mergers and acquisitions.
- Appointing and discharging members of the operating board, the "Vorstand."

The Operating Board: The "Vorstand"

The operating board, *"Vorstand,"* is the top management of a German AG. The law does not specify the number of members. One of the members, a full-time *"Arbeitsdirektor,"* *must* be responsible for personnel and human resource matters. Beyond that, any number is allowed.

One member, the *"Vorstandvorsitzender,"* which corresponds roughly to the CEO of a U.S. corporation, is designated as the speaker of the operating board. This was my job at Porsche. In theory, this position is one among equals, the other members of the operating board are technically not subordinate to the speaker.

I have not observed this equality in actual practice. The speaker acts as a CEO, but there are at least three major differences from the authority of a CEO in a U.S. corporation.

The speaker of a German operating board cannot hire and fire other members of the operating board, only the supervisory board can do that. If the speaker wants to hire or fire an operating board member, the facts of the case must be presented to the supervisory board for action.

The supervisory board has no legal authority to tell the operating board or its members what to do. They can suggest.

They can fire members of the operating board, but are not allowed to interfere in the direct management of the company.

No member of the operating board can serve as a member of the supervisory board. No exceptions are allowed.

These structural rules are the laws of the land. *There are no exceptions.* Coming from the very different corporate structure in the U.S., the necessary adjustments were a bigger challenge than table manners and social mores.

Many U.S. CEOs might cringe at the thought of reporting to a board controlled equally by owners and employees. The challenge of being formally and structurally accountable to both owners and employees is a significant departure from U.S. practice.

Restrictions on Formal Power

It is not possible for the operating CEO of a German corporation to dominate the supervisory board in the manner that some CEOs dominate the board of directors in U.S. corporations. This includes staffing and compensation of top management.

Beyond that, in a country where labor unions are strong and have significant representation on supervisory boards, it is virtually impossible for a manager to become a member of an operating board, much less the speaker, without the consent of unions and company employees.

My first confrontational experience with a labor union had taken place in Antioch, California, in 1974. My brother was managing a paper mill for Crown-Zellerbach. The local union called a strike that had dragged on for over 30 days with no settlement in sight.

I was working for Cummins at the time and was scheduled to make a trip to the San Francisco Bay area. My brother asked if I would be willing to visit the Antioch mill and try to mediate the strike situation. Believing my sales experience might be applicable, I agreed to take on the task.

A meeting was arranged for management and union at a local motel on a Monday morning.

I spent Sunday night at my brother's home in Walnut Creek, California, about 40 miles from the meeting site. Upon arising Monday morning, my brother informed me that he would not be going to the meeting with me. "You are going to be killed," he said, "and I cannot handle it."

I was met at the meeting site by the local union leader and his companion, a mountain of a man. Both were angry and belligerent. They led me into a meeting room filled with about 80 angry people. I was scared!

My presentation lasted about two hours and addressed the following subjects:

- We are in this together.
- Unless a win-win solution is formulated *together*, we will *all* lose, *together*.
- We have different agendas, but share a common fate.
- All must be prepared to settle for more than nothing and less than all.

The reaction to these comments was truly amazing. The strike was resolved within a week and the mill was back at work.

Beyond that, the militant leader of the union quit his post and his job at the mill. Claiming he had "seen the light," he started his own business, a small tavern close to the mill where his former union members would convene after working hours. I visited him, and we had a few drinks on the house. He explained how the strike and subsequent meeting at which I spoke, followed by negotiations with management in a new climate, had changed his life.

This served to build my awareness of how building honest and open relationships can overcome divisive situations.

These factors were to play a significant role in my tenure as an operating board member during my time in Germany. They also helped shape my views of leadership in general. I think it is easy for the CEO of a U.S. company to rely (perhaps overly) on formal authority, since the structure provides more opportunity to drive decisions from the executive office. An autocratic style is far more difficult to implement in Germany. The situation compelled me to continue developing my ideas about how to create driving force through a participatory leadership style.

During my initial struggles to get a solid footing at KHD, Paul Bleffert, the chief union steward and a member of the KHD supervisory board, became my good friend and supporter. My open relationship with union members at KHD became the basis for a close working and personal relationship with this man. Without this informal partnership between the peoples' representative and me, I do not think I could have been as effective in my leadership role. Bleffert later helped me build a positive relationship with the union leadership at Porsche.

From St. Louis to Cologne

During my tenure at Cummins, my friend Leo Brewer who had been the head of manufacturing, bought the Cummins distributorship in St. Louis, Missouri. Cummins managers who distinguished themselves with outstanding service would on occasion become eligible to acquire a Cummins distributorship as a reward. Cummins Engine Company would co-sign loans and provide other financial guarantees to make such an acquisition possible. At that time, becoming a Cummins distributor meant you would become a millionaire, usually within a few years. Before Brewer could profit from his new investment, he had to make some significant improvements and overcome a number of challenges. He was short of the capital needed to turn his new business around. Leo had exhausted both his personal wealth and borrowing capacity just to get into this business.

Shortly after the acquisition, Brewer came to visit me in my Columbus, Indiana, office. He had a problem. The business he bought was in bad shape. Above all, the entire facility was dirty and neglected, and Brewer sensed that until he cleaned it up and made it look like a successful business, neither his people nor his customers would lend their support to his efforts to turn it around. Unfortunately, Brewer did not have the resources to pay for the cleaning and painting that was so sorely needed.

We cooked up a plan and Brewer returned to St. Louis to implement it. He went back to his facility and gathered the entire distributorship crew in the shop area.

He addressed the gathering:

> *Look around. What do you see? I'll tell you what I see. I see a pigpen. No way would I want to work in such a filthy and neglected facility. I will also tell you that I cannot afford to have this place cleaned up and repainted. This coming Saturday morning, my wife Shirley, my children, and I are coming here at eight o'clock. We are going to clean this place up ourselves; anyone who wants to help can show up and pitch in. I will provide all of the necessary tools and materials; all I need is your help.*

"*I need your help!*" I have come to learn that those are the most powerful words in the world. (Right after "I love you.")

Saturday at 8 A.M., Leo, Shirley, and the teenaged Brewer kids were hard at work on their hands and knees, scrubbing the shop floor. One by one, employees came by and peeked into the shop. Upon seeing Leo and family working, they went home, got their spouses and kids dressed in working clothes, and returned to help.

By the time the sun set that day, the shop and office areas were sparkling clean.

Brewer announced, "Next week, we are going to paint this place. Once again, I will supply all of the needed tools and materials. Each of you can paint your own work area in any color you like."

The following week, the entire distributorship looked brand new, it had literally been reborn. The camaraderie of those two weekends resulted in more than just a clean shop. *It established the basis of a new culture*, a new relationship between management and labor, and the company took off to new heights of performance.

I recalled this story when, several years later, I found myself leading the Deutz Diesel and Gas Turbine Division of KHD. Behind the main plant was *"Reperaturwerk West,"* an engine rebuilding facility. A visit to this facility disclosed that, just like the Cummins distributorship in St. Louis, it was a filthy and neglected mess. The appearance of the people working there was equally shabby.

I gathered the entire crew in the middle of the shop and told them the Cummins St. Louis distributor story. After the story, I turned on my heel and left without any further instructions. (I mentioned in the introduction that a leader needs to be a good storyteller. This is one of the times when I felt the best way to communicate my point and plant an idea was to tell a story instead of issuing orders.)

A few weeks later, the supervisor of *Reperaturwerk West* came to my office. He asked if I could spare a few moments and accompany him to his shop.

The place was incredibly clean and neat. In the center of the shop was a huge aquarium with goldfish swimming happily in their beautiful new surroundings. The entire plant was spotless. People were dressed in clean work clothes and also spotless. In the small yard behind the plant was a recreational area, with a table, chairs and sun umbrella.

In front of the gathered company, the foreman poked my ribs with his elbow and asked,

Better than St. Louis, eh?

Turning Up the Heat

It was customary for the members of the operating board of a major German corporation to have a company car and an assigned driver. I was not used to this sort of luxury. I made use of a company car, but never got into the swing of having a chauffeur drive me around. Every member of the operating board at KHD received a budgeted amount to spend on a company car, adjusted to the loftiness of the individual's position.

I had a choice of drivers, but decided on Herr Eupen, who had been assigned to my predecessor at KHD. Herr Eupen was a good-hearted man in his 60s, close to retirement. I delegated the task of specifying my company car to Herr Eupen. In order to stay within our budget, he specified the usual Mercedes S class sedan, but one with a six-cylinder, instead of an eight-cylinder, engine. The six-cylinder engine, although less prestigious, was enough lower in price so that he could include a *"standheizung,"* a gasoline-fueled car heater that could warm the car when the engine was not running.

This heater was the subject of ridicule among my peers who would not think of giving up the prestige of an eight-cylinder engine for an accessory they viewed as useless; the driver always had the car thoroughly warmed up before they got in.

The entire operating board would often attend business meetings away from the KHD headquarters building. On those occasions, all the board members would motor to the meeting with their company car and chauffeur. In the cold of winter, the drivers would wait outdoors with their respective cars. They were not allowed to run the car engines while waiting for many hours, and it could be freezing cold.

Since Herr Eupen equipped my new car with an auxiliary heater, all the drivers would crowd into my car to stay warm while they waited.

This became known far and wide in the company and enhanced my reputation with employees and union people. It is an example of the power of a simple gesture to transform leadership climate, sometimes having positive repercussions beyond any the leader might have anticipated. A leader's impact is often the result of the *little things* they do and the small decisions they make, decisions they may not even realize have resonance beyond the immediate issue at hand. People take note of the details of a leader's behavior and draw conclusions that affect their willingness to cooperate.

Dining with the Doctor

I knew little about the history of the company, so I did some research. I learned that one of the predecessors of the current CEO was a gentleman by the name of Dr. Jacob, who still lived in Cologne. My research disclosed that Dr. Jacob left the company under confrontational circumstances more that ten years before. A traditional German of the old school, he had vowed, "I will never again set foot on KHD property." The entire issue was bitter and acrimonious.

I decided to visit Dr. Jacob, who was then in his 80s, at his home. I introduced myself and asked if he would be kind enough to share some KHD history and tradition that preceded the existing management. Once he started he could not stop; a great deal of history came pouring out. It was clear that this old gentleman still cared a great deal about the company and its people. I learned a lot about company history that enabled me to communicate better with people at all levels of the organization.

Upon returning to the company, I suggested that we invite Dr. Jacob and his wife to the upcoming Christmas party, a rather large annual affair. At first this was rejected out of hand. "We will not give the old ____ the pleasure of turning us down," was the prevailing attitude. I insisted. "I do not believe we will be turned down. I am convinced Dr. Jacob would love to be reacquainted with many people in this company."

Dr. Jacob was invited to the 1978 KHD Christmas party, and it was sensational. He sat to the right of the CEO (a big deal in Germany) and beamed. This reunion was an almost spiritual experience, particularly for numerous old timers in the union for whom Dr. Jacob had been an inspirational leader during the "*Wiederaufbau*," the rebuilding of German industry and KHD after World War II. Many KHD people never forgot my role in this event. It solidified my relations with them, particularly with members of the union.

Caring

These events served to establish my reputation with German labor unions. I learned that building useful relationships at all levels of a business is often not a question of giving anything away. It is not just a question of money or benefits. Money and other perks yielded in a grudging contentious manner are not effective. It is a question of giving and caring in a visible manner and enjoying the giving. It costs no more, but yields more in the way of results.

What goes around *does* come around, and these relationships paid huge dividends for me during my subsequent years in Germany.

Paul Bleffert became an officer in the headquarters of the I.G. Metal Union in Frankfurt and was always one of my loyal supporters. The I.G. Metal Union represents all union members in the entire German automobile industry, manufacturers as well as suppliers.

Corruption

Doing business outside of the United States introduced me to a number of practices that differed considerably from what I had become accustomed to. I described some of the differences in etiquette I encountered, and over time, I was able to adapt to those differences. I found it more difficult to cope with what I viewed as corruption. Many practices were standard in KHD's markets that would have been totally unacceptable at Caterpillar, Cummins, and other U.S. firms.

At KHD, there were no set prices for the various engines. Every customer negotiated a proprietary price, most often set by the fringe benefits, which were offered at several levels of the company. (This practice would be unlawful in the U.S.)

Here, I recall a typical annual price negotiation with a major OEM customer.

My spacious office on the top floor of the large KHD office building had an adjacent conference room with a large wooden table. On the day of a typical price negotiation, the door between my large office and this conference room was closed and locked. The conference table was covered with expensive gifts, including Rolex wristwatches, fine leather jackets, and many other luxury goods.

Our negotiations followed the typical pattern for such events: Both customer and company representatives exchanged lies about how difficult times were. I had a member on my staff who could bring tears into the eyes of the toughest customer with his tales of problems. The OEM had a capable counterpart. Each of them put on their best performances as a part of the ritualized negotiation process.

When we finally agreed upon a price, champagne bottles popped and the door to the conference room was opened. Customers lunged at the gifts, their personal reward for a tough negotiation. It was like a scene from the television program *Supermarket Sweep*.

These negotiations took place at our headquarters in Germany, where things were relatively tame compared to the customs in some of our other markets. Negotiations in places like Algeria and Jakarta defy description and comprehension. It is a whole different culture.

Upon returning from my first trip to Indonesia, I gave a great deal of thought to the deep and seemingly hopeless poverty that I observed there. Only the mild climate made it survivable. There was no electricity and running water outside of the bigger cities. Perhaps it was the bad taste left in my mouth from observing the prevailing business practices that led me to feel that we, as a company, could be giving something more, something that might make a positive impact in this impoverished society.

It occurred to me that if this population had the benefit of some electric power, their lives would improve significantly. At KHD, we built and sold electric generator sets that could supply such power. Natural gas or diesel fuel would be needed to fuel such units. These fuels were not readily available in Indonesia, and even if available, could not be afforded by these people.

I recalled reading that Volkswagen automobiles had been powered by gas created in wood-burning generators mounted in the rear of such cars during World War II. There seemed to be a generous supply of wood and other biomass in all parts of Indonesia.

I convened a meeting in the KHD technical center and asked, "Does anyone still work here who was involved in gas generated from burning wood during the war?" It turned out several people were familiar with the technology.

We assembled a small team to build a skid-mounted KHD gas-powered generator set coupled to a newly designed and upgraded version of a World War II Volkswagen wood-burning gas generator. The end product was a container into which wood was fed in one end, and electricity came out of the other.

One such unit could supply power to an entire Indonesian village. The equipment could be readily built in the licensed KHD engine factory in Surabaya, Indonesia. I had one such unit built in Cologne and took it with me on my next trip to Indonesia. (I was bringing the fire truck to school.) I had visions of improving the lives of millions of poor Indonesian people.

I proudly presented the unit to the Indonesian minister of industry, convinced that the application would be obvious. My efforts were received graciously. The minister was impressed with KHD technology. He was most grateful for our thoughtful efforts on behalf of the people of his country. Many nice words were said, but there was not much action. The generator ended up on the minister of industry's country estate, and that was that. "Many thanks to you and your KHD colleagues, Herr Schutz."

This reminds me of another incident that illustrates what I perceived as rampant corruption. The local KHD representative and I were headed to Surabaya from Jakarta, Indonesia, on

Garuda, the Indonesian national airline. Upon arriving at the airport, we found that our scheduled flight, Garuda ABC, due to depart at 14:30, was fully booked.

My associate placed a DM 100 bill in front of the young woman at the check-in counter.

Suddenly, an announcement blared over the speakers throughout the airport. "Garuda flight ABC, to Surabaya, has been cancelled. Garuda flight XYZ, to Surabaya, will leave at 14:45. Tickets are for sale at the check-in counter, first come, first served." We, of course, were able to buy the first two tickets.

What a way to do business!

KHD was truly a worldwide operation. There were licensed factories in Surabaya, Indonesia; Zagreb, Yugoslavia; Algiers, Algeria; and the United States and Canada. I traveled around the world in the line of duty and got priceless exposure. I gained valuable lessons as a "driving-force manager." I had seen how effective it could be to reach out to groups of people, in the labor union on a formal basis or in smaller groups informally. (I learned the same principles can apply in Cologne as in St. Louis.) This was true even on an individual basis, as in the case of the driver of my company car. I felt blessed by the kind and enthusiastic support of the many people I had reached out to during my tenure at KHD. In spite of this, I felt my adventures at KHD might be coming to an end.

It *was* truly a great adventure, but I found this company, particularly its top management, did not offer a culture, a set of operating values, with which I could ever become comfortable.

This is not a judgment of their business. I simply did not fit with the values and principles of that organization. As I continued to gain experience, the significance of such things became increasingly clear to me. With my eyes and ears open for other opportunities, I was prepared to return to the good old United States rather than continue at KHD.

Then, a wonderful opportunity came along during the summer of 1980. I was offered the position of Porsche CEO.

Hans Epple

SALARIED EMPLOYEE REPRESENTATIVE,
(*LEITENDE ANGESTELTE*), PORSCHE
SUPERVISORY BOARD, (*AUFSICHTRAT*) RETIRED

*A*s a long-time employee of Porsche, I had the good fortune to have Peter W. Schutz as a leader and accompany him on a portion of his professional career.

Peter Schutz lost no time in making the most of Porsche tradition to reestablish company success.

As a representative of salaried employees on the supervisory board I can attest to the deep understanding that he had for the plight and needs of company employees.

The book title, The Driving Force, *adequately describes the passion and commitment Mr. Schutz generated among all connected with Porsche. Driving Force describes the passion Peter brought out in me.*

8

Porsche Arrives at a Crossroad

In 1980, Porsche AG, the sports car builder domiciled in Stuttgart, West Germany, had come upon difficult times. The decade of the 1970s had been a trying time for the automobile industry, in particular the sports car and performance segment. Heightened concerns for the deteriorating environment had resulted in legislation that forced technical improvements in noise and exhaust emission levels and strained available technology beyond the achievable. In the latter part of the decade, oil shortages and concerns for safety added to the challenge.

The result was a deterioration of automobile engine performance levels and reliability and a massive negative image of performance automobiles and automobile racing. Most automobile manufacturers had withdrawn from active racing competition; sports cars and high performance automobiles were at a low ebb.

Porsche sales had declined. 1980 was the first money-losing year in the company's history. A significant number of new unsold Porsche sports cars were parked in a field behind the Zuffenhausen assembly plant, some more than a year old. The company had significantly withdrawn from motor sport competition.

Origins

In Germany, many titles are honorary, bestowed upon people for business accomplishment, social, or political reasons. Therefore, many people addressed as *"Doktor"* or *"Professor"* often carry such honorary titles. As we proceed in this book, when I refer to "Professor Porsche," I am referring to the son of the original Professor Ferdinand Porsche senior.

Professor Porsche, Sr., was a technical genius. In the early years of the 20th century, he invented a number of revolutionary vehicles, including an electric wheel concept that gave rise to road trains. These consisted of wagons that had axles individually powered by electric motors and could be coupled together like a railroad train. Most roads in that era were poorly paved and became impassable in the rainy season. This concept made it possible to negotiate terrain that offered impossibly poor traction for conventional vehicles.

After designing a number of advanced automobiles, he became chief engineer at Daimler-Benz in the late 1920s. He was the designer of the magnificent Mercedes K series of automobiles, some of the most powerful and beautiful cars ever built.

A brilliant engineer, story has it that he was a difficult and headstrong personality. Feeling held back by the corporate establishment at Daimler-Benz, he left that organization to start his own engineering company in the early 1930s. A number of automotive achievements during that time were crowned by his design of the Volkswagen, the "people's car," during the Nazi era.

After World War II, the French detained Professor Porsche, Sr., for alleged activity during the war years. In his absence, his son Ferdinand took over the rebuilding of the

Porsche Engineering Company. He gathered surviving members of the organization in Stuttgart and headed the engineering effort to support the production of the Volkswagen in the Wolfsburg manufacturing facility.

It was during this period that Ferdinand Porsche conceived the first Porsche sports cars. These vehicles were basically a Volkswagen with a new two-seater streamlined body, the vehicle that became the Porsche 356. I have been told that the creation of a Porsche automobile was never in the plans of the senior Professor Porsche; his son was the father of the Porsche sports car.

Enter the Porsche 911

In the mid 1960s, the company introduced the Porsche 911 as a successor to the 356. Among a number of famous specialty cars, it was the 911 that became the foundation of a successful Porsche automobile business. The car was light and powerful and had rather unique handling characteristics. It was not easy to drive; it had a tendency to spin around in a fast curve if mishandled. In the hands of a capable driver, it was extremely quick.

Beyond that, its unique rear-mounted air-cooled engine made unusual noises that became theme music for true Porsche lovers.

During this period, Ferdinand Piëch, a son of Ferdinand Porsche's sister, was in charge of engineering at the company. Ferdinand Piëch is one of the great technical automotive geniuses of the 20th century. Before retiring at the end of 2001, he had risen to be CEO of Volkswagen, an organization he took to international prominence. In those early Porsche years, it was Ferdinand Piëch who put Porsche into international motor sport prominence.

Among all the great racing Porsches, it was Piëch and the Porsche 917 that established Porsches as something more than cute little cars that were giant killers, winning races against much bigger and more powerful opponents. With the legendary 917, Porsche arrived in big-time racing.

In the early 1970s, the Porsche family withdrew from active management of the company. The first head of the company who was not a family member was Professor Ernst Fuhrmann, a brilliant engineer. Professor Fuhrmann was the engineer behind the high performance Porsche cars of the 1970s, including the awesome 911-turbo, a monster of a sports car in its time. A legacy of racing successes resulted from the 934, 935, and 936 Porsche racing cars that dominated this period.

Replacing the Porsche 911

During his tenure, Professor Fuhrmann also undertook the task of replacing the Porsche 911 with two water-cooled front engine cars, the Porsche 924 and 928. These cars were technically advanced for their time, although the 924s were underpowered. Both featured a transmission mounted at the rear axle of the car. With the engine mounted at the front, this resulted in excellent front-to-rear weight distribution, important in a high performance sports car. Among other things, this was intended to alleviate a cantankerous characteristic of the rear-engine 911, which was a tendency for the rear of the car to swing around to the front in a fast turn if the driver released the gas pedal suddenly.

Both the 924 and 928 featured a number of innovative designs that set new styling patterns. These included retracting headlights, plastic covered bumpers, wheels without hubcaps, and beautifully streamlined body styling.

The popular Porsche 911 was scheduled to be discontinued at the end of the 1982 model year. The prevailing opinion at the company was that the rear-mounted air-cooled engine could not be brought into compliance with anticipated noise and exhaust emission legislation. A decision had been made to move Porsche beyond the air-cooled, rear-mounted engine era. The new Porsche era was to be built around the 924 and 928 models powered by liquid-cooled front-mounted engines.

Professor Fuhrmann had moved Ferdinand Porsche out of the main Porsche plant in Zuffenhausen (Stuttgart) to the parts warehouse and sales facility in Ludwigsburg, about ten kilometers away. I was given to understand by Professor Porsche that Professor Fuhrmann wanted to "put his own signature on Porsche," a signature that did not include Professor Porsche and the Porsche family.

Sales, profits, morale, and Porsche culture were on shaky ground. The car that many people viewed as the heart of Porsche was about to be discontinued.

Such was the posture of Porsche in the spring of 1980 when the Porsche family decided to replace Professor Ernst Fuhrmann as CEO of Porsche AG.

Dieter Rickert

EXECUTIVE RECRUITER

*A*s executive search consultant I have recruited more than half of all significant managers in Germany in the past 25 years. When I am asked today who are the most impressive people you have encountered in the worldwide automobile industry, four names come to mind: Bob Lutz, Daniel Goeudevert, Helmut Werner, and last but not least, Peter W. Schutz.

Of all managers that I know, Peter Schutz is the one that has the clearest grasp of psychology of leadership. Beyond captivating the passion of his people, he is also a born marketing man, who understands better than anyone I have encountered how to ascertain and articulate customer expectations.

As he took over the Porsche leadership he was confronted by a demotivated company. Within one year, no one doubted that Porsche was back as a winner. I recall that as he decided to accept the Porsche challenge, Peter had specific ideas for leadership and took Porsche on as an experiment to verify his leadership concepts. The results of the years that followed have confirmed the validity of these concepts.

I am most pleased that Peter Schutz has documented these concepts in his book, The Driving Force.

9

Taking the Wheel
at Porsche

I n April 1980, the telephone rang in my office at
Klöckner–Humboldt–Deutz. A man by the name of Doctor
Schubart was calling to ask if I would be interested in inter-
viewing for the position of CEO of a major German corporation. He was not at liberty to disclose the name of his client
company, but mentioned it was in the automotive business.

Dr. Schubart, from his office in Frankfurt, had done his
homework. He knew I was an airplane pilot, although I had not
piloted an airplane in over two years. He announced that he was
a pilot and would be ready to fly his airplane to Cologne to meet
with me and discuss his client's interest. I replied, "Of course,
you would let me fly your airplane while you are here, right?"
"Of course," he replied.

Dr. Schubart came to Cologne. I flew his airplane and we
talked. After some hesitancy, he disclosed that his client was
Porsche AG, the world-renowned sportscar builder. I saw myself
as totally unqualified for such a position; I was a diesel engineer.

Somewhere I had learned: *Never turn any job down until after it has been offered.* Since I had not heard an offer, I responded, "Why not?"

Soon after, I found myself at the Porsche estate, a beautiful mansion on a hill overlooking Stuttgart, confronted by the ten owners of Porsche AG: Professor Ferdinand Porsche, his sister Frau Piëch, the professor's four sons, and Frau Piëch's three sons and daughter. All of them were shooting questions at me. I was not doing very well with answers, until I finally decided to end the interview saying, "I do not believe I am qualified for this job; I am a diesel engineer!"

The response was, "Herr Schutz, you do not seem to understand our situation. We already have people who know how to design automobiles. We have people who know how to build them and sell them. We have people who understand the purchasing infrastructure that you say you are not familiar with. That is not our problem. *Our problem is we are not making any money!*

"We have listened to people in the company, the managers, the dealers, and the customers. We have listened to our suppliers and knowledgeable advisors familiar with the automotive industry. We have received diverse and confusing responses. Everyone seems to have a different idea of what is wrong and what should be done to correct our problems.

"We are looking for someone who can get these capable people to march in the same direction and work together. In those circumstances, we are quite sure good things would begin to happen."

"Well," I said, "now that you put it that way, I believe I might know how to do that."

The response was, "We are very glad you see it that way Herr Schutz. The reason you are here today is because we believe that as well; we have done our homework and are familiar with your career. We plan to interview an additional 12 candidates for this job, so please do not call us, we will call you."

Possibilities

Upon returning to Cologne, I told Sheila that it had been a great day. I had met some really great people, however, it was unlikely that anything would result in the way of a job offer.

During the summer of 1980, there was a series of meetings with Porsche AG owners, members of Porsche management, union members, dealers, etc. On September 1, I received a phone call: "You can have the job if you want it." I replied, "I'll take it!"

On January 7, 1981, Sheila and I went to Stuttgart as husband and wife and became a part of the Porsche team.

It was now time to get down to business and begin the task of rebuilding Porsche. In many discussions with Porsche employees, owners, and customers, I had learned enough to have an inkling of what was wrong. Whenever I talked with anyone, eventually the conversation came back around to one subject that seemed to be on everyone's minds.

Two major challenges—the lack of profitability and the poor morale—appeared to have their foundation in the same development: *the planned and imminent discontinuation of the still-popular Porsche 911 sports car.*

The Porsche 911 Reconsidered

There were a number of practical reasons to discontinue the 911. Detailed technical analysis had determined that the air-cooled engine that had powered this automobile for over ten years could only meet upcoming regulations for reduced noise and exhaust emissions with great difficulty. The 911 was not as easy to drive as more modern concepts. The Porsche 911 had its origins in the Volkswagen beetle. Although highly evolved from that machine, the 911 retained some of the cantankerous handling characteristics of its ancestor.

The 911 was challenged on numerous occasions. Why did Porsche persist in propagating these strange handling characteristics, when state-of-the-art engineering could facilitate far more civilized performance?

The Porsche Australian importer visited me in my Stuttgart office and put the question to me: "Why did Porsche continue to build such a difficult handling car, a car that required a driver with above-average skill to drive well?"

My answer had its basis in my flying experience. I have been an airplane pilot for several decades. Most of the aircraft I have flown and owned over the years have been equipped with a tail-wheel landing gear as opposed to the more modern tricycle landing gear.

A tail-wheel airplane has more cantankerous ground handling characteristics than its tricycle gear counterpart (in which the third wheel is placed near the front instead of the rear). A tail-wheel airplane will ground-loop, careen in a sharp circle, and in some instances, end up on its back if not handled with skill and respect. One such airplane I owned and flew for a number of years was a Fairchild PT-23, a World War II Army Air Corps training plane.

I explained to my Australian visitor that when I flew this airplane to a small airport and did a chandelle after a high-speed pass over the runway followed by a perfect wheel landing, *every eye on the airfield would be waiting to see who got out of the airplane.* They knew it took a bit more than average flying skill to carry that series of maneuvers off well. It was a point of piloting pride.

In like manner, when a Porsche 911 owner drove their car well, it garnered the respect of peers, a point of driving pride.

The point had been made. A few weeks later, I received a gift from several Porsche importers: an aircraft tail-wheel mounted on a beautiful wood plaque with the inscription: *To the Porsche tail-wheel philosophy.*

Professor Fuhrmann was responsible for introduction of the models 924 and 928 Porsche automobiles intended to replace the 911. The 928 cars were powered with modern liquid-cooled V-8 engines, and the smaller model 924, with an adaptation of four-cylinder liquid-cooled engine designed and produced by Audi.

The Porsche 928 was an outstanding technical achievement, unquestionably a vehicle at the cutting edge of technology in its time. The 924 did not gain acceptance as a *real* Porsche. It lacked the power and performance expected by Porsche customers. When I got to Porsche, work was well underway to improve the somewhat tame styling and re-power the car with a more powerful Porsche designed four-cylinder aluminum engine. As the model 944, this car became successful and continued in production profitably for more than ten years.

A great deal of sound technical thinking went into these new Porsche automobiles. One objective was to eliminate the perceived instability or nervousness of the rear-engine 911.

This characteristic, the *directional instability*, can be described in positive terms as *maneuverability*. It is a function of the driver's point of view. Some drivers love a car that is stable, a car that continues to go straight until the driver takes action to make it turn. It goes in the direction in which it is steered.

On the other hand, some drivers love a car that will change its heading as a function of things other than just steering. Highly maneuverable racing cars and sports cars can be steered with the engine throttle and brakes in fast turns.

The Porsche 911 was this kind of car.

The 944 and 928 were not.

A well-balanced car will have about the same weight carried by the front wheels as the rear wheels a 50 percent–50 percent weight distribution.

When an ice-skater twirls with arms extended, the rate of rotation is slow. If arms are pulled in close to the body, the rate of rotation will speed up. This is dictated by the conservation of polar momentum. The energy of rotation is the product of rotational speed and polar moment of inertia of the rotating body. When the skater pulls arms in closer to the body, the polar moment of inertia is reduced.

Because the total energy of rotation must be conserved, the rotation must speed up. All of this has been decided by God; it is a fundamental law of nature.

If outstanding maneuverability is the objective, the heaviest components of the car are concentrated as close together and as near the middle of the car as possible. This is why racing cars and many high-performance automobiles have the engine, transmission, and occupants placed as close together as possible. It enhances the car's maneuverability.

The Porsche 924, 944, and 928, the vehicles intended to replace the nervous 911, were like figure skaters with their arms extended for slow spins. The engine in the front and transmission in the rear were designed to optimize stability instead of maneuverability. This resulted in stable touring cars that were outstanding technical achievements, but not real Porsches in the eyes of the hard-core Porsche faithful. *Neither of those new vehicles was able to replace the about-to-be-discontinued Porsche 911 in the hearts of Porsche customers and dealers.* It was essential for us to recognize what our faithful hard-core customers were looking for and make sure we gave it to them.

Saving the Porsche 911

A deep sense of loss, a grieving that was almost heartbreaking, was gathering like a storm. The new Porsche offerings could not replace the revered 911. To me, a newcomer, the feeling of impending catastrophe was overpowering.

The decision to keep the 911 in the product line occurred one afternoon in the office of Professor Helmut Bott, the Porsche operating board member responsible for all engineering and development. I noticed a chart on the wall of Professor Bott's office wall. It depicted the ongoing development schedules for the three primary Porsche product lines; 944, 928, and 911. Two of them stretched far into the future, but the 911 program stopped at the end of 1981. I remember rising from my chair, walking over to the chart, taking a black marker pen and extending the 911 program bar clean off the end of the chart. I am sure I heard a silent cheer from Professor Bott. In his calm reserved way, he let out a loud hurrah! I knew we had done the right thing.

The Porsche 911, the company icon, had been saved, and I believe the company was saved with it.

Vaughn Beals

VICE PRESIDENT OF ENGINEERING OF CUMMINS ENGINE COMPANY AND CEO OF HARLEY DAVIDSON (RETIRED)

I hired a well-recommended young Caterpillar engineer named *Peter W. Schutz. What I did not know was that buried in there was a great marketing talent! Both the engineering and marketing talent served Cummins and Porsche well.*

10

Imagining the Future

A major step in the rebirth of Porsche had been achieved. More was needed to get the company moving forward. Something *exciting* had to be added to the product offering. Many customers who were candidates to buy a new Porsche already owned one. Beyond that, existing Porsche cars frequently lived a better life than their owners. They never went out into the rain and stayed home in cold weather. How could loyal Porsche owners be moved to buy a new car?

It was time to do some marketing and new product development.

We initiated an intensive questioning of customers, dealers, and importers. We listened to Porsche management, people, and suppliers. We heard the following:

- Porsche cars are too darned expensive.
- Porsche quality is not adequate.

So, according to customer research, all we had to do was reduce prices and make cars with fewer defects. I could not bring myself to believe it would be that simple. I could not see myself, the new leader, getting up in front of the organization and inspiring them to cut costs and improve quality. It was not sufficiently compelling to re-energize the company. I had to get beyond that.

Sharing a Dream

Subsequently, Professor Porsche and I sat together, as we often did, to discuss the future of the company.

I recall asking him, "Tell me Professor, what ever moved you to take a Volkswagen Beetle, remove the body, replace it with a streamlined two-seater body, call it a Porsche, and charge five times as much money?"

He replied, "I did not listen to any salespeople; I did not question any customers or listen to my engineers. I simply built my dream car, figuring that others would share my dream."

This had a hauntingly familiar ring to it. Where had I observed this before? It was Clessie Cummins and his truck diesel engine all over again.

I learned the difference between a change from a short-term focus of *exceeding* customer expectations to a longer-term focus of *re-defining* customer expectations. The differences are profound and have major impact on a business and its structure.

An effective way to present what I have learned is to address the impact on the four major activities that are basic to any business:

Core Function	Exceeding Expectations	Redefining Expectations
Customer interaction	Sales	Marketing
Adding value	Production	Developing new products
Accounting	Bookkeeping	Finance
Personnel	Personnel department	Human resource development

Exceeding customer expectations in the short term is called selling. It has to be professional selling, based on a clear understanding of what customer expectations are, coupled with an offering that can exceed them. But it is still sales and its orientation is to go out and engage in transactions based on what customers currently want and need.

We must keep our eye on the customer and not the profit and loss ledger. There is nothing happening on the ledger. If we take our eye off the customer to look at the ledger, we will miss the sale. I love the song by Kenny Rogers about the gambler: "You never count your money while you're sitting at the table, there is time enough for counting when the dealing's done." After the customer contact is over, you can look at the ledger. This may be useful in order to plan sales tactics, etc., but if we take our eye off the customer to check profit while the customer contact is active, we can miss the sale.

Exceeding customer expectations (selling) requires full concentration on the customer at hand. If we become distracted by other events, we will miss the sale. That is why I define it as focusing on *customer interaction* in the above table.

Since the objective of selling is to exceed customer expectations in the short term, it seems clear that we must focus on customer expectations, not as they might have existed in the past, not as they might exist in the future, but expectations as they exist right now, today.

How do we determine customer expectations, as they exist right now, today?

We ask and listen. *If you listen closely enough, your customers will explain your business to you.* Selling is a very customer-focused activity.

Selling and other activities that focus on exceeding existing customer expectations are fundamentally *reactive* in nature.

In business, this strategy can be expressed as follows:

Until the situation that confronts us has been thoroughly investigated, documented, and confirmed by appropriate

127

authorities, we will not commit the resources of the business to action. It sounds like a good, careful, responsible way to manage. However, it has one drawback that sometimes proves fatal. It is a reactive *strategy.*

A popular solution in business is to appoint coordinators or middle managers to assign responsibility and organize accountability. We might end up with a number of departmental coordinators. Next, we might need a coordinator to coordinate the activities of the coordinators.

What is wrong with this picture?

Nothing is wrong if you find you can operate profitably after paying all those coordinators and managers. Beyond costs, this can give rise to complex interactions that can get in the way of performance. It is a common consequence of applying a reactive strategy to a changing situation.

In the good old days, deciding what to do next was not so much of a challenge. Customer expectations tended to be relatively unchanging. Once we figured out what they were, basic business challenges were reduced to lower prices and higher quality.

That has changed dramatically. Today, technology and resulting customer expectations are changing rapidly. Our efforts to cope with such a challenge in the good old reactive style can lead to complicated, top-heavy, and difficult-to-manage expensive business structures.

A *proactive* strategy is needed in today's less predictable business climate.

Taking the Initiative

We cannot predict the most likely expectations of our customers after change has occurred. *It is not possible to determine future expectations of customers by listening to them.*

We must use our vision and imagination to:

Decide what customer expectations are likely to be *after* change has occurred.

It is a difficult task. No one can predict the future, in spite of all best efforts. That is not the problem. Since no one can foretell the future with any reasonable degree of reliability, it would be foolhardy to bet the business on such predictions.

The important element in this activity is less a case of predicting the future, but rather of considering the following:

Are you, the manager, prepared to take the risk of getting the business into position to meet future customer expectations with your best effort?

That is how you can become a successful market leader.

There is risk associated with any proactive business activity. There are no guarantees. With our best efforts, we can fail to predict the situation correctly. Having made the investment in time, money, and energy, we can find ourselves in the wrong place, at the wrong time, with the wrong product or service offering.

If you have taken a risk, turned out to be wrong, and are now hopelessly out of position to serve the customer, it may be tempting to decide:

"Never again will I take such a risk and look this foolish!"

This can result in once again becoming reactive, and the consequences previously presented will result. If we defer action until we know where the market is heading, we will be constantly chasing after it.

If we are chasing after the market, we are not thinking about being a leader. Instead, we are just trying to survive.

A business that employs a reactive strategy in times of accelerating change will frequently find itself in an unending battle to just survive. Salespeople will find themselves fighting to match competitors' offerings. The company can descend into the trap of being a commodity business, competing on price and quality.

This can be a difficult thing to remember when you are in a tough situation, as Porsche certainly was. It is easier to fall

129

back on reactive strategies. They feel safer, but will rarely produce a winner.

We must be aware of competition, operating environment, and our own capabilities and limitations. *We must take a risk and become proactive.*

Become proactive and redefine customer expectations—known as marketing and/or new product development.

If there is little or no change going on, present customer expectations and future customer expectations are the same. This can lead to the conclusion that selling and marketing are basically the same thing.

The greater the rate of change, the greater the difference between *selling and production (exceeding* customer expectations) vs. *marketing and new product development (redefining* customer expectations).

It is not possible to ascertain future expectations of customers and redefine them by listening to anyone engaged in sales and production-focused activity. No one engaged in *existing* activity, neither sales people nor dealers, can get this job done well.

Activities, such as customer surveys, are useful in *selling*; they are a good way to determine customer expectations as they exist *in the present*, in the short term.

Understand that customer surveys are rarely useful in marketing and new product development.

Customer surveys will frequently result in two responses:

1. *The product or service is too expensive.* Many business organizations will expend their limited resources in efforts to reduce costs and achieve a lower selling price. There is nothing wrong with achieving a lower cost structure and thus a lower selling price, but it is a reactive short-term activity. It will not address the redefining of customer expectations.

2. *There is a quality problem or deficiency.* Many businesses will expend their limited resources in efforts to improve quality and solve quality deficiencies. There is nothing wrong with striving for better quality, but it is a reactive short-term activity. It will not address the redefining of customer expectations.

I would like to illustrate this important point with a fictitious example: Imagine it is 20 years ago and a company, let's call it Music Man, is in the business of manufacturing and distributing phonograph records. You remember those big vinyl disks that played music? Business is good. The company is making money and exceeding customer expectations.

At some point, a decision is made. Wouldn't it be great if the company could do some marketing and get a fix on what customers would like in the future? What are the customers expectations in the long(er) term likely to be? Is it possible to redefine customer expectations?

A customer survey is initiated and customers are asked, "What kind of phonograph records could Music Man provide for you in the future?"

There is a major mistake here. *It is not possible to be in the phonograph record business!*

Phonograph records are the contemporary product. *There is no phonograph record business.* The business is *reproducing sound.* We know this now of course, because we have the advantage of hindsight, but it was certainly not clear to many people who depended on sales of phonograph records for their living.

Never define a business around the product or service when striving to redefine customer expectations.

If the customer survey proceeds, responses might be as follows:

- *The phonograph records are too expensive.* Many companies exhaust their limited resources in efforts to reduce costs and offer a lower price to the customer. This will serve to further exceed customer expectations, but will not redefine them.

- *The records scratch too easily.* This is a perception of deficient quality. Many companies exhaust their limited resources in efforts to improve quality. This will serve to further exceed customer expectations, but will not redefine them.
- *There is an unpleasant hissing background noise.* This might suggest the development of a lower friction vinyl. Again, this will exceed customer expectations, but will not redefine them.
- *Needles need to be better. Soft needles wear out; hard needles wear records out.* The solution might be to develop better needle materials.

These are all good ideas and might help a company do better in the short term. How many customers must be interviewed before the following expectations would emerge?

- Offer a compact laser disk for which customers are prepared to pay half again as much as they are currently paying for phonograph records.
- A desire to box up the entire phonograph record collection, deposit it in the attic, and replace it with a new collection of higher-priced compact laser disks.
- Discard the phonograph record player for which customers paid a great deal of money a few years ago and replace it with new equipment to play compact laser disks.

It is not likely that these expectations would surface in a customer survey, at least not one conducted on this planet. Such customer expectations, ones that redefine the business, are not likely to emerge from a customer survey.

We cannot do good proactive marketing or new product development by listening to our customers.

It is helpful to keep in mind that there was no customer demand for the

- transducer
- airplane

- automobile
- Internet
- microwave oven
- Clessie Cummin's truck diesel engine

No one asked Steven Jobs to invent the personal computer.

Proactive marketing and new product development activities that redefine the business require a totally different approach. This has major implications for organizational structure, as well as the process employed for marketing and new product development.

Taking the Lid off Product Development

No one, but no one, had asked for a convertible in all the questioning and surveying that I initiated at Porsche; responses had been about price and quality.

After the meeting with Professor Porsche that opened my eyes about marketing, I decided Porsche should make a convertible version of the 911 coupe.

Why? I liked the idea. I thought a convertible would be an exciting new product.

I met with Professor Bott, the head of engineering, and asked him: "Porsche once built a beautiful 356 cabriolet. Does the man who built that car still work for us?" I was told: "Yes, he does. His name is Herr Bauer, who is 65 years old and about to retire." "Could we get him up here to join us?" I asked. Herr Bauer joined the meeting. After telling him how much I liked his 356 cabriolet, I asked if he could make a convertible out of the Porsche 911. "Give me six helpers and eight weeks and you will have your convertible 911," he replied.

Herr Bauer built a truly classic cabriolet out of the 911 Targa. The car was in production within eight months, an incredible performance in its time.

Let's recap the product strategy for Porsche's turnaround because it is still a compelling and somewhat surprising one that has served as a good model for other companies I've interacted with in succeeding years. What exactly did we decide to do? *Instead of responding to the customer request for a less costly and more trouble-free car, we built a convertible with a price (note that I purposefully did not say cost) approximately 20 percent higher than the contemporary coupe. It also created a whole new set of quality problems (challenges) that we never had before.*

Some tops leaked and some of the window seals whistled. In a standard quality survey, this new car would not have ranked at the top of the list. New models seldom do; they frequently have some kinks that need to be worked out over time.

The problems proved inconsequential because the product was unique.

Dealers and customers loved it. The Porsche 911 Cabriolet redefined customer expectations without tarnishing the Porsche image. It also gave some of our loyal customers a good reason to purchase a new Porsche.

By saving the Porsche 911, we also saved an invaluable company icon. *The Porsche 911 was in a position to lead the company to new heights.*

For a business to redefine customer expectations and move to the next level, it is vital that such proactive activities be implemented.

To bring about efforts that carry with them a probability to redefine the business and perhaps an entire industry requires extensive inspiration. Major effort and a lot of perspiration will be required to translate such an opportunity into success.

Success that goes significantly beyond that which can be achieved through cost reduction and quality improvement of contemporary activities will be a competitive edge until the world inevitably catches up.

Inspiration can lift a business to the next level, moving out of the commodity business and into a differentiated business that opens the opportunity to become a leader in the industry.

Perspiration is the basis for *exceeding* customer expectations. Redefining customer expectations is in large measure the result of *inspiration*.

Inspiration is frequently based on the achievement of an individual that will only come to full fruition from the perspiration of a diverse team of people working together.

With the saving of the 911 and the creation of a convertible, we were well on our way toward redefining Porsche customer expectations. We had a better idea of how to turn the corner and bring the company to new levels of success. We still had a lot of work ahead to make it happen.

Bert Jones

FOUNDER OF PERCEPTION PROFILES, INC.

*W*e have known each other, both professionally and as friends, for many years and you continue to amaze me. You write and talk about how much you have learned from others and how important it is to listen to what others have to say. If the truth be known, it is I who have learned so much from you. Our conversations have always been inspirational and educational and never cease to be fascinating.

11

Creating a Culture of Excellence

I n 1979 and 1980, Porsche had slow sales years. Several hundred new unsold automobiles, mostly 924 models, were parked in a field behind the factory with weeds growing around them. Some were over two years old.

This was a serious situation. It showcased the lack of sales and was a constant reminder of what was clearly a failure to perform. It was depressing in that it drove home the poor profit performance and had a negative impact on company morale.

It was clear to me that until that situation was rectified, the company would continue in the doldrums. Anything I did to boost morale was going to be diminished by this depressing sight. Nobody was motivated to put out major effort in the face of this all too visible inventory of unsold automobiles collecting dust in the field behind the factory.

We *had* to shed this millstone of inventory.

As I looked into it, I realized that the *cost* of creating this inventory was buried in the expenses of the previous years. It was the expense that had given rise to the lack of profit. Accountants had already punished the company for this unsold inventory and we were punishing ourselves all over again by staring at it every day.

The cars had been built, but not sold.

The answer seemed simple: *Sell them!*

We had a meeting of Porsche importers and dealers and involved them in the solution of a major problem that was *our* problem.

We showed them the inventory of unsold Porsches behind the plant before the meeting. The question I put to the assembled group was simply, "What would it take to make those unsold cars go away?"

The answer was, "Give us a DM 2,500 discount off the normal dealer price and they are gone!"

Within a week, these cars were shipped and the obstacle was history.

The unexpected consequence, something that had not entered into my thinking, was that all the revenue went right to the bottom line. We had immediately turned a profit in the current year.

In terms of the turnaround, we had sold cars that were "free" as far as the current year was concerned. The full amount of revenue generated from the inventory liquidation went to the bottom line as cash flow and profit.

Porsche finished the 1980–1981 business year (June 30 to July 1) with a DM 12 million profit. Of course, part of the profit was stolen from the past, but this was not just about money. It put Porsche back on its feet. We had taken a step to jettison the past.

The company was in position to move on. It was time to rebuild the Porsche culture.

Company history and culture had been a most important component of past Porsche success.

On a number of occasions, I have been asked how it was to return to Germany, the country from which my family and I had fled so long ago, losing everything we owned in the process. People also asked how it came to pass that such a traditional Austrian/German company would hire a Jew. I never looked at the situation that way. All that was in another life and I never looked back.

There are numerous pictures of Ferdinand Porsche, Sr., with Adolph Hitler during the World War II years. I have seen them on History Channel World War II television documentaries on a number of occasions. I often heard that the senior Porsche was one of Hitler's favorite engineers.

The Porsches were caught up in the events of the era, doing the work they loved: engineering. I do not believe they personally supported Nazi philosophy. I heard more than once that Professor Porsche, Sr., and his son refused to wear Nazi uniforms.

It was the son, also named Ferdinand Porsche, and the rest of the family, who hired me in 1980 to become the CEO of the family business. On two occasions, Professor Porsche addressed me in private with tears welling in his eyes: "You cannot know Herr Schutz, how much it means to me to have a Jewish refugee running a business that is my life work."

During my years at Porsche, another of my staunchest supporters was Hushke Von Hanstein, a close friend of Professor Porsche. Hushke had been an S.S. Colonel during the Nazi era. He had been a racecar driver and Porsche's director of motor sport and retired a few years before my time at Porsche. He used his considerable influence in my behalf on a number of occasions during my Porsche tenure.

The fact that I was of Jewish descent and working for a traditional German company was more of an issue for the press and others living in the past than it was for me.

Reconnecting the Roots

The relocation of the Professor's office to the parts warehouse in Ludwigsburg and his resulting absence from Porsche headquarters contributed to a general feeling that Porsche was no longer what it once was.

I remembered the impact of bringing Dr. Jacob back into the consciousness of KHD.

Across the hall from my office, at the Porsche Zuffenhausen headquarters, was the accounting department. We moved the accounting department to another location at the plant and built a new office for Professor Porsche. His office was twice the size of mine. There was enough room for trophies and honor awards and his own private secretary.

Although he was in his 70s, Professor Porsche would come to his beautiful new office every morning at nine sharp and stay until noon. If I was in town, I always crossed over to his office after his arrival and we shared time over a cup of coffee. I learned a lot about company history from Professor Porsche in these sessions, a perspective that no one else was capable of passing on to me. He told me about the service, manufacturing, engineering, and racing managers that helped him build Porsche and make it great. I sought some of these people out and got a wonderful Porsche history briefing.

Professor Porsche was a shy and humble person who shunned the spotlight of publicity. I, on the other hand, believed it essential that he, not I, assume the public posture as leader of the Porsche organization. It took real effort to get this quiet gentle man to face reporters and journalists.

I recall one interview in which Professor Porsche did not want to participate. He urged me to hold the interview without him, but I insisted he attend. "I will not know what to say," was his expressed concern. I assured him that I would back him up.

He was asked, "Tell me, Professor, what is your absolute favorite Porsche of all time?" Professor Porsche was groping for an answer and I broke in with, "We haven't built it yet!" "That is right," the Professor added. I said, "Now, do you understand why I admire this man so deeply?"

The quote became his in that instant. We supported one another flawlessly in all public appearances.

Professor Porsche's acceptance of the role of figurehead, something that was not in his nature since he did not relish public exposure, was an important element in the rebuilding of Porsche culture.

This section of Porsche culture would not be complete without mention of Dorothea, or Frau Porsche, Professor Porsche's wife. She was one of the most widely loved persons I have ever known, a wise, humble woman, with incredible strength, heart, and will. She and Professor Porsche were a devoted couple. They made a great team. With Frau Porsche's passing on July 25, 1985, the world changed for many of us, including yours truly. I always felt that a part of Professor Porsche died with his beloved Dorothea.

The relationship that existed between Professor Porsche and me in that time period was one of the great experiences of my professional life. He was a truly remarkable man. His unwavering support made it possible for me to reestablish and grow the *Porsche magic,* and revive an outstanding company culture.

Balancing Interests

Why are we in business? What is the purpose of a business? What is the objective of a business?

I have spent many fruitful hours debating these issues with friends and valued business associates. If we don't know what we are trying to do, it is unlikely we will accomplish our goals.

The subject came into focus during my first business meeting with the Porsche supervisory board after I was named CEO of the company. Herr Gottschlecht, the vice chairman and a union representative on the supervisory board, asked, "Herr Schutz, what do you see as the most important challenges facing the CEO of a company such as Porsche. What are your priorities?"

This question, coming from a union leader in the presence of the company's owner representatives, could not be taken lightly. Beyond that, it put some of the differences of managing a company in Germany rather than the United States into perspective. In the United States, it is unlikely that both employees and owners would be represented in the same room when such a question is posed.

I answered that I believe there are at least three purposes for which a business can exist.

1. To provide goods and services for the common good, *to add value for customers.*
2. To *provide a satisfying life for its employees,* for the people who have invested their lives.
3. To *provide a satisfactory return for shareholders* who have invested their money.

Which of these is most relevant or correct? Which is most important?

I have come to acknowledge that all three of these purposes, as well as some of their variations, are indispensable. It is possible to draw a parallel to the survival of a human being.

In order to survive, we must

- *Breathe,* analogous to adding value, sales;
- *Drink,* analogous to support by employed people;
- *Eat,* analogous to support by the company's owners.

Failing to do any of these things would leave us just as dead. Once our bones are buried, it makes no difference whether we died of asphyxiation, thirst, or starvation. The results for a business are much the same.

Yet, there is a difference in urgency. We can only live a few minutes without breathing, a few days without drinking, and perhaps a few weeks without eating. In the end, failing to do any of these things adequately will bring about the same result.

In business, adding value for customers is analogous to our breath; without it, we or a business will die quickly.

Without drinking, a person would live a bit longer, but survival is not possible. Without committed effort on the part of its people, a company would die a bit more slowly, but would still die.

Profit, to assure ownership interest and support, provides the nourishing capital upon which the business is built. It is analogous to eating. We might survive for a number of weeks without eating, but starvation is inevitable. A business might survive for a considerable time without profit, but in the longer run, the resulting lack of ownership support is fatal.

Because the customer's support is felt immediately, it is the critical path to future success. We cannot maintain healthy employee and owner relations without sales.

Making money (generating revenue) confirms customer problems have been solved and value has been added.

Just as a person cannot live without breathing, a business cannot survive long without adding value for customers. Failing to add value for customers will cut the lifeblood of any business quickly.

Making money puts the business in position to provide secure and prosperous employment for its employees.

A person cut off from drink might survive for about ten days. In like manner, a business might survive for an interim period with dissatisfied employees. Failing to meet the expectations of its employees, it will likely fail in a competitive business environment.

Making money can satisfy the need for owners to realize a return on their investment.

A person can survive the better part of a month without food before starving to death. Failing to earn a satisfactory profit for its owners, a business may survive (after a fashion) for an extended period, but no business can succeed and prosper without making money for its investors.

Making money is what makes a business a business. Adding value for customers is the activity that generates revenue and makes money. Without revenue, a business cannot make money. There is much more to running, a successful business than generating revenue, but I submit that it is not possible to run a business without it.

Revenue is a confirmation by the customer that value has been added. The amount of revenue is a good indication of the extent to which it has been accomplished.

The profitable years at Cummins confirmed that adding value for customers will be rewarded with revenue.

If a business focuses on activities necessary to make money, it will focus on the activities that most of us can agree are the objective(s) of a business.

I believe most of us got into business to make money. Even if we are engaged in a charitable activity, it is necessary to generate some sort of revenue. The ability to do that will depend on solving customer problems and selling the value that is added to the source of our revenue—the customer.

We struck an implicit deal. If union people would commit to help the company make money, I would commit to help them achieve their objectives.

The Plight of the "Middleman" in Business

The economics of modern business put a great deal of pressure on middlemen. Included in this category are enterprises such as travel agents, wholesale distributors, and retail dealer outlets. The pressure to eliminate such activities is particularly severe in commodity businesses. How can such middlemen survive and prosper in a competitive economy?

First of all consider the thesis: *In business, we are all middlemen.* Few businesses can supply the necessary value-added for customers from cradle to grave. Most business consists of an interdependent chain of middlemen.

The key to the survival and success of any middlemen in the chain of business is to add value. Any business in the supply chain that fails to add value forfeits its right to make money and is thus doomed to extinction.

Sharing the Glory

Shortly after my deal with the Porsche union had been struck, I invited my good friend and ally, Paul Bleffert, the chief union steward from KHD, to Stuttgart for lunch with Porsche union stewards and me. This added to the important working foundation that grew between the union and management at Porsche.

I knew that to make our business work, to get the people whole-heartedly behind efforts to generate more revenues at Porsche, I would have to win their committed support. I knew I had to reach out in many ways to tap into the potential power of these people and engage their driving force in our turnaround plans.

After squeaking a profit out of the 1980–1981 business year, we drafted a profit plan for 1981–1982 *together*. Porsche management shared all numbers and plans with our union colleagues.

The 1981–1982 Porsche business plan forecast a profit of DM 32 million after taxes. The owners did not believe it was realistic or possible. "We have never earned that much money. It is not necessary or expected," described their position.

It turned out they were correct. We did not earn DM 32 million after taxes. We earned DM 42 million!

It became evident that Porsche was headed for a record profit year as early as May 1982. I approached the Porsche family and suggested we share some of this profit with our people. "I would like to take DM 5 million out of June operations and pay it out to the people who put out the extra effort necessary to realize our ambitious plan."

The owners replied, "That is not done in German industry, Herr Schutz."

"It is not done in America either," I replied. "If we committ to share success with our people it would be a confirmation of our contract with them."

The owners agreed.

I called Franz Blank, our chief union steward, to my office and told him: "The owners of the company have agreed to share the results of the outstanding effort that your people have put forth. They have agreed to return DM 5 million to our Porsche people."

He replied, "You cannot do that, Herr Schutz. Here is how we must do this: You offer DM 3 million, I will demand 8 and we will settle on DM 5 million."

What was going on here? The office of chief union steward is an elected office. Franz Blank is an outstanding politician and was aiming to solidify his hold on his elected office. What was wrong with that? I had invested in my relationship with him, so let him shine for his people, big time. It would help an ally.

I had to set my ego aside. I agreed with one condition. His initial reaction was: "Uh-oh, here it comes." I then said, "I want *you* to decide how the DM 5 million is distributed among our people."

Franz Blank could not believe his ears. Not only did he have DM 5 million, he had the opportunity to play the benevolent king. He could distribute money as he saw fit.

He quickly found out how difficult it is to give money away. He returned to my office sometime later and said, "You have most of our people mad at me. Everyone has a different idea of what is fair. I have gotten myself crosswise with most everyone."

Franz Blank had gotten a good taste of what we face as managers.

Rather than some complicated allocation based on seniority or whatever, I suggested: "Every person in the company contributed to our success. You have DM 5 million and 5,000 people. Say thank you, give each DM 1,000, and you are done."

We had established a principle that when we win at Porsche, *we win together.*

I believe we often reward performance unfairly in business. We pay big bonuses to people who are already making a lot of money, frequently a percentage of a rather high pay level. Usually, such people are well compensated for their special talents or seniority. When the organization has a good year or operating quarter, it is the effort of the entire organization that makes it possible. When a top salesperson closes a big profitable deal, it is most frequently the culmination of efforts at virtually all levels of the company. Pay such salespeople a salary for skill and experience, but let the whole organization share in the total accomplishment.

This act and others like it established a strong and clear culture among Porsche people.

John Weitz

Clothing Designer and
Bestselling Author

*P*eter and I share many things.

We were both born in Berlin, Germany, and became American citizens because of Hitler's racial mania. We were both fascinated by the automobile, especially the romance of the fast sports cars and their racing stars. We both understood Germans and Germany and had a warm affection for our new home, America.

What a coup for Porsche to hire someone of Peter's background and knowledge to run their business.

Peter quickly saw that he would have to use a romantic approach to widen Porsche sales. Driving a Porsche was a frame of mind. It was not just "the fastest way to get from point A to point B." He also had some revolutionary ideas about servicing Porsche customers and dealers.

These notions were far ahead of their time.

During his time at Porsche he also expanded the vast fund of design knowledge Porsche's superb engineers could provide. Everyone knows about the cars, but few people know of the technical expertise Porsche supplied in aeronautical and military fields.

The Schutz era was a highpoint in Porsche's history and certainly helped it to its way to its present preeminent position.

12

Prospering Among Giants

Porsche is a small company among giants. This meant we were not going to succeed by doing what our competitors did. An unorthodox approach was needed in several aspects of Porsche operations.

Spreading the Word

In the vital area of building a brand through advertising, we were at a significant disadvantage. In general, our competitors set their advertising budgets as a percentage of sales based on a far larger level of sales. To compete on a dollar-for-dollar basis, we would have had to commit all our revenues to advertising, an obvious impossibility. Many smaller competitors face a similar dilemma and the most effective solution is to find a way to reach customers *differently* than the giants who dominate conventional advertising media. You cannot afford to out-shout them, so the trick is to find other ways to communicate the value of your brand.

Since there was no way we could afford an advertising and public relations budget to support our selling activity as measured by industry standards, our solution was to use our racing success and advanced technology to keep Porsche in front of our public. As long as we were making headlines as a leader in these areas, we were worthy of positive editorial coverage which money can't buy. We did not have to buy much expensive advertising space. Small businesses can often find newsworthy activities and a competent publicity campaign to effectively supplement a modest conventional advertising program.

In the United States, the International Motor Sport Association (IMSA) provided the competition to place the Porsche name before the public. In the rest of the world, it was the International Sports Car Championship Series. In 1984, 1985, and 1986, world championships in the Formula I series were added.

The benefits arising from racing transcended public relations. Racing was also profitable and stimulated our company morale as well as our engineering endeavors. Beyond that, it played a key role in Porsche's ability to attract and hold some of the best and brightest people in the industry.

Turning Costs to Profits in Engineering

A major challenge facing businesses offering a technical product or service is the management of engineering and development costs. For Porsche, it was a problem of scale. The cost of engineering is the same for one car as it is for millions of cars. A small business is at a serious disadvantage. We got around the problem of scale by selling engineering and testing services to other automakers and technically based companies.

Porsche had performed engineering services for Volkswagen before building Porsche automobiles. It was the key to Porsche's early existence. After Volkswagen designed the Golf automobile to replace the Beetle, Porsche gradually lost much of the Volkswagen engineering business.

The cost of the Porsche engineering complex could not be supported by the revenue and profit of the limited-volume Porsche car business. On the other hand, the company could not survive as a supplier of high-tech automobiles without it. A solution came from an experience out of the Cummins years.

Cummins employed a company doctor. Doc Richards was a dynamo. In an era when it was not yet the norm, he instituted annual physical examinations for Cummins managers.

The facilities for this were minimal and Doc Richards sought improved modern equipment and facilities. Grudgingly, management yielded to these demands until the cost escalated to a level the company was no longer willing to fund.

Undaunted, Doc Richards became an entrepreneur. With dogged persistence, he managed to get a new facility built and equipped to perform state-of-the-art physical examinations. He offered other businesses in Columbus, Indiana, the opportunity to send their people to his new facility for physical examinations. The revenue thus generated more than covered the cost of the new facility.

As this activity grew, the local hospital relieved its strained capacity by sending patients to Doc Richards' facility as well.

The Cummins Medical Center did not cost. It paid.

We applied the Doc Richards plan to Porsche engineering and development. The opportunities offered by safety and environmental challenges faced by the automotive industry were extensive. Porsche contract engineering revenues grew to hundreds of millions DM per year. Efforts went beyond the automobile industry. Porsche received a contract to design the first airliner cockpits that were not an evolution of a World War II heavy bomber; the first "glass cockpits" for the Airbus 300. This modern technology is now state-of-the-art. It was profitable business.

Beyond generating vital profits, contract engineering introduced a management discipline that impacted all Porsche engineering activities. The need for professional job cost estimates, schedules, and performance milestones, established a discipline that proved to be indispensable in managing engineering and development costs.

Porsche engineering did not cost. It paid.

Turning Costs to Profits in Racing

In the 1980s, Porsche sold competitive ready-to-race cars, unique in the industry. In 1984, A.J. Foyt, an icon among Indianapolis race winners, approached me at the Indianapolis racetrack. He said, "I think I would like to race a Porsche in the IMSA series. Is it possible to buy a Porsche 962 IMSA racing car?" We sold A.J. a ready-to-race Porsche 962, which he campaigned successfully for a number of years.

No one else would supply a competitive car on that basis. Most racing teams have to source components and engineer a competitive car.

Every year there is a major sports car race in Japan—the Fuji. A race team owner, John Fitzpatrick, took his entire racing team to Japan to compete in the 1985 Fuji 1,000 kilometer race. It was very hot. The Fitzpatrick Porsche 962 blew a tire during qualifying and was damaged beyond on-site repair capability. John was in Japan with his entire racing team and no car.

In 1984, a Japanese museum owner, Mr. Matsuda, bought a Porsche 962 to display in his outstanding Porsche museum in Japan. (Mr. Matsuda also has an outstanding Ferrari museum in Japan.) Fitzpatrick called Mr. Matsuda and asked if he could rent the Porsche 962 displayed in the Matsuda Porsche Museum to run in the Fuji race.

Fitspatrick arranged the rental and qualified the Matsuda car *as received* off the museum floor on Friday. He drove his *rent-a-car Porsche 962* in the big race on the following Sunday and finished third behind two Porsche factory cars.

After the race, Mr. Matsuda returned his racing Porsche 962 to his museum exactly as it finished the race. The grime and grease that covered much of the car was a badge of honor.

Porsche sold competitive racecars that were identical to factory team cars in every major aspect. We could sell them and conduct a profitable business because the cars could win; they were competitive.

If you win, racing does not cost. It pays.

Learning from Experience

Porsche learned a great deal about developing innovative new technology from racing.

In the early 1980s, fuel injection transitioned from mechanical injection to electronic systems. At first, the new electronic systems were balky and difficult for drivers to manage. This was particularly true of the turbocharged Porsche racing engines. Our racing program was an important development tool for this new technology.

At first, being assigned to drive a car equipped with the new electronic system was a sentence for a driver. I recall a race in Kilami, Africa, in which Derek Bell was assigned an electronic fuel injection car. Jacky Ickx drove a car with mechanical fuel injection.

Bell went ballistic, "This (blankety blank) system is impossible to manage, particularly in traffic." It was true; not enough was known about the detailed settings that became possible with the new systems. Bell struggled mightily, but because of Herr Bott's relentlessness, stuck with it. Within two additional races, the new system became far superior, and no one ever wanted to drive the old mechanical system again.

In 1983, Porsche teamed up with McLaren to race in the Formula I world championship series. Porsche contracted to design, develop, and build engines for the McLaren chassis. The new and untried TAG engine was installed in a racecar for the first time and entered a Formula I race in Zandvoort, Holland. The car did not do well; it overheated badly. Herr Bott pointed at a spot on the car body and suggested, "Cut a hole in the car right here and rig an air scoop out of heavy tape and cardboard."

I thought the McLaren chief designer was going to have a cow.

"What!" he roared. "You are proposing to cut a hole in my car and rig a scoop out of what?"

The unusual Porsche approach was too much for a famous race chassis designer. We were used to learning and experimenting in order to perfect our ideas; it was a natural by-product of our commitment to excellence. When you are committed to success, you can easily become inflexible, but the longer-term orientation of a commitment to excellence encourages flexibility and constant learning.

The Porsche culture is:

"The sooner you get something new on the road or track, the sooner you know where the challenges are. Do not correct things that are not a confirmed problem." It was Nashville music, not New York City.

Herr Bott taught me:

Do not put a designer in charge of a new development concept. It will take forever to complete the job. Instead, put a test and development engineer in charge and it will get done in a timely manner.

Sharing our Culture

Several incidents in racing demonstrated the winning Porsche culture.

Porsche was teamed with McLaren in the Formula I championship racing series during the era of the turbocharged 1.5 liter engine. Ron Dennis, the McLaren boss, had contracted for Porsche to design, build, and supply engines to the McLaren Formula I racing team.

This was a rather innovative (for the time) little aluminum engine. It sported two tiny turbochargers and was contracted to produce about 700 horsepower. In the course of winning three world championships, one with Nicki Lauda as driver and two with Alain Prost, this engine produced a great deal more power as development progressed in those three years.

In the first full season of racing—1984—Nicki Lauda was unbeatable. The most serious contender—the Williams racing team with Honda power—was plagued with poor engine reliability. Other teams were hardly competitive. Porsche's extensive experience with turbocharged racing engines proved untouchable, and Lauda became world champion.

In the 1985 season, Williams and Honda made significant progress. Nigel Mansell and Nelson Piquet were excellent drivers for the Williams team, and the Honda engine was much improved. Nonetheless, Alain Prost became world champion in the McLaren TAG powered car. The engine was not called Porsche because unlike other racing teams, McLaren paid Porsche for the TAG engines; other racing teams received engines on a gratis basis. The Porsche family was not eager to supply engines to Formula I. They agreed to do it reluctantly on a paying basis much like any other contracted engineering job.

1986 was to be the last season for turbocharged 1.5 liter engines in Formula I. Starting in 1987, a new engine formula that required 3.0 liter naturally aspirated engines would take effect.

As the 1986 season got under way, it became clear that Honda had done its homework with a vengeance. Honda had designed a totally new turbocharged engine for just one season of racing. With all of the lessons learned in two previous seasons, this Honda iron engine was much stronger than previous aluminum units. McLaren and Porsche were not prepared to make such a massive investment in an engine that could only race one year.

Thus, in 1986, Porsche had a disadvantage in engine reliability—it was marginal. The Porsche aluminum engine was beginning to come apart at the power levels attainable in 1986.

The 1986 season played out as fiercely competitive between McLaren-TAG and Williams-Honda. It came down to the final race of the 1986 season in Adelade. Nigel Mansell in a Williams-Honda only needed to finish third to become world champion.

With ten laps to go to the finish, Mansell was running in third place behind Prost in second, and Piquet leading the race. The fourth place car was a distant two laps behind the three leading cars. I was in Germany watching the race on television when the left rear tire on Mansell's car exploded. Mansell did a masterful job of bringing the crippled car to a safe stop, but he was out of the race, his chance for a world championship gone.

Prost now had to catch and pass Piquet in the other Honda-powered Williams to become champion.

With an incredible effort, Prost caught and passed Nelson Piquet two laps before the finish.

*Prost won that final race of the 1986 Formula I season and became world champion by **one point**.*

The 1986 season was the end of the Porsche-McLaren team effort. Honda offered McLaren engines on the customary gratis basis for the 1987 season. Porsche chose not to respond in kind and a productive association came to an end.

In January 1987, we held a bittersweet gathering in Weissach. Engineers, mechanics, and drivers who had been a part of the McLaren-Porsche team attended. We simultaneously celebrated the 1986 world championship and acknowledged the end of a wonderful relationship with heavy hearts.

I had not seen Ron Dennis, the McLaren boss, since the race in Adelade. Upon greeting Dennis at this gathering, I congratulated him for winning the world championship. I remember telling Dennis, "It was fantastic how Alain Prost won the world championship by one point in the last race of the season." Dennis replied, *"No one ever won a world championship in the last race of the season."*

He went on to explain that Alain Prost really won the championship during the *second* race of the season. It was the race at Spa, Belgium. On an early lap of that race, Prost had a tire failure. After limping back to the pits for repairs, he reentered the race in 21st place. In Formula I racing, this is an impossibly crippling event; there is little chance to accomplish anything useful from that position.

Because he is a true champion, Prost drove one of the best races of his career that day and managed to finish fifth.

Fifth place is worth two points!

I have found the same thing to apply in business and my personal life. Just when things look the darkest, when everything seems to be stacked against us, *that* is the time to really turn it on.

In the previous chapter, I described the culture of excellence I was trying to create at Porsche and some of the actions we took within the company to bring this about. The racing program was an important element of this culture. It provided a highly visible arena in which our commitment to excellence could be tested and shared with the world. Past and future customers, our employees, suppliers, and even shareholders, were all spectators when Porsche went to the races. Whenever our performance demonstrated the qualities of a culture committed to excellence, all of these important groups of people got a powerful message about Porsche and what we stood for.

What exactly was the message? What were we trying to say about ourselves and our company through our turnaround efforts and, in particular, through our racing activities? It is something I thought about long and hard. I realized it was not as simple as just committing to success on the racetrack. Everybody who went racing did that. What would make us special, would give us a competitive edge, and would communicate the special driving force of our company most effectively to those who watched us race?

I realized our driving force, on the track and off, had to come not from a simple pursuit of success, but from a deep commitment to excellence in all that we did, whether we were in first place or twenty-first.

The Culture of Excellence

A business culture built on excellence will most frequently outperform a culture in which success is the singular objective. It is easy to conclude that excellence and success are the same, but they are not.

Success in business is often measured by material accomplishments, money, and assets. The criteria change constantly and are often compared to the perceived success of others. People focused on success can be burdened by an obsession for it, frequently leading to a focus on short-term results. For such people, the daily stock price and performance of the business in the most recent quarter becomes an overriding objective.

Managers focused on success, particularly short-term success, will frequently fail to mobilize the real driving force, the committed passion of people that can result in extraordinary performance.

For such impatient and compulsive managers, the future is short term.

Success must come quickly and may be fleeting and fickle.

Managers focused on success want to be known as winners above all. At times, they look for a single transaction to catapult them into fame. The pressure for short-term results, particularly in the eyes of others, is exhausting and can cost such a person their health, to say nothing of happiness or fulfillment.

Excellence is lasting and dependable.

Excellence is largely under the control of the manager. Managers striving for excellence and quality tend to be patient because their focus is on the longer term. They lead with a quiet confidence because they know they will win in the longer term. This is due in part to the fact that their opinion of themselves matters more than the opinion others have of them. This can, at times, be perceived as an inner arrogance that may be difficult for others to understand.

Such managers do not obsess about success in the short term. The daily bottom line results do not cause them to rejoice, panic, or scream. They will frequently shrug off a short-term setback and focus on the lessons to be learned instead. They know that a focus on excellence and quality will more likely activate the driving force of the business and bring positive results in the longer term.

Managers focused on success are frequently so competitive that they feel threatened by the success of others, even members of their own business team. They may actually resent real excellence.

In contrast, a manager committed to excellence and quality is invigorated by these qualities in others. Being surpassed is not feared but nurtured in the effort to excel.

An obsession for success can burn up the manager that seeks it.
Excellence will build the manager that strives for it.

Catastrophe in business news is often the result of a business success story gone wrong. The difference between excellence and success is not always easy to grasp. A business that has focused on success to the exclusion of excellence and ethics can fall prey to disaster.

At Porsche, we were striving for a culture of excellence above all. When I admonished the racing group that we would never enter a race we didn't intend to win, I was calling on them to embrace a quest for excellence. If I had said, "we will never *lose* a race," it would have been a call to success rather than excellence. We might have won the first race, but it could have been a short-sighted pursuit of success. Excellence is the appropriate focus of leaders who wish to create and sustain driving force.

A Champion Never Quits

In the 1984 Le Mans race, Jacky Ickx spun the number one Porsche 956 at the end of the Mulsanne-straight on the very first lap. Al Holbert, driving the number three Porsche 956, passed Ickx to take the race lead. Holbert and Hurley Haywood led the race from that point on, but not without major challenges. In the middle of the night, Holbert was at full speed on the Mulsanne-straight when the right door of his 956 came open. Beyond creating incredible noise, the partly open door deflected cooling air away from the right side radiator. The engine overheated; the door had to be closed.

The car came into the pits and the badly damaged door was bolted shut and taped over. Holbert returned to the track and was immediately ordered back into the pit area by the race marshals. Doors on cars had to be mounted so they could be opened in case of an emergency; it was not acceptable to bolt the door shut.

The door was remounted with an emergency hinge. Shortly thereafter, the door simply disappeared at full speed on the Mulsanne-straight. It flew off at over 200 miles per hour into the bordering woods. To the best of my knowledge, that door was never found.

A new door was installed. It would simply not stay shut. It rode slightly open, about an inch or so. This was enough to interfere with engine cooling on the right side of the engine. (Each side of the flat six engine had its own radiator.)

Holbert managed to hold Ickx off and maintain the lead of the race. Inevitably, he lost ground to Ickx. Holbert's 956 was clearly losing power. Lap after lap, Ickx closed in on Holbert. With two laps to go, Ickx had Holbert in sight and was gaining steadily. Holbert battled back with his badly overheating and clearly failing engine.

Coming through the two chicanes before the straight stretch to the finish line, Holbert's tired engine gave up and seized.

Holbert disengaged the clutch quickly to conserve as much speed as possible, put the transmission in low gear and reengaged the clutch. This broke the engine loose and gave him at least a little power to work with. With thick black smoke pouring out the right exhaust stack, he crossed the finish line just before Ickx caught up and flashed by.

Holbert had won the race by a few yards as a result of his last-minute efforts to keep the car moving.

This never-give-up performance typified the Porsche culture.

Keeping the Faith Through Highs and Lows

Racing is dangerous and we had our incredibly bitter moments.

Two racing driver fatalities had a major impact on the Porsche racing program. Rolf Stommelin lost his life in a horrendous crash in Minnesota in 1983. The Porsche 935 he was driving was hit by another car and lost the rear wing (spoiler). Losing control of the car at over 200 miles per hour, Stommelin impacted a concrete barrier with incredible force.

The "cage" surrounding him was not penetrated. There was not a single scratch on him and all of the restraining belts were in place and intact. Every safety device had functioned perfectly, but Stommelin was dead!

One of the brightest young stars among race drivers in the 1980s was Stefan Bellof. There was little question that he was headed for stardom in Formula I racing, the top of the race driving profession. Bellof was fast, as fast as any of our drivers.

Bellof often drove for the Porsche factory team. In Spa, Belgium, he drove a privately owned Porsche 956. Ickx drove one of the factory team Porsche 956s. Ickx, the veteran champion, and Bellof, the up and coming young tiger, were incredibly competitive. The Spa racetrack was one of our favorites. It is set in the beautiful hilly forests of northern Belgium and since Ickx is Belgian, *it was his track*. This raised competitive fever to a high pitch.

At the end of a downhill straight run past the pits is a rather difficult curve followed by a climb up a steep hill. The curve is the famous Aux Rouge curve. The Aux Rouge *cannot* be driven side by side. Ickx and Bellof roared past the pits toward Aux Rouge alongside each other. Someone would have to yield. Bellof attempted to intimidate Ickx, but Ickx would not be intimidated. They entered Aux Rouge side by side.

Both lost control of their cars. Ickx spun up the hill past the curve. Bellof hit a concrete barrier at full speed and died instantly. There was little left of his Porsche 956. Our Stefan had no chance of surviving and was killed in that incredible impact.

To the best of my knowledge, Ickx never raced again as a driver after that accident; we lost both Beloff and Ickx that day in Belgium.

The deceleration was so great that his heart and brain could not handle the impact, killing him instantly.

Helmut Bott, Porsche director of technology, decided: "That's enough!" He initiated a study of racecar deceleration upon impact with an unyielding barrier.

About seven Porsche racecars were driven into a concrete barrier with the following energy-absorbing materials placed in front of the concrete:

Tire stacks consisting of five tires banded into a stack
- Empty
- Filled with bags of sand
- Filled with plastic foam.

The amount of energy that could be absorbed was significant. The foam-filled tires worked so well, that we at Porsche decided, *we would no longer expose our drivers to the hazards of a track in which concrete retaining barriers were not protected by energy absorbing devices.*

The NASCAR accident that cost Dale Earnhart his life also involved an unprotected concrete barrier.

Restraining the driver, providing energy absorbing crash zones in the body of the car, and other means of keeping the driver in the car during a crash are important, but when the deceleration exceeds a certain value, the human body comes apart internally. Extensive (and more sophisticated) tests at the University of Nebraska have confirmed much of what was learned at Porsche almost 20 years before. Modern electronic instrumentation resulted in credible data about performance of available energy absorbing materials and their effective reduction of deceleration forces.

At the running of the 2002 Indianapolis 500, energy absorbing material was installed at critical points of the track retaining walls. An increasing number of tracks are equipped with sand traps and other measures to increase the survivability of racing accidents.

I am confident that in the face of increased speeds, automobile racing is safer today due in part to the safety measures Porsche initiated in the middle 1980s. The loss of two of our drivers was the low-water mark, at least for me. There were plenty of highs too. A high-water mark of Porsche sports car racing in the 1980s was the Le Mans 1983 finish. In 1983, our advertising and poster said it best:

LeMans 1983

Nobody's Perfect

1st	Porsche
2nd	Porsche
3rd	Porsche
4th	Porsche
5th	Porsche
6th	Porsche
7th	Porsche
8th	Porsche
9th	BMW—Sauber
10th	Porsche

The Porsche 956 and its successor, the 962, raced competitively for another decade. The world was beginning to catch up with the standard of performance that Porsche had set. What mattered at the time was that we had successfully harnessed the excitement and drive of a winning racing program as we worked to rebuild Porsche, one person, one customer, and one attitude at a time.

From time to time in its history, Porsche created special automobiles that were industry leaders. These vehicles commanded significant exhibition space at automobile shows worldwide. During the years I was there, Porsche designed and built a vehicle called the Porsche 959. It featured an innovative series-turbocharged flat-six water-cooled engine capable of developing almost 500 horsepower. The styling was striking. Over 15 years later, the integrated rear spoiler is still used on many contemporary vehicles. One of the most advanced features was a four-wheel drive system that is still part of the Porsche product line. The Porsche 959 body was made of Kevlar, a light high-strength material now the standard structural material of top high-tech racing cars.

For three years in the 1980s, the Porsche 959 was the centerpiece of automobile shows worldwide. We got a lot of press attention as a result, not all of it to my liking to be sure. On balance, it proved an essential component of our turnaround.

I had a great deal of contact with the press during my Porsche years. Most of it was productive and positive. Some was not. I recall an occasion where a German car magazine published a story that included information about me that was demeaning and totally untrue. When the Porsche press manager confronted the magazine editor in my presence, I was told,

"If a story sells magazines, it need not be true!"

Fortunately, most of the publicity we got was more responsible and helped us share our driving force philosophy and commitment to excellence with others around the world. The largest selling issue of most automobile publications featured some sort of Porsche on the cover. Porsche was exciting news and stood for excellence on several continents. What better advertising and publicity could a leader wish for?

Richard M. Riley

CEO OF GRAND X RAY, INC.

I met Peter W. Schutz as a member of the Porsche Club of America attending a Porsche parade in Asheville, North Carolina, in 1981. At that time Porsche was planning to replace the Porsche 911 with the 928. Not many attendees at that parade were happy about that development. In hindsight it would have been a disaster for Porsche. Schutz reversed that decision and made the 911 series one of the most successful production cars in history.

When Peter arrived at Porsche, production facilities were antiquated. The Weissach development center consisted largely of a number of old huts.

When he left Porsche there was a new assembly plant, a new paint plant, and a new parts delivery system in place. Weissach had a modern wind tunnel, new design facilities, and numerous new test facilities.

Employees enjoyed a beautiful new cafeteria, and apprentices were trained in a new training center.

The insight and foresight that Schutz demonstrated at Porsche is what today's executives need in an ever-changing marketplace.

When this man writes a book, it is a must-read for everyone in business.

13

"Cars Don't Win Races"

Our racing activities brought many benefits to the company and were an important part of our turnaround effort. But the story of our turnaround and subsequent successes is not a story about cars; it is about people and what they built together. As mentioned in the introduction, this book is a story of *people* who turned Porsche around.

Cars don't win races, people do!

Taking Porsche to the Next Level

The basic turnaround was behind us. Porsche had two profitable years in 1981 and 1982. It was time to get serious about managing the company for the longer term. Drawing on my experience to this point, it was clear that Porsche, as well as most other businesses, had few superstars. I was an ordinary person faced with getting a tough job done with a whole organization of mostly ordinary people. We had to produce some extraordinary results with the people we already had. I had no desire to go out and hire some so-called "superstars."

Extraordinary Results with Ordinary People

Calling the people at Porsche ordinary is not intended as a put-down to anyone. We had good, caring people; we had some smart people, and there were a lot of people from those years at Porsche who will always be special to me. But were we so much smarter and better than the people and managers of other automobile manufacturers that we could out-compete larger competitors just because of who we were or what we knew? I believe not.

The real power of driving-force management is that it does not require everyone to be above average. Like many leaders, my challenge, and that of my management team, was to produce exciting products and superior results by virtue of how we led people, not because of any innate superiority we hoped to possess.

The challenges of maximizing our driving force became more difficult and complex as we began to accelerate out of our first turn. We were no longer in crisis mode. During the turn-around period, most decisions had been rather clear to see and subsequent implementation was facilitated because the consequence of failure was evident. We were fighting for our survival. It had been a time of decisive leadership; I had to be the toughest fighter on the block.

In fact, I had to become more than just a tough fighter; it was time to become a true leader, an effective chief executive officer.

I have come to believe that there are at least two distinct approaches to being an effective leader and manager.

Imagine that the task is to lead a tribe of Native American warriors in the old West.

One approach is to be *the strongest warrior in the tribe.*

Leading from this posture of strength, a leader must always wear "war paint." They must continually reaffirm the fact that no one in the tribe can defeat them. They will be challenged repeatedly. If any member of the tribe can defeat them in a fight, they will no longer be the leader.

One disadvantage of this leadership concept is that a great deal of time and effort will be expended reaffirming the leader's posture instead of improving the tribe's performance.

Another disadvantage is that such a leader will be reluctant to bring new warriors into the group who are, or could become, better fighters than the contemporary leader.

Members of the organization are limited by the quality of the leader.

Another approach to leadership is to *be a good enough warrior to earn respect, but not the best warrior.*

In this instance, the right to lead is based on excelling in a capability that is not directly related to fighting. There is then little incentive to challenge the leader to a fight. The result would be a foregone conclusion.

The strong warriors accept the leader because the leader brings something else to the party that allows the tribe to achieve higher goals.

I have learned the following:

- To lead a sales organization, it might pay to be the best engineer or finance expert, *not* the best salesperson.
- To lead an engineering organization it might pay to be the best salesperson, *not* the best engineer.

Leading to *Their* Strengths, not Yours

The challenge I faced at Porsche was to demonstrate I could be the best *leader*—not engineer, salesperson, or manufacturing genius. It was important for me to avoid the temptation of meddling in the engineering function, for example, even though I knew something about engineering. I could not lead by trying to be the strongest engineer. I would only damage morale if I started competing with engineers. Similarly, even though I thought I knew quite a bit about selling, I could not afford to

171

get into a battle of wills with salespeople without impairing our sales potential.

When a leader exercises sufficient restraint to stand to the side and let others be the strongest, they have taken an important step toward awakening the full driving force of an organization.

Imagine that the leader of a tribe is not the best at *any* of the daily activities of the group. Perhaps the leader is a wise elderly woman who cannot see well enough to gather food and has not the strength or skill to fight. Nor has she the dexterity to weave baskets or mix medicines. What can she *possibly* do to justify her position of leadership? She can see that others, those with the needed qualities, become the best at what they do. In other words, *she leads by virtue of being good at leading, at bringing out the best in others.*

If she can do this successfully, if she can succeed simply by being a great manager, there will be no leader stronger than she. There will be no group stronger than the one she leads. It is the next level of challenge for leaders.

When we, as leaders, focus attention to help people achieve extraordinary results, we are aspiring to a higher level of leadership.

The Porsche Operating Board Team

The challenge I saw as we began to return to profitability was

to achieve extraordinary results with existing Porsche people.

To do so, I knew that it would be essential to put the right people in the right places on the team. One of the keys to being a successful manager is to make sure you are using people to full advantage. Many organizations are held back because people are not in positions where they can apply their full talents most effectively. I found it helpful to give special attention to staffing decisions, especially the staffing of leadership roles.

The Porsche supervisory board had decided to replace the personnel and manufacturing members of the operating board before I became CEO. I had the opportunity to participate in finding and installing their replacements.

During my tenure at KHD, I had faced the challenge of building a great number of variations of basic engines for the industrial engine market. This was contrary to what most of the automotive industry was striving for. In most instances, the manufacturing objective was to build as many units as possible to the same specification.

KHD customers wanted to install Deutz engines in a large variety of machines and many different engine arrangements were needed to accomplish that. We hired Professor Rudy Knoppen, a university mathematics professor. His mission was to design an inventory management system that could support the varied engine assembly operations required to service KHD engine customers. Professor Knoppen did that job well.

Professor Knoppen came to Porsche to head manufacturing. He restructured the Porsche assembly plant after the KHD pattern. It put Porsche into a posture that served us well in building a large variety of customized Porsche sports cars with acceptable efficiency. This activity ran counter to the general trend in the automotive industry at the time.

Porsche was also able to attract Dr. Heiko Lange to take the post of human resources manager on the Porsche management team. Dr. Lange made significant contributions to Porsche management excellence. He left Porsche in 1987 to become manager of human resources for Lufthansa, the German commercial airline.

Professor Helmut Bott, the head of Porsche engineering, was a technical giant in his field. He had been with Porsche forever. He was an outstanding people manager. The team at the Porsche Weissach Technical Center and I loved and respected him deeply.

Heinz Branitski was the chief financial officer. Like Bott, Mr. Branitski had been with Porsche for many years.

Lars Schmidt served as head of sales and service.

This team of rather diverse people tackled challenging business situations well enough to achieve acceptable success. I do not know if they would have been brilliant in other contexts, but each brought unique skills and knowledge to their roles. Everyone did their share to achieve extraordinary results.

The Need for a Management Process

It is one thing to assemble a team, and quite another to manage it. We needed a management process that could support our culture of excellence and help us produce extraordinary results.

As an engineer, I tend to take an engineering approach to most challenges that have confronted me. Before addressing the subject of management process, allow me to clarify what it is we are talking about. It has been pointed out to me that for the purpose of understanding the management process, it is useful to simplify it. In my opinion, no one has done that more clearly than Ichak Adizes, one of my mentors and a true genius in the field of management theory. My ideas and activities at Porsche reflected much of his thinking.

What is management? What do managers do when they manage? These are not easy questions to answer. I recall when I served as general manager of the KHD Deutz Engine division, a reporter came to interview me and asked my secretary, Frau Poschman, "What does Herr Schutz do all day long?" She replied, "He has meetings, and he talks on the telephone." Well, that was at least a simple answer. But it did not help me understand the management process any better.

If we were to make a list of what managers do, it would include a number of things. One of them would certainly be communicating—an important part of the job to be sure and (for my secretary at least) often the most visible part. But there are many other important things on that list.

Have you ever felt like a teacher when managing? An important part of the job is like teaching, but actually it is *more* than teaching or even coaching. It is more like being a *parent* than anything else I can think of. It is a nurturing process, getting in touch with people's capabilities and ambitions and somehow finding a way to help them grow to be all that is possible for them.

It is also essential that we plan and monitor performance to let the organization know where it is going and how it is doing.

Sometimes it is necessary to be a strict, tough, disciplinarian. I have known some managers who believed this was the fun part of the job. I never did, but it must be done.

At times, a manager also has to play the role of an accountant and a lawyer.

All this must be carried out with the attitude of a cheerleader. We need to be upbeat, encouraging, and enthusiastic, even if we don't feel that way when we wake up in the morning.

Management, as practiced today, is *a complex activity*.

In anything as complex as this, a bit of good luck certainly helps, as a story I used to tell at Porsche Club meetings illustrates:

President Ronald Reagan visited the Pope on a trip to Italy. While in conversation with the Pontiff, he noticed a golden telephone on the desk. Reagan asked, "What is that golden telephone?" The pope explained, "That is a direct connection to the Lord; we talk every day." Reagan was amazed. "Do you suppose I might make a call?" "Certainly," replied the Pope. "But it is very expensive—$25,000 per minute and no credit cards are accepted."

"That is too bad," was Reagan's reply. "I don't have that sort of money with me, but we'll do it next time."

Later that week, Reagan came to Stuttgart to visit Professor Porsche. While in Professor Porsche's office, he noticed a golden telephone on the desk. "Is that a telephone like the one I saw in the Pope's office recently?"

"It certainly is," answered Professor Porsche. "If it were not so expensive, I would sure like to make a call to Heaven," said Reagan. The professor said, "Please help yourself; it only costs 25 cents per minute."

"What?" exclaimed Reagan. "In Rome, it costs $25,000 per minute."

The professor responded, "You see, from here, it's a local call."

When I entered my office on the day following my telling of that story to Professor Porsche, there was a golden telephone on my desk.

When You Don't Have a Golden Telephone

For the purpose of understanding the complexity of management without trusting to luck or a golden telephone, I have found it useful to define management in a different way, consisting of just two basic activities. As managers we must,

1. Decide

Make timely decisions of high quality.

We must *do the right things*. If we do the right things, the business will be **effective**. We will be making good decisions.

Doing the right things is not enough to succeed in business. We may be doing exactly the right things, at exactly the right time, but if we are not doing them well enough (cost effectively), someone else will do things at a lower cost and be in a position to offer a more competitive price to the customer. We could fail.

2. Implement

Get things done with optimum use of available resources.

To implement means *we must do things right*. If we do things right, we will be cost effective. Our business will be **efficient**.

*In order to succeed in business we must be both **effective and efficient**.*

This constitutes the first major challenge facing a manager. There is a hidden problem:

Effective and efficient are not compatible.

About the time that things are really working right, when suppliers are delivering on time and to the correct specification, and people know what to do, it is time to do something different. Every time we do something different, our hard won efficiency declines. The question then is: How far does efficiency decline and how long will it take to get it back into an acceptable range?

It may be strategically smart to be on the cutting edge of industry. That would mean every time there is an opportunity, we will choose to do something better or faster, to exceed customer expectations in a new and better way, to be out in front. But each of these opportunities also creates problems if we pursue it.

If we change direction too often, we can end up with chaos at the operating level.

Roger Frock

PRESIDENT OF QUEST MANAGEMENT, INC.
AND RETIRED FEDEX EXECUTIVE

I can't think of anyone more qualified than Peter W. Schutz to expound on how a leader can take an organization beyond success to excellence. I find it interesting that a book covering this material will be published at this time. It seems that more and more, we are experiencing greed and corruption in the world of big business, particularly in the capital markets. I believe the subject of excellence in business is very timely and needs to be brought to light by someone of Schutz's experience and reputation.

14

Establishing Credibility

D uring the time that it was my privilege to be CEO of Porsche, I found that managing a company in Germany was different from managing a similar company in the United States in a number of significant ways. Some were of questionable merit. Others, if applied properly, could have significant positive impact on the way businesses are managed in the United States or anywhere in the world. I came home with some helpful insights that I have shared with U.S. businesses and have seen them work here also.

A major difference in the conduct of business in Germany is the top management structure described in Chapter 7. While I don't recommend we adopt similar legal requirements in the United States, I do recommend that managers strive for employee as well as owner representation and provide for their input at all levels of decision-making.

Being a Target

Law mandates that a German AG must hold meetings with all its people, a "*Betriebsversammlung,*" several times each year. The law requires that this event be orchestrated by employees, *not* management. It is a meeting in which the when, where, and what, is spelled out by the employees, not the employer. Furthermore, these meetings must take place on company time, with full pay and no time limit.

At Porsche, this meant that several times a year, Franz Blank, our chief union steward, would come to my office. He would not come to make polite inquiries about my schedule or availability. He would simply march in and announce, "We will meet next Wednesday and here is the agenda."

We held four meetings with our 8,500 people. One was attended by about 4,000 first-shift factory personnel and a second attended by about 3,000 second-shift factory people. The first two meetings would be held in the main cafeteria. Tables were removed and chairs arranged theater style. A third meeting took place in Weissach, the Porsche Technical Center, attended by about 1,000 technicians and engineers, followed by a fourth meeting in Ludwigsburg, the parts warehouse and service center, where about 500 people would attend.

The agenda for these meetings was always pretty much the same: Management (yours truly) would be asked to make a short presentation about what had transpired since the previous meeting, the status of the business, and finally the outlook for the immediate future. After this, anyone could ask any question and there was no time limit and no place to hide! There was no way to be saved by the bell or manipulate the meeting.

It was a time to be accountable to employees.

The first time I found myself in these circumstances I was scared out of my mind, almost paralyzed by tension and fear. I found that in such situations you learn quickly.

How to give short, clear, easily understood, completely honest answers to questions.

I found this easier to do once I got it through my head that I was nothing special. I was no different, certainly no better, than any of these people. I had the job; that was the difference.

After I got that straight, I learned two very important lessons.

1. *I had nothing to fear from these people!* It is amazing what people are prepared to accept, as long as they are sure that you are telling it exactly how it is.

2. *You will build credibility.* A credibility that I found to be a strong foundation upon which we as an organization could address issues and actually resolve some of them. Credibility made it possible to resolve issues that previously might have been considered untouchable.

Credibility and Vulnerability

I emphatically am *not* suggesting that the United States implement such a law to intrude into the inner workings of management. There is no law to forbid it and managers are free to do whatever they want.

What I *am* suggesting is that if a manager has not already done so, steps should be taken to build the kind of credibility and accountability I have described. I believe that is the first step in getting extraordinary results with ordinary people.

Does this mean that managers should begin to have meetings with their people such as I experienced in Germany? Perhaps, at least in some organizations, but I have long since learned that there are no pat answers. No two organizations are the same. They have different histories, cultures, and personalities. There are any number of ways to achieve credibility and accountability, but no matter how a manager goes about it, I believe that there is one indispensable component.

One way or another, managers must put themselves into a position where they are vulnerable.

This cannot be done with a newsletter, video communication, or bulletin board announcement. No form of one-way communication can get this job done effectively.

Managers must put themselves on the line.

There is simply no substitute for giving people an opportunity to confront leaders directly, look them in the eye, and ask the tough questions that are on *their* minds, knowing the managers can neither run nor hide. They must be in a position to ask the tough question, knowing that the managers must deal with the issue face to face.

Any way that this is accomplished will serve to build the required credibility.

The Care and Feeding of Credibility

Once credibility has been achieved, it must be nurtured. It is perishable.

In the summer of 1948, the Russians blockaded Berlin in an attempt to starve the population of the city into submission. The Allies countered this effort by flying coal, food, and medicine into Berlin with a fleet of leftover worn-out World War II airplanes. It was known as the Berlin Airlift and was the subject of a movie called *The Big Lift*.

This event played out through the winter of 1948–1949. Winter flying weather in Berlin is frequently bad, with low ceilings and poor visibility.

All this took place before the days of modern instrument landing systems. The way aircraft were landed in poor weather back in those days was with a system called ground control approach (GCA).

GCA employed a radar set and radio operator on the ground. The pilot in the airplane could see nothing but fog and rain through the windscreen. In the earphones, the pilot would hear the droning voice of the radio operator on the ground: "You are on the glide-path, continue your approach— you are 50 feet high on the glide path adjust your rate of descent—you are drifting to the right _____." The operator would literally talk the aircraft all the way down to a safe landing on the runway.

Experience showed that the single most important element in that system was that

the operator on the ground must never stop talking for more than five or six seconds.

If they did, the heart rate and blood pressure in the cockpit would go right through the overhead (the cockpit ceiling in the language of pilots).

In the *absence* of uninterrupted communication, the pilot will begin to fantasize, has the radar set quit? Has the radio operator given up on me?

Suddenly the freezing and starving people of Berlin no longer matter. The pilot no longer thinks about landing the airplane. Instead, the pilot now thinks about how to survive. It suddenly becomes simple and personal. Instead of trying to land, the pilot pushes the throttles to the firewall and pulls the airplane up in an effort to get out of the experience alive.

The lesson is:

managers must never stop communicating.

I have found that many managers stop communicating when things are going wrong.

Just as in the Berlin Airlift, if managers stop communicating when things are coming off the tracks, the tension levels and anxiety in the organization can go sky high. Instead of trying to solve business problems, people will focus on their personal survival. Performance will deteriorate further and anything (bad) is possible.

Managers must never stop communicating. Credibility must be nurtured. Even if things are going well, take time to say something like, "You are on the glide path, continue your approach," or "You are on plan, continue the good work!"

I confess that I usually looked forward to those big meetings with Porsche people (*Betriebsvesammlungen*) after I established my credibility with them. I was excited by the opportunity to hear what was on people's minds. I enjoyed a reasonably trusting relationship with them and wanted to be accountable.

This relationship was not without an occasional jousting. Accountability can be uncomfortable at times. I learned to not view these things as burdens.

In contrast, I knew of some German managers who had good reason to dread those confrontations. Perhaps they had something to hide or could not deal with the prospect of acknowledging they did not have total control. The concept of control is frequently an illusion anyway.

Credibility is indispensable if managers are to get extraordinary results with ordinary people.

Credibility and accountability are foundations of the driving force.

Donald Krull

ASSISTANT CHIEF ENGINEER,
CATERPILLAR TRACTOR CO. (RETIRED)

*P*eter W. Schutz developed the ability to interface as a boss, business colleague, and salesman that resulted in a relationship where all perceived him as a friend. They came to look on him as a teacher and guide in developing their leadership methods.

As a longtime friend I realize that most of those that have had the opportunity to interface with Peter W. Schutz, no matter how casual the contact, perceive that the contact has made their lives fuller and more rewarding.

15

Making Democratic
Decisions

While in Germany, I sometimes heard Germans say, "Governing Italy is extremely difficult and totally unnecessary." Some things are difficult to do, and it is reasonable to wonder if it is necessary to do them.

If managing is so difficult, why is it necessary?

A recurring question at mandated employee meetings would be:

> *Tell us, Herr Schutz, why is it that this company has grossly overpaid managers, such as you? Hundreds of them, sitting in beautiful offices, doing Lord knows what, when it is we, out there in the factory, who build these funny little cars with the motors in the back that are sold and generate revenue. Why don't we dispense with much of this overrated expensive management? We could do our thing, ship the cars, collect the money, and divide it among us. It would be a simple business.*

That is not a throwaway question. In any event, if you should ever find yourselves in the circumstance I have described, I would strongly advise that you not take this question lightly. It is a good question that weighs heavily on the minds of many people who work hard every day in order to feed, clothe, and shelter their families.

Why, indeed, is it necessary to manage?

What would happen in a business if we actually did what was suggested and eliminated a good deal of the expensive overhead we call management? Would our businesses fall apart tomorrow? The next day? Next week? Next month?

I would suggest the most likely answer would be, it could work for a while.

How long could it work? Well, that all depends. Depends on what? It depends on

change.

If there is no change, there is little need to manage. As the old saying goes: "If it ain't broke, don't fix it." ***Good advice, if there is no change, but deadly advice if there is.*** As soon as anything changes, inside or outside the business, there is an immediate need to

decide what to do, or what not to do.

And then *implement*—get it done.

I had taken the opportunity to listen to a number of successful old-timers in the industry. They would relate how they managed when they built the business. While they talked, I would get the feeling they were not talking about the challenge(s) that were facing me. Somehow, it must have been easier in those good old days.

If we think about that and ask, what was the rate of change in those days compared to today? The answer, of course, is that the rate of change was a great deal slower. So it really was easier.

The interesting question to consider is:

What will the rate of change be in the years that are now ahead of us?

I believe most managers would agree that

the rate of change will continue to accelerate.

The speed of racecars increased significantly during my time at Porsche. They were travelling at higher speeds, but often on the same tracks. This meant that turns and decisions came up more quickly and accidents were more difficult to avoid. At higher speeds, the skill of the driver is more critical. The quality of workmanship and responsiveness by the entire team that builds and drives the car is more important.

When we acknowledge an increasing pace of change in business, I submit we have addressed and answered an important question:

What will be the role of management in the years ahead?

Management will become more important. There will be more need for increasingly professional and competent management. The penalty for mismanagement will escalate.

An Invisible Role

Mismanagement is often highly visible, at least in retrospect. Everyone knows about a crash, but the drivers who navigate a course without incident seldom get acclaim. When things go wrong, everyone is eager to point the finger. The same is true in business. Good management is not as visible. Ideally, management should be so good that major problems are avoided and major opportunities are pursued in a timely manner so that the organization can achieve stability in spite of the fast pace of change around it.

During the time Sheila and I were at Porsche, we were one

of the few American couples active in the upper levels of German industry. During a good deal of this time, Richard Burt was the U.S. Ambassador to Germany. The ambassador's residence and the U.S. Embassy were in Bonn. He and his wife, Gahl, represented the United States in an outstanding manner; they were a couple that made Americans in Germany proud. On several occasions, Sheila and I were invited to attend official events at the residence. Henry Kissinger was present on one of those occasions. He made an interesting statement over dinner regarding leadership: "If you, as the leader, make a timely decision of high quality and subsequently get it implemented efficiently, you will rarely, if ever, receive credit or acclaim for your achievement. Instead, you will be challenged sometime later in a manner that approximates the following: Please don't misunderstand, the results are excellent, but do you recall that advertising campaign last fall? It was very expensive. Was it really necessary?"

I was asked that question often during my time at Porsche.

Was all of the money spent on racing really necessary?

Who knows? We cannot go back and create a controlled experiment in which another strategy was used to see which might have worked better. I believe racing activities were vital to our turnaround and subsequent growth on many levels—both internally and externally. Increased profits and improved morale were enough to satisfy me; I learned to ignore such rhetorical questions.

Quality management is difficult and frequently not appreciated. Management that makes timely decisions of high quality and gets them implemented efficiently and averts crisis is not recognized or rewarded in the manner that short-term crisis management is. Crisis management decisions are usually easier to implement.

The more timely and higher the quality of the decision, the more difficult it is to implement at all, much less efficiently and the manager will frequently not receive recognition and acclaim.

Why is it that quality decisions that carry a real probability of redefining our business are usually the most difficult to implement?

Seeing the House

Today, I live in beautiful Naples, Florida. Sheila has a real talent for finding "fixer-upper" houses in settings with great potential. She will buy an old house, tear the place apart, hire subcontractors to do a complete redo, sell it, and actually make a profit. Remarkable!

When she buys such a house, she takes me out to see it, and asks, "Well, Peter, what do you think?"

What do I think? I think this place is a dump! I can't visualize what she sees. She can already see the way it will be when it is finished, new landscaping and all.

Because many people in the organization do not share the manager's ability to visualize the consequences of great managerial decisions, the best decisions are frequently the most difficult to implement.

In my personal experience

- *making decisions is the fun part of being a manager, and*
- *the difficult part of management is implementation.*

I have made a number of wonderful decisions in my career; many of them were never implemented. *There is little question in my mind today that efficient implementation is the key to achieving results and also the tough part of management.*

The Road to Implementation

The following elements impact implementation:

- authority
- power
- influence

Leaders need to think long and hard about these three elements that to most people are just so many words, but which, to the leader, may hold the key to success, or failure.

Authority and Bureaucracy

Authority is the legal right to decide no, and *the legal right to decide yes.*

If someone has the right to decide either yes *or* no, but not both, they do not have authority. They have an illusion of authority.

Let us say you walk into a typical automobile dealership. There is a beautiful new Porsche on the showroom floor. The price sticker reads $50,000 (which proves this is an old story). A salesperson approaches and you say, " I will pay $45,000 for this car." Can the salesperson say no to such an offer? Of course, they can say no to anything, but before they can say yes, they have to check with the sales manager.

In this example, the salesperson does not have authority. It is an illusion of authority. If you are a smart negotiator, your response might be, "Since you do not have the authority to sell this car, may I please speak with someone who does?"

Empowering someone in the organization to decide **no**, but **not yes**, can constipate the system; it can obstruct implementation.

This can be the foundation of an obstructive bureaucracy. In a typical bureaucracy, there will be multiple layers of management, each of which is allowed to say no. To say yes, they have to check with the next level of management.

If there is little or no change going on, this can work. After a period of time, most of the questions likely to arise will have been asked and answered; but if we introduce real change into such a situation, the operation can be paralyzed.

Who has authority (*real* authority to say yes as well as no) in the business?

- Not the chairman
- Not the chief executive officer
- Not the president
- Not the manager (unless they own the business)

The owner(s) have authority.

I recall a story in Lee Iacocca's first book. It described an incident in which Iacocca was embroiled in a controversy with

Henry Ford II. At one point, Mr. Ford walked across the conference room, took Iacocca by the shoulder, pointed out the window at one of the huge Ford Motor Company buildings and said, "I want you to look at that building. It does not say Iacocca on that building!"

Never forget who put the name on the building.

Clarifying the Limits of Authority

Authority can and must be delegated. Some of the most rude awakenings in business occur when a manager with delegated authority discovers the brutal fact that only the owners have unlimited authority.

When authority is delegated, we must strive to clarify its limits.

A story I have told many times illustrates the challenge of explaining the limits of delegated authority.

Imagine you have responsibility for sales and service at XYZ Engine Company. A fleet of dump trucks on Long Island is using your engines. The truck drivers on the job are tearing up the engines and you are faced with a catastrophe. XYZ Company convenes a meeting at headquarters to deal with this looming disaster.

Someone in the meeting comes up with a great idea: "If we could convince the drivers to treat the trucks as though they owned them, then perhaps we would get better results with the engines."

So, a contingent goes to Long Island, puts on a fantastic show for the assembled drivers and succeeds. The drivers leave the meeting actually believing they own the trucks.

So they sell them!

How can we create heightened awareness of the limits of delegated authority in the organization? Constant change makes it difficult to define limits.

I believe it is advantageous for a manager to become a good storyteller. This can serve to make a point with a minimum of judgment or confrontation. In this book, as well as in my speeches, I often tell stories to make a point.

Here is another example.

Many years ago, I learned to fly. I learned in a little fabric-covered 65-horsepower marvel called an Aeronca Champ at Mt. Hawley Airfield in Peoria, Illinois. Back in the 1960s, this was a grass field. Most pilots will agree that landing an airplane on the grass instead of concrete is like sleeping in a feather bed; it is a sensuous experience.

At the north end of Mt. Hawley Airfield were some tall trees. When the wind blew out of the south, which was common in the summer, a landing approach had to be made over these trees.

One day, while I was learning to land, I was making an approach over these trees. I turned to Donald Krull, my flight instructor (to this day one of my best friends), and asked, "How do I know that I am high enough over the trees during a landing approach?"

I will never forget Don's answer: "If you can see the trees, you are too darned low."

When making decisions, I always check to see if anyone else's authority is in sight and try to clarify the limits. If I can see the trees, I know I am flying too close to someone else's (or my own) delegated authority limit.

If you have the thought: "Will what I am about to do exceed my delegated authority?" and you do not know the answer, pick up the telephone *before you act* and make a short call to clarify the situation with the person who has delegated authority to you. You can save a great deal of grief for yourself and others in the organization.

Understanding Power

What is power?

Power is the capacity to grant and withhold cooperation.

That definition is different from what many people might say. In my experience, it gets at the most important aspects of power.

Power is easily misunderstood. Why do we, as managers, have an organization? We have an organization because *there is a job to be done that we cannot do alone.*

Most managers have a task to perform that they cannot do alone. If they can do it alone, it is not a management task. If they can't do it alone, they will need the cooperation of an organization of people.

Who has power in the business?

Anyone whose cooperation is needed has power.

This can be frustrating to a manager, particularly one who has a tendency to be a control freak.

You can't have your cake and eat it too.

If managers have authority, they cannot *have power.*

This is central to my thesis.

Imagine that you are raising a five-year-old. You, the parent, have decided spinach will be eaten for dinner. As the parent, you have the authority to decide the dinner menu; there is no controversy. But does that mean spinach will, in fact, be eaten?

Now, it is clear where the power is.

If a manager had both authority and power, they would not need anyone's cooperation to accomplish a task. It would not be a management challenge. They could simply do it alone.

> *The higher up in the organization managers are, the more authority and the less power they have.*

In order to implement, a manager must have the cooperation of those with power. Managers frequently have authority. They can decide what *should* happen, but it only *will* happen if those with power are willing to cooperate and *make* it happen.

A management problem arises when those with power choose not to cooperate. In that instance, significant mismanagement and failure to perform can occur.

A valued associate who is frustrated by failure to gain the cooperation of those with power might approach the manager. "Boss, I have the responsibility, but lack adequate authority to _____."

What is a proper response?

If the boss decides to address the issue, it will be necessary to redefine and re-delegate the authority requested. This is a complex task that can easily impact authority that has been delegated to others.

The real issue is something quite different anyway. Suppose the manager attains the authority that is sought. What can be done with it? Can authority be used to force cooperation that is not forthcoming?

Intimidation and Bribery

Attempts to gain cooperation with authority usually come in two flavors: intimidation and bribery. (Neither tastes good.)

Efforts to gain cooperation of those with power by using authority can involve intimidation. In this mode, the manager with authority threatens those whose cooperation is sought.

The parent, who has authority, decides the child should eat spinach. In order for this decision to be implemented, the child, who has power, must cooperate. If the child refuses to cooperate, the parent might threaten the most horrible consequences imaginable to intimidate the child into cooperation.

What do five-year-olds hate to do more than anything in the world? Go to bed! So the parent might threaten, "Either you eat the spinach, or you will go to bed at seven o'clock every night for a week."

If this works it is quick, clean, and easy. But if it does not, the situation can get messy.

In the business example, the manager may threaten to fire the noncooperating individual. The manager may have the authority to do that. If the manager actually fires the employee, *who has been punished?* Who has a problem?

The manager needs the cooperation of the individual who has been fired to implement the business decision.

Having fired them, the manager must do the following:

First: find a replacement

Second: hire the replacement

Third: train the replacement to do the job

Fourth: hope the replacement will cooperate.

This all gets the manager nowhere fast! Many businesses spend a great deal of valuable time and energy in such unproductive activity, striving for employees who will have a more cooperative (or more easily intimidated) nature.

In the case of the child who will not cooperate and eat the spinach, it gets even more difficult. You cannot fire the child. (This is a shortcoming of nepotism in business.)

If intimidation can get the job done, it is a no-brainer. It requires little management skill.

The opportunity to manage in that manner exists in any number of underdeveloped third-world countries. In these circumstances, people need the job to survive. Such people might tolerate intimidation and respond to it. A number of major corporations have moved some of their operations to such areas. But even there, intimidation will lose effectiveness over time.

If intimidation fails to get the job done, another alternative might be *bribery*. In this mode, the manager with authority attempts to gain cooperation by offering a bonus or special perks.

The parent offers the child a reward: "If you eat the spinach, you can stay up late, have dessert, etc."

The manager on the job may take the following approach: "I know that you do not want to do what I am asking. Tell you what, do the job and you can have a bonus and an extra week of vacation."

You have bribed them.

If this works, the individual being bribed may decide, "I hate this job, I don't like the boss, and I don't really want to do this, but I cannot afford to walk away from whatever has been offered."

This may get a specific job done at the time, but will not likely produce extraordinary results or a competitive edge.

In this era of accelerating change, when we must alter course frequently, authority is a poor and hazardous way to strive for the cooperation of those with power. I say hazardous because having failed to achieve the desired cooperation with the means that authority offers, the manager is frequently out of options. There is no place else to go to gain indispensable cooperation.

Every management has the organization it deserves.

There is another road the leader can follow, in which the focus is having positive influence through motivation.

Influence

Influence means to persuade those with power to do what we want done, to cooperate, because it is in their interest to do so.

Willie Sutton, the legendary bank robber of the 1930s, was allegedly once asked, "Tell us Willie, why do you rob all those banks?" Willie replied, "Heck, that's where the money is."

Willie understood the mechanics of his profession.

But Willie was also quite a philosopher. He is quoted as saying, "You can get further in this world with a kind word and a *gun*, than you can with a kind word alone."

Willie had it right, but he was not faced with the prospect of needing sustained (and frequently, loosely supervised) cooperation. Even Willie acknowledged that there was more to success in management than a gun. He also recognized the value of a kind word.

When a manager persuades those with power to do what the manager wants done because it is in the interest of those with power, it is called motivation.

The motivational approach with the five-year-old might be, "I am not asking you to eat the spinach because it will change *my* life. The spinach is not for me, the spinach is for you, so you can grow up to be big and strong and athletic like Michael Jordan." That is why we put Michael Jordan's picture on the Wheaties box. "If you eat what is in this box, then maybe you too can grow up to learn how to shoot baskets, retire at age 30 as a multimillionaire, and make a successful comeback whenever you feel bored."

The response might be, "WOW! Give me two helpings of that stuff."

When those with power are motivated, they do what is asked because it is in their interest to do so.

Motivation is not just the most effective way to gain the full cooperation of those with power. It is the only way.

Motivation or Manipulation?

Motivation has a sinister relative, a most dangerous and destructive one. When those with power are persuaded to do what the manager wants done because it is in the manager's interest for them to do so, instead of their interest, it is not motivation, but *manipulation*.

Such managers are sometimes characterized by a rapid rise in the organization, followed by a sudden full stop. It occurs when those with power who are being manipulated discover they are being used and exploited and refuse to cooperate further.

The most dangerous and disruptive managers I have encountered are those manipulators who are so clever that the people (with power) being manipulated feel motivated.

How to Achieve Genuine Motivation

In order to get things implemented in an optimum manner, a manager must motivate those with power to cooperate.

When a manager is faced with a new venture, specifically with a venture that includes activity that has not been addressed before, consider the following: (Let me point out, that the rate of change is so rapid today, even some activities that have been dealt with before may no longer be the same.)

Focus on gaining the cooperation needed for efficient implementation instead of addressing the many things that managers have learned to do so well, such as: How much might it cost, how long might it take to recover the initial investment, what new equipment and facilities might be required, etc. Set these issues aside for now. It will be necessary to deal with them in great detail at the appropriate time.

When you make cooperation the primary concern, you will focus efforts on pursuing the cooperation from all those with power who are needed for implementation.

Remember, implementation is the difficult part of management.

Step 1. The List

Make a list of those with power, those who must be persuaded to cooperate if your proposed action is to play out in the manner in which you have pictured it.

The first step in the process is to make a list as complete as possible of all those with power.

This list will usually contain individuals and organizations outside the scope of the manager's authority. It will often involve people outside the company, such as:

- suppliers
- bankers
- legislators
- various public officials
- activists of various sorts

Caution! Do not leave anyone off the list if you need their cooperation. If you do, they can achieve a posture to sabotage implementation.

Step 2. The Interests

Determine the diverse interests of those with power.

In order to determine the diverse interests of those with power, it is necessary to ask and listen. This requires skill.

Once upon a time, when I was much younger and still believed I was smarter than I in fact turned out to be, I was convinced that if I could just get these stubborn (stupid?) people to pay close attention to the description of my wonderful proposal, no rational person could possibly choose to oppose me. WRONG!!! The more I talked, the more stubborn these people became in refusing to cooperate.

Motivation is not about talking and explaining, but about asking and listening.

These may be among the most important management skills.

Step 3. Representation

Provide for adequate and effective representation of the diverse interests with power.

Representation means to condense the number of individuals involved to a manageable number. It is important to provide for adequate representation of diverse interests by representatives who enjoy the trust of those who will have to be motivated.

It will not do to **appoint** *such representatives, they must be chosen,* **elected***, by those holding the power, those whose cooperation is required for implementation.*

Step 4. Accommodation

Accommodate the diverse interests of those with power to earn their cooperation.

This does not mean that it is expected to get people and organizations with power to *agree* with the undertaking. It is not necessary to get agreement. All that is needed is cooperation. The objective is to negotiate an accommodation.

Often the parties see the situation differently; it may be impossible to reach agreement. That is not the problem. The question is: is it possible to sit down as adult human beings and negotiate an accommodation, so that in spite of any differences, it is possible to act in concert?

203

In 1983, Porsche needed to build a new paint plant. Additional car painting capacity was needed. There was a need to supply a greater diversity of colors in order to satisfy customer requests. New environmental regulations had rendered the existing plant untenable. The old paint plant had been built adjacent to the chassis assembly plant at a time before the area became residential.

The challenge was to build the new paint plant adjacent to the existing chassis assembly plant where the old plant had been. It is not practical to ship finish-painted chassis components across town. Inevitable damage will occur. The problem was that the new plant had to be built in what had become a residential district of Stuttgart Zuffenhausen.

A paint plant in a residential area presented a number of serious challenges. It can emit noxious odors and be noisy. In addition, people who lived in the area anticipated inevitable additional automobile traffic during shift changes after the new plant went into operation.

It was at this time that I became acquainted with the Green Party in Germany. Members of this organization were very knowledgeable about odor and noise, as well as several other environmentally damaging consequences of a paint plant. These concerns were expressed eloquently and often.

I also got to know the head(s) of local home-owner associations, local politicians, etc.

It took 18 months of negotiations to reach the accommodations necessary to proceed. In the end, Porsche received a DM 10 million grant from the German government on recommendation of the Green Party. In the view of the Green Party, Porsche was doing it responsibly.

It cost us 18 months and more than the DM 10 million received from the government in noise and odor reducing hardware, but we got our paint plant built where we needed it.

Such is the nature of this process.

There is a form of government designed to utilize these four steps. It is called:

Democracy, U.S.A. style.

The elements that make U.S. democracy unique for application to management include a chief executive with veto power and a nonpolitical supreme court to assure compliance with a constitution.

In a democracy, the diverse interests whose motivated support and cooperation is necessary are accommodated.

In Germany, I learned the power of decision-making with a democratic twist. By including all relevant people and groups in the decision-making process, I sometimes took months to produce a flawed decision rather than making a decision with my staff and advisors in a much shorter time. By including those with power in the process, I found I could make decisions they could understand and support. This proved essential to maximize the driving force of the Porsche organization. A higher-than-ordinary level of involvement was the key.

I learned to take an exceptionally open, participatory approach to decision-making. My role as a leader was not to be the smartest decision-maker, but was instead to design the best decision-making *process*. Democracy makes decisions slowly and laboriously, but optimizes the probability of efficient implementation.

In driving-force management, it is imperative to open the decision-making process. It requires sharing information and goals and encouraging input to a higher degree than is customary. Often, leaders do the opposite, they decide what to do and then inform those with power and expect cooperation.

Christoph Schug

GERMAN EXECUTIVE

I worked for Peter W. Schutz when he was CEO of Porsche. I was a young manager in the Porsche finance establishment. Peter developed a close cooperation with a number of young executives from all parts of the company whom he called his "tigers." At that time, I was in my late twenties and early thirties.

I owe Peter a lot, on the personal as well as professional side. Even under great pressure, Peter would always motivate me, because he always helped me to do what was good for me. He taught me about building complementary teams and putting people in position to perform.

Over the years, I developed my career further. Today, I am the CEO of a large organization and have come to appreciate the value of Peter's insights. I have thrived on the things I have learned from him and pass these principles on to my younger colleagues.

I view Peter as the best leadership teacher in the world. I am happy that he finally decided to share his experiences with the public in his book, The Driving Force.

16

Implementing Like
a Dictator

Many managers would agree that people who are
involved in a process are more likely to support it. As
a result, leaders often invite participation during
implementation. They might announce a decision and then ask
those with power how they plan to achieve it. This is a common
approach and reflects the widespread assumption that in order
to implement successfully, it is desirable to employ a democratic process.

In earlier times, when the rate of change was slower, democratic implementation might have gotten the job done. No
more! Not today; not tomorrow.

A democratic process is not suited for efficient implementation. The democratic process is clumsy and requires an incredible amount of skill and patience. It is inherently corrupt; such
is the nature of man. It has one redeeming feature. It works. I
have found that if you take a participatory, democratic,

approach during implementation, it can undermine an organization's driving force.

Take Two!

The nature of implementation became clear to me as I observed one of Sheila's projects. She has taken part in activities that frequently are more interesting and diverse than mine. One was movie production.

Production of motion pictures is an interesting exercise in management.

The producer is the CEO. This role bears responsibility for the story, script, getting performers under contract, arranging financing, etc.

The director is the chief operating officer, responsible for implementation.

In 1985, Sheila joined the production crew of a movie directed by one of the truly great directors of our time, John Frankenheimer. The movie was The *Holcroft Covenant* and starred Michael Caine, Victoria Tenant, and Lily Palmer. (This was a big thrill for me; I had a teenage crush on Lily Palmer.)

In the business of making movies, a shooting day is implementation. On a typical shooting day, you might have:

- Arranged the location of the camera and sound equipment
- Hired the technicians needed to operate everything (at "union scale")
- Performing stars on site, complete with wardrobe, make-up, etc.

You have arranged to use a gate at JFK International Airport and leased a Boeing 747 to taxi up to the gate. At a time such as this, all the spigots are wide open; you may be spending money at the rate of $200,000 per hour. If we engage in a democratic discussion at a time like this—perhaps the camera angle could be better, or the leading lady decides to renegotiate her salary—we would be over budget and out of business in no time.

Implementation is a time to do, not to talk.

Experience has demonstrated that democratic implementation is unsatisfactory in a competitive operating environment. It can be a disaster.

In order to achieve results in today's business climate it is necessary to *implement with a dictatorial process.*

John Frankenheimer was a nice man and a good personal friend; he passed away on July 7, 2002, as I was writing this book. In the role of director on a shooting day, he would become a ruthless dictator. There is no other way to get that job done. Someone must be in complete charge during implementation.

Managing a business is no different. When we are implementing, we have paid for inventory and are paying employees and suppliers, and it is a time to do, not talk. My experience at Porsche reaffirmed the nature of implementation.

In the Racing Pit

A fun part of the Porsche job was racing. During the time I was privileged to serve as CEO, I made it a priority to attend all the 24-hour races at Le Mans and Daytona, as well as the 12-hour race at Sebring and as many of the other races as I could fit into my schedule.

On these occasions, I would spend almost the entire race in the pit area. I did not have a job to do there, I was only there in the role of a cheerleader.

If you have ever been to an automobile race, or watched one on television, you may have observed that from time to time, during the course of the race, the cars will come into the pits to be refueled, have the tires changed, etc. That activity, my friends, is implementation. At that time, there is not much talking; everyone seems to know exactly what to do, and the job is done in seconds. It is a time to do, not talk.

When something went wrong, there was one person in charge. It was not me; I was only the CEO of the company. It was not Herr Bott, our technical director. In charge at this time was a person called the crew chief, who was one of the mechanics the others had decided to accept as their leader in the race pit.

In Germany, the chief executive of a company is treated with a great deal of deference and respect. (They are not paid as well as a U.S. CEO, a poor trade-off.) This deference and respect was forgotten in the heat of the moment during a pit stop. If something went wrong, the crew chief might scream at me, "HEY YOU!!" Here I was, the (revered) chief executive, and this person is screaming "HEY YOU!" He might point at some big heavy looking object back in the garage area and yell, "Get that thing over here right now!"

I would leap into action and comply instantly, even if it meant getting grease all over my clothes.

Why did I respond in this manner under those circumstances? *It was the only way to be competitive.*

Imagine what would happen if, as the car rolled to a stop in the pit during a race, the individual charged with changing the left rear tire chose that time to say, "There is something that I have been meaning to bring up to the group. Is OSHA aware of what is happening in this pit area? Why do I have to change the rear tire, which everyone knows is heavier than a front tire? Beyond that, I have some new thoughts about our health-care plan."

If you are going to entertain such activity in those circumstances, you might as well pack up and go home; there is no way you could hope to win a race.

What have I just described here? What is going on in this pit? This is not a democracy. It is a dictatorship. I don't mean a benevolent dictatorship; this is a *tyrannical* dictatorship.

If you want to implement efficiently in a competitive environment, you must implement like a dictatorship.

Nothing else is focused and efficient enough to produce results in a competitive business environment.

Since a democratic process is not useable during implementation, the alternative is to employ the democratic process in the decision-making phase of management. To manage well in this era of accelerating change and competition, we must learn to

> *decide like a democracy, so that we can subsequently implement like a dictatorship.*

Avoiding the Usual Patterns

As managers, we frequently get this sequence backwards in that we tend:

- to decide like a dictatorship,
- and then get stuck with democratic implementation!

Why does this happen? One reason might be that many managers have been trained to make decisions. They learn to do that well and want to use that skill in management of the business. Making decisions can be fun. It can be an ego trip.

I recall a story about a factory that was built in an area with high unemployment. The building was finished, the tooling was in place, and it was time to staff the venture. There is a line that explains,

> *"We sought workers, but people came instead!"*

When people came, they brought something with them:

their diverse interests.

These people had power. Their cooperation was necessary for successful implementation and their diverse interests had to be accommodated in some manner.

Unless provision is made to accommodate these diverse interests democratically in the decision process, they will be accommodated democratically in the implementation process. This is far too inefficient in an era of rapid change.

Why do managers decide like dictators and saddle themselves with this problem?

- It is fun; it satisfies the ego.
- We are trained to be decisive.
- It is timely.
- It frequently yields a high-quality decision.

The third and fourth items are particularly troubling. A democratic decision process is certainly much slower and cumbersome than a more direct, autocratic, dictatorial process. Even more upsetting is the unquestioned fact that a dictatorial decision will most frequently yield a decision with superior quality.

In the process of accommodating the diverse interests of those with power, it is often necessary to subordinate at least some of the interests of those with authority.

This accommodating can compromise or dilute a decision the manager has authority to make unilaterally. *There is little question that the manager has the legal right to decide.* Giving up this right is frustrating.

It will take more time to formulate a decision democratically, but the time consumed to accomplish the total task, including implementation, is frequently shorter.

A quick dictatorial decision can result in a timely decision of high quality that ends up not getting implemented at all.

Implementation is the difficult challenge in management.

What good is a timely decision of high quality if it is not implemented in a timely and efficient manner?

Equally frustrating is the fact that in addition to sacrificing time, a democratic decision will frequently sacrifice some quality. In a dictatorial decision, the diversity of interest(s) that must be accommodated is limited, usually to those of the owners and their representatives. A democratic decision will introduce additional diversity into the mix and the decision quality will be diluted by the accommodation(s) necessary to build adequate cooperation and support.

If we get in a hurry, or are not prepared to accept the limitations that democratic decision-making imposes, we risk getting stuck with democratic implementation. That can be a disaster.

When democratic implementation hardens into a formal process, we have a name for it: a (traditional) labor union.

A traditional labor union can come about when the diverse interests of those with power have not been adequately addressed and accommodated in the decision process.

The diverse interests of those with power **will** *be accommodated.*

This will happen either right away in the decision process, or later, in the implementation process, which can have devastating results.

The competitive edge in the era of accelerating change and competition is to mobilize the driving force, getting extraordinary results with ordinary people. A key to accomplishing this is to learn how to ***decide like a democracy and implement like a dictatorship.***

One More Time: Democratic Decisions

The success of dictatorial implementation depends, in large part, on the foundation of support built during the democratic decision-making process. If everyone involved enters the implementation phase together with a clear purpose in mind, they will follow orders and do whatever it takes to win the race. When leaders bungle the effort to open the decision-making phase, they sow the seeds of disaster to be reaped later when they are burning through their cash and struggling in vain to implement what may well have been a brilliant decision. Learning how to make decisions democratically is difficult. It will rarely yield decisions that are timelier than dictatorial decisions and time is money. It will become evident that the quality of a democratic decision is rarely better than a dictatorial decision.

Why then, have I come to believe that it is necessary to make decisions democratically?

So that we can implement like a dictatorship. Period!

Democratic decisions will be less timely, and due to the need for accommodations inherent in the process, will frequently lack the crisp quality of a dictatorial decision. In a dictatorial decision, we must only accommodate one interest, that of the owner(s) (manager). In a democratic decision, we must also accommodate the diverse interest of those with power.

Missing Skills

Making decisions democratically requires skill. It requires some skills that I had neglected in my personal development, such as learning how to disagree without being disagreeable.

Reading a book, taking a course, watching a video, or watching a skilled person do something can result in acquiring knowledge. Knowledge is wonderful, but skill is different.

For example, it takes skill to ride a bicycle. I do not know of anyone who ever learned to ride a bicycle by studying physics, centers of gravity, and dynamic interaction. How do you learn how to ride a bicycle? You must get on the bicycle and be prepared to fall, *to fail!* Failure is an inseparable part of learning any new skill.

When we first undertake the task of making democratic decisions, we will probably fail. We will fail until everyone involved in the process has acquired adequate skills.

There is a huge difference between knowledge and skill. It is profound and significant to management.

If you have ever taught a five-year-old girl to ride her new bicycle, you may recall you had to remove the training wheels. In the presence of a safety net, you can acquire knowledge, but you cannot learn a new skill. You can go through the motions, perhaps acquire some knowledge, but in order to learn a new skill, the safety net has to go. It is necessary to deal with cruel reality. In many instances, we make the learning of a new skill needlessly difficult by creating unrealistic expectations.

Many of us have learned how to sell. Can you still remember when the most welcome sound in the world was a busy signal? Or when you were informed that the customer would not be available for the whole week? There was an incredible sense of relief; you did not have to put yourself on the line just yet.

Once we have learned to sell it is not such a big deal.

How do many companies "train" new salespeople today? Some send them to a weekend seminar—"official training"— and then hand them a manual, and say, "Go get'em tiger, *and don't be scared*. Oh, and by the way, you are on commission. If you don't sell, you don't get paid."

It is not very productive advice. The new salesperson thinks: I *am* scared—there must be something wrong with me." We have made a difficult job more difficult. Not only must they deal with the lack of skill, but now they believe there is something fundamentally wrong with them.

If we are to teach difficult skills effectively, we must be honest about our own experience and not act as if a task is easy when it is not. Many managers present themselves as infallible and miss an opportunity to show their own vulnerability.

We must deal with reality: "I can imagine that you are scared. I was scared when I was in your position." Now the perception changes. "You, the big boss, you were scared? Maybe there is hope for me after all."

Don't try to tell me that those old butterflies are no longer there. In professional or personal situations, *when it is really on the line*, we are still scared. If we are to teach difficult skills effectively, we cannot stay on our high horse and act as though the task is easy. It is not easy.

So, you sit the youngster on the bicycle, grab the back of the seat, and hold them up as they ride down the street. You tell them to pedal and steer. Pedal and steer at the same time—that is not natural. It is like when we first learned how to swim. Move your legs one way, and your arms another; it does not work until we acquire the necessary skill.

Sooner or later, you must release the seat; the first time you do, maybe the whole operation falls apart. The knees may be skinned; the tears may be flowing; mother gets very upset. "You are killing my child, that is enough for today!" But it is not enough. If you want that child to learn how to ride the bicycle, you must get them back up. It is OK to dry the tears and give a few words of encouragement, but that is not the main event. This is a time for tough love. The sooner we get the youngster back on that bicycle, the sooner they will acquire the skill.

When I was an engineer at Caterpillar, I had three young children at home: twin boys, Mitchel and Michael, and their older sister, Lori. Engineers were not paid a whole lot of money. I was moonlighting as a flight instructor to support my little family, teaching Bradley University students to fly airplanes. Some of my young students would catch on to this rather complex skill quickly; they had a great deal of natural aptitude. Others seemed to have an inordinate amount of difficulty.

I discovered that there was no perceptible correlation between how quickly a person would catch on and how proficient a pilot they would ultimately become. *Some people simply learn faster than others.*

I also learned that too much natural aptitude, too much talent, can be a handicap on some occasions. Another dimension is persistence or wanting it badly enough. Some of the best pilots I ever trained were youngsters who were not fast learners. They did not have outstanding natural aptitude. They had that piercing persistence that is essential to excel and become a professional.

It seems as though I have been talking about children who want to ride bicycles and young adults who want to fly airplanes. Not so. I am talking about leaders who want to learn the skills needed to master the difficult process of democratic decision-making. Business leaders today need a higher and wider range of skills than their predecessors and acquiring them can be a painful process with more than skinned knees to show for it. Too often, managers retreat behind their authority, close their doors, and avoid painful interactions until they become absolutely necessary. Avoiding difficult conversations and ducking an unpleasant confrontation only postpones the time when one must deal with the lack of support for implementation of a *dictatorial* decision, a big mistake if you want to maintain driving force.

In accepting the challenge to make decisions like a democracy, we must expect to *fail* until we become skilled. Some people learn more slowly, so patience is necessary. It is not easy.

Sooner or later, every child catches on and rides the bicycle. Some will fail more than others, but suddenly, something clicks and they go down the street on their own, a bit wobbly at first. Mother now really hits the panic button. "Where is she going? My God, we never taught the kid how to turn a corner; we never taught her how to stop and get off." Suddenly, the entire family is running down the street trying to catch her before she gets to a busy intersection.

Each time I began to seriously develop my skills in a new area, I was much like that young girl. Now that a new skill had been acquired, it would take her to places she never knew existed. Just like that young girl who would never again be satisfied to simply play in the backyard when there is so much uncharted territory to explore on her bike, I was on my way.

As I became serious about developing my management skills, they took me to exciting places I never knew existed.

Tiger for a Day

The bad news is that learning the democratic decision process is not much like riding a bicycle. Instead, it is a great deal more like learning how to play golf. I do not play golf, but my friends who do have told me that few ever get really good at the game. They told me the worst thing that can happen to a golfer is to have a really good day and decide, "I have finally caught on to this game!" The next time out could well be a disaster.

Making democratic decisions is much like that. Few are ever good at it consistently. The more we work at it, the better we become. Time and again we experience failures. All we can do is take our lumps, learn from them, and hope for a better day tomorrow.

Ground Rules

A democracy has its foundation in the belief that

rules are more important than people.

The best example of a democracy that works well is not a democracy at all. The United States of America is a *representative republic.* A democracy functions with every member of the society having a vote; the majority rules. In a representative republic, the population elects a limited number of representatives who then conduct the actual discussion, decision-making, and subsequent voting.

The concept for democratic decision-making that has proven to be most effective is embodied in a congress consisting of elected representatives of the general population.

In business, it is most effective to convene the elected representatives of the various interests with power to achieve a manageable group. At Porsche, I found the elected union stewards—twelve in number—comprised such a group.

It is important that the representatives of those with power not be appointed *by management,* but elected *by those whose interests are to be represented.*

I recommend an informal structure in which each company department is represented.

The foundation of such a democracy is a constitution, a document that defines the basic rights of the members and the system of rules by which the process is conducted. This constitution applies to *all* members of the organization.

All members are created equal under the rules, and rules are more important than people.

Veto Power

Another indispensable component of U.S.-style democracy is a chief executive with veto power.

The chief executive must sign off on all decisions. If the CEO deems the democratic decision of the elected representatives of the organization inappropriate or inadequate, the CEO is duty-bound to veto it. Only the CEO, the leader, is responsible for results.

The manner in which a veto is handled can be decisive. A veto can have a traumatic impact on the entire process. Instead of vetoing a democratic decision, the following steps can be constructive:

- Explain the concern as clearly as possible.
- Share the possible consequences of the decision if implemented as submitted.
- Ask the representatives to reconsider the decision from that point of view.

If this does not resolve the conflict, explain that the decision will receive approval under the following conditions:

- Results will be monitored closely for a proposed time period.
- This will focus specifically on the perceived shortcomings of the decision.
- Performance will be reviewed at prescribed intervals, with specific focus on the points of concern.
- If the points of concern prove to be valid, the decision will be revisited with a view to clearing the problem issues.

In other words, it is often best to withhold a veto, even though it is warranted, and instead create a situation in which the decision is methodically tested.

- In some cases, my concern was unfounded.
- In some cases, the organization took action to overcome the shortcomings of the decision without further discussions.

- In rare cases, the representatives conceded the shortcomings and revisited the entire decision.

In many of the cases where I was tempted to veto a decision, it later proved unnecessary.

Avoiding the confrontation that a veto can precipitate will go far to preserve the always tenuous process of democratic decision-making.

Interpretation

Finally, the implementation of a democracy requires a mechanism to *interpret the constitution*. A decision that violates the constitution, the rights of participants, or the culture of the organization, must not be implemented.

In the United States government this activity is carried out by members of the Supreme Court, who are appointed for life and thus not beholden to any political faction or re-election. In a business this activity can be exercised by directors of the board or the equivalent. Just as in the U.S. government, this works best if these board members are *not* involved in the management of the business.

Business management is charged with enforcement of the rules, not interpretation and judgment of their constitutionality.

Mutual Respect

Rules alone do not make for a successful democratic process. The democratic process is also based on mutual respect.

This means to *acknowledge the sovereignty of another person's thinking and feeling.*

As long as mutual respect and credibility exist between the representatives in a democracy, the process can be productive. When mutual respect breaks down, partisan bickering and gridlock result. In those circumstances, the entire process can break down.

At its best, democratic decision-making is always time-consuming and difficult to manage (compared to making decisions dictatorially). At its worst, it can be chaos.

Why do I advocate such a flawed decision-making process?

So that we can implement like a dictatorship.

One of the most important lessons that I had to accept was:

A flawed decision that is well implemented will yield more in the way of results than a perfect decision that is not implemented well.

One of the best friends I have in the world is Jack. (A friend is someone who loves us even after they get to know us.) Jack worked at Cummins with me. Earlier in life, he played football professionally. He was a reserve player on Vince Lombardi's Green Bay Packers in the 1960s, when the Packers were at the top of professional football. Jack served as a green beret in Vietnam and was wounded so gravely that his football-playing career never came to fruition. Instead, he has excelled as a high school football coach. To date, his teams have won state championships in four states.

Jack loves to tell stories of his experiences as a member of the Green Bay Packers and I love to listen to them.

One of my favorite Packer stories is when he explains how Vince Lombardi would gather the entire team in the locker room a week before an important game with the arch-rival Chicago Bears or Detroit Lions. This would be a democratic meeting. Everyone on the team would have an opportunity to explain how he thought this game should be played. Lombardi would diagram football plays on a blackboard in response to this input—you know, the Os and Xs.

One of the key players on the team was a big man who played tackle on offense; we will call him Tony. Tony was 265 pounds of muscle, bone, and gristle. He could flatten any linebacker in the National Football League. The problem with Tony was that he was not the smartest player you could wish for; sometimes he had trouble understanding the play that was diagrammed.

After completing his explanation, Lombardi would always turn to Tony and ask: "Tony, do you understand this play?" If Tony returned a blank look and responded, "Well coach, I'm just not sure—," Lombardi would respond, "All right, forget this play. It may be a great play, but if Tony does not understand the play, it will not work for us."

Those who follow football know that the Green Bay Packers, the champions of their era, were not characterized by brilliant play concepts. They made *good* decisions, not *brilliant* decisions. What characterized those teams was flawless execution of the fundamentals; *brilliant, flawless implementation* was their unique specialty. When that Packer team was on the opponent's 15-yard line in a critical part of the game and it was third down and six yards to go for a first down, there was no mystery about what would happen next. The whole world knew it would be Jim Taylor in a power sweep over left tackle; Tony would flatten the linebacker and Jim would explode into the end zone for a touchdown.

The whole world knew what was coming. They could not stop it because of the perfect execution of the fundamentals.

It is the flawless execution of fundamentals that will most frequently be the basis of positive results in business.

After the Green Bay Packers had won the world championship, there would be a team meeting at the beginning of the following season. Vince Lombardi would walk into the meeting holding a football. The meeting and the new season would begin with,

Gentlemen, this is a football.

For Lombardi and his winning team it was all about fundamentals and flawless implementation.

If you do not have "Tony" on board, understanding and supporting the decision, do not "pull the trigger" to initiate implementation.

Finding "Tony"

In virtually all undertakings, there will be a Tony.

The question is, ***Who is Tony in your organization?*** If the discussion in a meeting deals with financing, the star salesperson may be Tony. If the subject is customers and their expectations, the chief manufacturing genius may be Tony. There will be times when the leader is Tony. It does not matter who Tony is. What matters is

until Tony is on board, do not initiate implementation.

There is a reality that many managers have to face in this era of rapid change. The rate of change in most aspects of business is so vigorous today, that it is increasingly impossible for a manager to stay on top of every detail. This is particularly true as the organization (and its managers) move to the "next level of performance," which I describe in Chapter 20.

Many managers will become Tony as they move up to the next level and strive for excellence.

When I first joined Caterpillar out of engineering school, I was employed as a test engineer. In time I was promoted to head a group of test engineers. No problem. I knew the details of every task my organization was assigned.

Problems occurred as I was promoted to greater responsibility. With every promotion, the ability to be on top of every situation that arose became more difficult. I became Tony step by step with increasing responsibility.

In Chapter 1, I related my experience of being Tony as I joined Porsche. I was conditioned for this experience during a visit with my son Mitchel, who was an engineering student at Purdue University. I had just accepted the CEO job and as explained previously, was a diesel engineer rather ignorant of many Porsche specifics.

Mitchel invited me to meet with some of his fellow students who were Porsche fans at Purdue. I met with about a hundred young people in one of the University lecture halls.

I spoke for about 30 minutes explaining my new assignment as Porsche CEO and then solicited questions.

I was in over my head with the first question. Someone asked something like, "Why did Porsche change the alternator mount on the 1956 Porsche 356?"

I had not the slightest clue. I was Tony.

I responded with, "Who here knows the answer to that question?"

A number of students raised their hands; I pointed at one of them. "Please tell us."

I received a marvelous education from those students that evening. The above process was repeated until we were asked to leave the lecture room late that evening. At the request of my audience, we reconvened at a local beer hall and continued the process for several more hours.

I did not contribute many answers, but the evening ended with those students believing I was one of the most knowledgeable Porsche experts they had ever met.

I discovered and became comfortable in the role of Tony.

Managing is not about being perfect. Instead, it is largely about allowing capable people to perform.

Alexander Rankin

Founder and Retired CEO of Vulcan Spring & Mfg. Company

*P*eter Schutz and I met during his career at Caterpillar. He was developing diesel engines, operating a flying school, and teaching thermodynamics at Bradley University. I was designing tires for earthmoving equipment and still learning to spell thermodynamics. As two entrepreneurial engineers we took different paths in our careers. Peter, with his managerial skills and engineering skills was able to be effective and succeed in the corporate world. I obtained some experience and left the corporate world after ten years to found the Vulcan Spring & Mfg. Company.

We had common interests—family, cars, engines, and excellence. Our goal was to be the best at what we did and bring ideas that were outside the "existing status box" to our industry.

Over the years, we have gained a mutual respect for each other's abilities and look forward to comparing our thoughts and philosophies when we get together

You will be enriched by the wisdom Peter has revealed in The Driving Force.

17

Learning from Experience

As I look back at my eventful Porsche years, two important decisions stand out in my mind as offering particularly valuable lessons in decision-making, implementation, and leadership. These cases stand out because they were difficult decisions. They taxed my own and the organization's abilities and offered ample opportunity for failure. In the end, we managed to survive and even profit from our experiences, but the road was not without its bumps and curves. Because of the many challenges we faced, I sometimes found it difficult to stick to my dictum of deciding like a democracy and implementing like a dictatorship. Departures proved costly.

In the first case, regarding the pricing of the Porsche 944, I found it necessary to exert strong influence over decision-making in order to break the organization out of traditions and assumptions that no longer served us. This meant challenging people to think harder and consider some new approaches. Sometimes the leader needs to keep the heat on during the decision-making process to make sure people do not take the easy way out and make a challenging decision without really thinking it through. Although I did not exercise veto power, I did push hard for an improved decision.

The second case involved efforts to change the Porsche dealer network in the United States and ideas to improve it. I went farther than I should have in attempting to drive the decision-making process. The result was a high-quality decision that did not have enough support and proved impossible to implement. I ended up having to revisit the plans and do significant damage control. This incident highlights the necessity of following my own advice and making sure all interested parties are fully involved in decision-making early on. It is too easy to slip into the trap of using leadership authority to drive decision-making without sufficient regard for those who truly hold the power—and their cooperation is needed to implement the decision.

Pricing

When the Porsche 944 was ready for market introduction, there was a major question about the proper price for this new product.

I recall sitting in the board meeting of a rapidly growing company. We, the directors, had just completed almost two hours of the usual cost analysis game. The sales manager gave a sales status report. Business was good, very good, with new orders, new customers, etc. The operations manager suddenly opened up and said, "That is all well and good, but I do not have access to the resources and production capacity to deal with this flood of new orders."

The gut reaction was to increase capacity.

This presented a number of significant difficulties:

- It would take time.
- It would take financial resources that were not readily available.

- It would require additional people. (Talent is difficult to recruit and training is expensive.)
- The "break-even volume" would be raised significantly.

I recall suggesting, "Let's raise prices. That could fix the capacity crunch in a hurry! It would reduce the excess demand (orders) and improve the profitability of what is shipped. We would make more money without increasing our break-even volume."

The response was, "It is not that easy." (That is correct; in a commodity business, it could be deadly.)

It raised an interesting point: Exactly how is pricing done in many companies? Who sets the price of products and/or services offered to customers? The answer to this important question is often unclear. Pricing is perhaps the most difficult area of business decision-making. It can test the quality of the decision-making process, sometimes to the breaking point.

One hears that pricing should be based on "what the market will bear," or that it should be "competitive." Competition sets the price. That may be true; however, in many cases, it is not what is done. Prices are often dictated by *costs*. Prices are set by the computed cost plus a margin for profit.

Pricing can be driven by the financial establishment in the business, a situation in which costs are never low enough.

Let me be emphatic: Controlling costs is vital. Failing to do so effectively can result in failure.

Setting prices is not often an appropriate role for the cost side of the business.

When I was a trainee at Caterpillar, the pricing concept was explained as: "At Caterpillar, there are some parts that are big and impressive—parts such as diesel engine connecting rods. These impressive steel parts might weigh as much as 20 pounds and cost as much as $30 to produce. Other parts, like fuel injection pumps, are small and unimpressive. Such a pump must be built to very close and exacting tolerances and weigh a few ounces, but cost almost $100 to produce. Customers, who can not be expected to understand why such a small part is so expensive to produce, might not be willing to pay $150 for a small fuel injection pump. So it is priced at $30, but customers will pay more than $150 for a big impressive part like a connecting rod, which is priced accordingly."

Today, pricing must deal with a much better informed customer. The market increasingly drives pricing.

Customer-Driven Pricing

I have found it useful to view pricing in two distinct categories:

1. Pricing a product or service that is a "commodity."
2. Pricing a "differentiated" product or service.

A commodity is defined here as a product or service that is available from a number of alternate sources—a basically undifferentiated offering. In this instance, pricing will be determined by the competitive market, the users of the product or service. As communication continues to improve, every sale can become an auction. Sometimes it will be possible to differentiate such a product by superior service, delivery, or other ancillary activity. It is important that such opportunities not be overlooked.

A product or service that is a commodity must be priced at the competitive level set by the market. The costs incurred to generate and deliver such a product or service are not determining factors in pricing.

If the costs exceed the market price for a commodity, the organization has a serious *cost* problem. Clearly, the key to success would be cost reduction. The ability to beat industry cost level is the basis for success in a commodity business.

Competing in a commodity market is not a price war, it is a cost war.

A differentiated product or service is defined as one that is unique; it cannot be readily obtained from alternate sources. The differentiation can be technical, delivery, timing, ordering process, etc. In this instance, an opportunity exists to price the product or service as a function of the value-added perceived by the customer. Such a value is more or less uncoupled from the costs incurred in generating and delivering the product or service. Again, it seems clear that the costs incurred by an organization to generate and deliver the product or service need not be the basic factors that will determine pricing of a differentiated product or service.

Costs do not play a fundamental role in pricing, regardless of whether the product or service is a commodity or differentiated. Yet many organizations do their pricing on a cost-plus margin basis.

Having covered how pricing should not be done, how might pricing be done to optimize the performance of the business? Pricing a commodity is clear; it must be competitive. The market will set the price.

Pricing the differentiated product or service is not so clear.

Getting a handle on the value-added to the customer is fundamental in pricing a differentiated product such as the new Porsche 944. It is a rather sophisticated activity requiring skill and knowledge of the customer's business.

A special circumstance exists when the subject is a new product or service with no prior history or existing direct competition. This situation may be faced by a young and struggling organization that might have an innovative product or service that is not a commodity. How might such a product or service be priced effectively? Certainly not by simply examining the costs and adding a margin.

Often a manager will bump into a mindset that insists on viewing pricing decisions from a cost basis. How can leadership change the way a pricing decision is approached without abandoning the democratic decision-making process?

Pricing the Porsche 944

In 1981, Porsche was faced with the opportunity to introduce the Porsche 944 automobile into the U.S. market. In its day, this constituted a significantly differentiated product. It offered unique performance and styling. The question arose: What is the appropriate price for this automobile?

We had a big pricing meeting. The sales department had done its homework. In concert with the financial establishment, a cost had been determined for the car. At the time, a production level of about 70 cars per day had been projected.

I remember posing the question, "What is the proper price for this new product in the U.S. market?"

Armed to the teeth with the best and latest financial cost information, the sales people responded, "$24,000."

I asked, "Why $24,000?"

"Because that is what it will take to make a reasonable profit," they responded.

I had reached a point where I had to be careful about what I did next. I could have disagreed, told them what I thought was right, and tried to use my authority to force the decision my way. Everyone would have been sure the new product would fail because Herr Schutz had insisted on doing it "his way" instead of "the right way." We might have taken a great leap backward in our efforts to make the best of the driving force in the organization. On the other hand, I could not let this decision be made in a way that I was pretty sure would not lead to maximum success for the new product. I did not disclose what I believed was the "right" answer. I challenged their thinking instead.

Specifically, I decided to put a spotlight on their reasoning and the statement that a price of $24,000 would "make a reasonable profit." I replied with, "That is not what I asked you. I would like to know: What is the *proper price* for Porsche to *optimize the return on the investment we have made in this car?*"

This response resulted in major confusion. Cost-plus pricing was an integral part of the company culture; it was the way it was done. Nobody had thought about how to optimize the business by selling large numbers of cars; they were thinking instead about how to achieve a reasonable margin on each car we might sell.

To clarify the issue, I rephrased the question by making my request more specific: "At what price would this new product generate a volume level of 150 units per day? At what price would this new product be a major success in the U.S. market and make full use of *available* production capacity?"

After some discussion, the answer was, "To accomplish that, the price would have to be $18,500."

"All right then," I replied, confident that people knew what they were talking about. "The price is $18,500."

A few days later, it was time for our periodic management meeting that included all of the company's top managers. The issue of the 944 introductory price was addressed.

To my amazement, the sales department said the price was going to be $24,000.

"How can that be?" I asked. "I was told that the proper price to make this product a success was $18,500."

"Well, at that price, the company will not make any money," was the response.

My chief financial officer was quick to side with the sales department, "At $18,500, we would lose money on every car sold," he said.

"Even if we build 150 per day?" I asked.

"Well, we really cannot compute such a situation; we have never built that many units per day," I was told. "But it is quite certain that even at that level, costs would not be covered by an $18,500 price."

We were trapped by:

- Viewing a new product as a commodity before it was introduced (a reflection of the company culture at the time), and
- The concept of cost-plus pricing.

It took a lot of effort to get out of that trap and get general agreement to experiment with a lower price in an effort to maximize the product's initial sales success.

The Porsche 944 was introduced to the U.S. market at a price of $18,500 in the summer of 1982.

The car was sold in significant quantities; it was a resounding success and a real bargain in customers' eyes.

As predicted, Porsche lost money on every unit delivered.

So, we fixed the problem. We raised the price in succeeding increments. The production volume reached 150 per day, resulting in significant cost savings on a unit basis. Within two years, the car was selling for $22,500; later, it sold for more than $24,000. Porsche earned a substantial profit.

What did I learn from this?

The proper price of a product or service is not a simple number. There is no such thing as the "right price." The price is a band, a spread around a mean value. In engineering, this is known as distribution tolerance.

Because of this and the unknown value-added impact of a new product or service, the most reasonable answer to the question, "What is the proper price for this new product?" is: "We do not know!" Until such an offering actually hits the market and is in the hands of a customer, it is not possible to know. Only the customer can determine the value-added impact of the new offering and thus the right price.

So how do we determine a price when we do not know? If we try to determine a price in isolation, we will quite likely not get it right.

We can run a potential problem analysis: What can go wrong, and what will we do when it does?

What happens if we err on the side of pricing the new offering too high?

We could make a *good profit on paper.* However, if we have priced too high, it will not generate significant volume. How do we resolve this dilemma? The sad truth is that we have not become any smarter. We know that our price is too high, but we do not know *how much too high.* Sales are sluggish and the offering is in trouble. What can we do?

We are forced to lower the price.

Once this is done, not much good can happen. The customers who have bought the offering at the too high initial price will feel embarrassed. It is unlikely that they will tell the world of their purchase. Others who buy the product at the reduced price will wonder, Will the price drop still further? The market will view the situation as an offering in trouble. Further price reductions will have only a minimal effect on volume until the price is at the lower level of the spread around the proper price.

A promising offering can be sabotaged by introduction at an initial price that is too high.

This circumstance can result if costs are too high.

Often it is the result of

- Arrogance. Somebody believes they know a proper price level when they in fact cannot know it—the offering is "new."
- Greed.
- Impatience.

What happens if we price a new offering at a price below the unknown proper price?

The offering is likely to sell in large volumes. It is perceived as a bargain. It *is* a bargain.

The problem now is, we are not making money.

The solution? *Raise the price.*

If this is done in discrete increments, we can anticipate the following results:

- Customers who bought the offering at the introductory price will tell the world. They will spread the word. What a great offering! What a great value! An existing customer will never be upset by a price increase.
- Sales volume will be maintained, or increase, as the word spreads.
- Volume will not moderate as the price is raised until we reach the upper level of the spread around the proper price.

- The offering will be perceived as a success, and the upper level of the price spread will likely generate an optimum profit level.

What did I learn?

- If the proper price is not known, strive to price at a level that is safely too low. The lack of profit can be solved by subsequent price increases.
- If the introductory price is too high, the lack of sales volume cannot be corrected by a price reduction and a distress situation can result.

The Porsche 944 situation is not unique. I believe Toyota followed the same pricing strategy in the market introduction of the successful and profitable Lexus 400. Porsche repeated this effectively in the introduction of the Porsche Boxter sports car almost 20 years later.

Nothing goes to the bottom line like effective pricing. Nothing can drain performance more destructively than improper, thoughtless pricing.

The low-price, sales volume-oriented concept for a new offering sounds risky and expensive. Nothing is in fact riskier and more expensive than the failure of a new offering introduced at too high a price.

What I am describing here is a pricing strategy. Strategies are often important aids and guides during decision-making. As the leader, I had an obligation to clarify the strategy to be used. When I did that, people arrived at a very different price than they had at first.

Was this a democratic decision-making process?

Management is never easy. Building a culture and introducing strategic concepts must be incorporated into the process.

I did not set the Porsche 944 price; I raised strategic questions. I relied on people in the organization to come up with sound answers. Beyond that, it established the merits of strategic thinking.

Much as I had done when I said, "We will never go to any race without the objective of winning," I now said, "We will not price a Porsche on a cost-plus basis as though it were a commodity or an appliance." I had set limits on the range of decision.

It is necessary for a leader to set a new direction by clarifying strategic issues involved in a decision. Asking questions about what the objective is or what will happen under different scenarios can help change the basic strategic framework with which people approach a decision. It is far better to exert influence on a strategic level than take control and force a decision on the organization without their understanding.

Porsche Cars North America

The business relationship between Volkswagen and Porsche started in the 1930s when Professor Porsche, Sr., and his son, Ferdinand, designed and developed the famous Volkswagen Beetle. Until the advent of the Volkswagen Rabbit in the 1960s, Porsche continued to do most of the engineering and development of Volkswagen cars.

After Porsche began to build Porsche sports cars, Volkswagen became the importer and distributor of Porsche cars in the United States under a contractual arrangement. This was accomplished by a wholly owned Volkswagen U.S. subsidiary called "Volkswagen of America." This arrangement served both companies well for a number of decades.

Over time, the United States became the biggest and most lucrative market for Porsche. In the early 1980s, Porsche sold about half of its cars in the United States with a rising potential.

After I became CEO, Porsche acted to optimize the U.S. Porsche business. A number of conflicts arose in the Porsche-Volkswagen of America business relationship. The focal points were the spare parts business, appointment of Porsche dealers, and advertising. Volkswagen appeared to be managing the Porsche business as a minor branch of the total operation, failing to optimize the Porsche potential.

Despite repeated attempts, we did not succeed in getting the cooperation we deemed indispensable to realize the full potential of the Porsche business in North America. The Porsche family decided to terminate the Volkswagen of America importer contract and take on the U.S. import and distribution of Porsche automobiles through a proprietary company. Money issues did not drive this decision. At the time, we did not know how profitable the Porsche U.S. import and distribution business was.

Of all the things that were implemented during my tenure at Porsche AG, terminating the Volkswagen importer contract and creating Porsche Cars North America (PCNA) to take over the import and distribution of Porsche sports cars in the United States was without question the single most profitable Porsche move. After the event, PCNA earned more money in March 1984 in the United States, than the entire company had ever earned in an entire year. PCNA continues to be a profit leader at Porsche.

However, the *implementation* of a good decision is critical to success. In this case, *my mismanagement of the decision process nearly sank me and much of Porsche with it.* Only the steadfast support by the Porsche family and a few important U.S. Porsche dealers allowed us to salvage the project.

I had long since learned that decisions should be made democratically and implemented dictatorially. Yet, I fell into the all-too-common trap of pushing through what seemed an obviously great decision without following that process.

When I first became vice president at Cummins, I recall a series of meetings with Cummins distributors. One such meeting took place in Tampa, Florida, with the southeastern U.S. distributors. I presented what I believed to be a brilliant plan.

A distributor by the name of Bill Blizzard took the floor. He was getting close to retirement and was a wise experienced man.

Blizzard said, "Son, let me tell you a story. A factory representative and a distributor owner were walking across a large grass field. Suddenly, an angry bull charged at them. The factory representative climbed a tree and the distributor jumped into a hole. As soon as the bull charged past, the distributor jumped up out of the hole. Upon seeing this, the bull charged once more. The distributor jumped back into the hole. This up and down went on for about 20 minutes before the bull tired of the game and walked off. The factory representative came down out of the tree and the distributor came up out of the hole. The factory man said: 'I will grow to be over 100 years old and will still not understand you distributors. What was all that silly jumping up and down? If you had gotten down into that hole and just stayed there, this whole episode would have ended sooner and I would not have been left hanging in that tree for 20 minutes.'

'You factory people are all the same,' replied the distributor. 'You don't understand the local situation. *There was a wildcat in that hole!'* "

There were wildcats in those holes, and we could not see them from Columbus, Indiana.

There were a number of wildcats in the holes of the Porsche U.S. dealer organization. Financial covenants with financing banks and investors could be severely impacted by some of the suggested changes proposed for dealer franchises. Pending dealership sales and planned mergers would be upset. The new plan was focused on operating efficiency and customer service. Without dealer involvement in the planning process, a significant number of key operational factors were overlooked.

Having learned and experienced all of that, how could I have mismanaged the Porsche North American Importer project so badly? To this day, I cannot answer that question.

I did not make the decision in isolation. I availed myself of the best and brightest advisors in the industry. I was convinced I had not rushed to judgment. My fellow managers and I believed that every conceivable element of the subject had been explored, researched, and checked.

The decision was brilliant.

The decision was decades ahead of its time. It included elements of "just-in-time inventory" for car dealers, elements of today's Internet trading, and factory-financed floor-planning of dealer car inventories.

Exactly what did I do wrong? I had made a dictatorial decision.

Although a great number of people were involved in the decision process, I failed to include the Porsche dealers. They had the power and without their involvement, the decision was dictatorial. The program never got off the ground.

I failed to include "the wildcat in the hole" for "legal reasons." Lawyers warned that without the inclusion of *all* dealers, Porsche would be open to legal action charging a conspiracy. I would not argue that such legal issues are/were not valid. But whatever the reasons, I had learned that without the inclusion of the parties that have power, without their democratic participation, the plan had little (no) chance of being implemented well.

To this day, I ask myself, How could I? But I did. It literally took me to the brink of disaster. I met with Professor Porsche ten days after the proposal presentation to U.S. Porsche dealers. I did not have to explain the catastrophe. A large number of Porsche dealers had already contacted him asking for my scalp.

We agreed to back off the proposed plan and set up a traditional dealer contract situation instead. One thing I had not forgotten: *Always have something to fall back on other than your behind.* Professor Porsche approved the proposed plan revision, and I got off the hook. But it was close.

I still recall Professor Porsche's remark: "Herr Schutz, the press will have a feast on this." In fact, he said, *"Sie werden von der Presse in der Luft zerrissen."* Literally translated, "The press will tear you into pieces in the air." This is a German saying alluding to a wild carnivore tearing prey to pieces in the air.

My response was, "I am a big boy, and I can take it. We must do what is best for Porsche, not Schutz."

"That is the difference between a politician and a manager," said Professor Porsche. "A manager puts the business first and a politician puts ego first."

We managed to handle the crisis and although it took some time, we regained dealer confidence and made a lot of money together.

I do not know how many times we must relearn some lessons, but trust me; I shall not make that mistake again.

Tom Fredericks

CEO, ECL GROUP OF COMPANIES

I *met and listened to Mr. Schutz at a business conference in Chicago, Illinois, in 1997. The conference had many excellent speakers. The one that most positively affected my thinking was Peter W. Schutz.*

Following that conference, we developed a new forward-going strategy for the ECL Group of Companies incorporating many of the philosophies that Schutz articulated in his Chicago presentation.

In 1998, we invited Peter to speak to our employees about achieving "extraordinary results with ordinary people." After a three-hour presentation in the morning Peter spent the afternoon with 20 of our senior management people discussing the challenges each was facing and formulating solutions. His personal approachable manner on business issues and the ability to communicate with a common-sense, uncomplicated approach, had a very positive impact on our management team.

As we develop our group's forward strategy to take us through the year 2005, we have invited Mr. Schutz to return to Calgary, Canada, to gain further insight into his views on leadership for the future.

When I learned of his new book, The Driving Force, *it confirmed that Peter is a forward thinker. I have yet to read a book that looks beyond success to excellence in that manner.*

18

The Star
Performance Model

W hy do some organizations perform well, while others with equal skills and talents do not? This has confounded many managers. What is the secret of performance at the next level—star performance? In a sense, that is the subject of this book.

The victory in the 1981 Le Mans race led the charge to reestablish Porsche as a winner. The number 11 Porsche 936 racecar, driven by Jacky Ickx and Derek Bell, was very visible. But it was the number 12 Porsche 936 car, the one that did not win the race, that played a major role in the way I have come to view management.

The number 12 car was mechanically identical to the number 11 car. It was driven by two Americans, Al Holbert and Hurley Haywood, and an Australian, Vern Schupann. Each lap at Le Mans is 8.5 miles. On the first lap, the number 12 car was down in power and came limping into the pits in last place. It turned out a spark plug was defective. This was easily corrected and the number 12 car resumed racing in last place after just one lap.

Twenty-four hours is a long time. The race started at 3:00 in the afternoon and by 8:30 PM, the number 12 car had passed all the other cars and was running in second place behind our number 11 car.

The two Porsche 936s ran one-two through the night, until at 4:30 in the morning the number 12 car came into the pits for fuel and was unable to resume racing. A clutch bearing had failed. This was a small part that looked like about a $2.50 bearing, but I found out that nothing on a Porsche costs $2.50. The problem was not the cost of the bearing, but the fact that to change it, most of the car had to be disassembled due to extensive collateral damage.

A Miracle in the Making

At 4:30 A.M., in the predawn darkness of southern France, I watched a team of mechanics who had not slept for 36 hours disassemble a Porsche 936 racecar, parts of which were so hot that their asbestos gloves were smoking; there was no time to wait for the car to cool. There were parts and wrenches all over the place. There was not a lot of talking; everyone seemed to know exactly what to do. *Fifty-two minutes later, that car was once again reassembled and ready to race.*

As Hurley Haywood pulled the car back out onto the track, it occurred to me that I had just witnessed a miracle. (Incidentally, the number 12 car did manage to finish the race, in seventh place.) I turned to Helmut Bott, the smartest car man I have ever known, and asked, "Tell me, Herr Bott, how long should it take to disassemble and re-assemble a Porsche 936 racecar? Not a racecar, parts of which are too hot to touch. Not in the dark, at the side of a racetrack, but in a well-lighted shop. Not by a group of mechanics who have not slept for 36 hours, but well-rested union mechanics (and these were all union mechanics). And, oh yes, it must be a zero-defects job."

His answer, after some thought, was, "I would estimate about six to eight hours."

I had just seen it done in 52 minutes!

Is 52 minutes a reasonable time for such a repair job? Of course not. It is something that one might experience once in a career. But how about four to six hours instead of six to eight? I had just seen it done in less than an hour.

It occurred to me that morning in France that *most people are capable of much more than even they believe possible.*

It is important to understand that this feat was performed by ordinary Porsche people. What is it that can cause such people to rise to such incredible heights of performance?

At Porsche, we typically raced with one car. Sometimes, we raced with two, but it was only at Le Mans that we raced with a three car factory team. In order to support three cars and a spare, it was necessary to recruit 20 or 25 additional people to supplement the normal contingent of race mechanics. Where did these additional people come from? They were recruited from the pool of Porsche people from the factory floor and office work force.

On the occasion of a *"Betriebsversammlung,"* the large employee meetings that took place from time to time, I might announce, "This year as in years past, we will be going to race at Le Mans with a three-car team. In order to do that, we will have to recruit an additional 20 or 25 people to help work the race. Are there any volunteers?"

Several hundred hands would be raised and I would explain:

- There will be no extra pay for this duty.
- We will not work eight-hour days. You might have to work three or four days with only an occasional catnap if that is what it takes to get the equipment ready to race. (It must be noted that I was addressing union people, people who might call a strike because a ten-minute coffee break is no longer adequate.)
- I can promise you neither hot food nor three meals a day. You might have to subsist on jelly sandwiches (there was

no peanut butter in Germany back then) and drinks out of a vending machine.

- We will be doing our work in tents that will be erected alongside the racetrack, and it rains in southern France in the springtime. You will be wet and cold and tired and hungry.

These were absolutely miserable working facilities and conditions. Did this change the number of people who volunteered? Not at all.

"Oh yes. One thing I forgot to mention, if you are selected for this duty, our sponsor will outfit you with a pair of racing coveralls. They will be white with a blue border around the sleeves and your collar, and a big logo on your chest— Rothmans Racing—and Porsche in big red block letters on your back. You get to keep those after the race."

More hands would go up.

These uniforms were a badge of honor. They were something that would be saved to show the grandkids someday.

Typical, committed Porsche people did that 52-minute repair job at Le Mans in June 1981.

Let me assure you that this performance was not the achievement of superstars. They were people who became superstars because of circumstances thrust upon them. I have wondered, what if I had approached one of these people as they were engaged in the job and asked: "You look tired, my friend, why not take a short break?" I believe he might have slugged me. He would certainly have said, "Are you out of your mind? We have a job to do! We will take a break after the car is back in competition."

I studied the situation. If I could not understand what was going on here, I would never reach my true potential as a manager by mobilizing the driving force.

Lessons from Larry Wilson

One of my mentors was Larry Wilson. Wilson is a genius, the founder of Wilson Learning Corporation in the 1960s, and one of the true experts in teaching selling and interpersonal relations.

Early in his career, Wilson was hired by a major automobile manufacturer that had a problem. The company had over 5,000 dealers in the United States and Canada. Each was a free-standing entrepreneurial organization. Some of these organizations performed well and others did not. The differences that gave rise to this variation in performance were not clear. What was the common denominator in organizations that performed well while others failed?

Wilson was hired to shed light on this mystery. He and his organization undertook a study of 1,500 automobile dealers seeking to identify the secret of success—the common factors that most frequently correlated with successful operations.

They found five questions. Five simple questions, which when answered adequately at all levels of the organization, most frequently correlated with good performance.

They also found two factors that did *not* correlate with good performance.

The first of these was money—*pay and financial incentives.* They found some organizations were well-paid, through creative incentive programs that performed well. But others, equally compensated, did not perform well.

Pay and financial incentives did not correlate with good performance.

Of course, pay is important, it must be competitive, and creative incentives are indispensable. If you do not believe it, try a little experiment: Stop paying people and see how long the organization performs. Pay and financial incentives are not the key to outstanding performance; they are the price of admission.

Pay and incentives will not transform a low-performance organization into a high-performance organization.

Second were *facilities and equipment.* Some organizations operated in modern, well-equipped facilities and performed well, while others, equally well-equipped, did not. On occasion they would find some hole-in-the-wall operation in an old building with old equipment in which numerous mechanics were vying for work and customers were making appointments for routine service two weeks out. Other organizations, operating in old facilities, were doing very little.

Are facilities and equipment important in an organization? Of course, they are. Any organization is capable of more and better work if good facilities and equipment are available.

You cannot transform a low-performance organization into a high-performance organization by moving into new facilities and buying new equipment.

Facilities and equipment did not correlate with good performance.

What *Really* Drives Performance?

Here then are the five questions that most frequently correlated with outstanding performance:

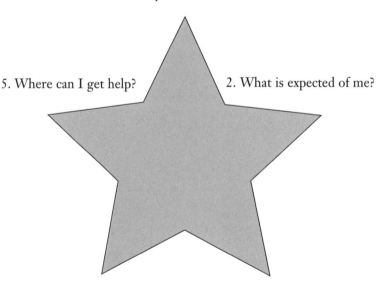

1. Why are we here?

5. Where can I get help?   2. What is expected of me?

4. What's in it for me?   3. How am I doing?

Groups most often performed well when every person in the organization could answer these questions. They are basic ingredients that can turn the driving force on and achieve extraordinary results.

Often, people cannot give adequate answers to all five questions. When that is the case, the manager has an opportunity to address some basic problems and see dramatic improvements in performance.

Over and over, this method was a powerful one that helped me lead the Porsche organization.

A good way to share these experiences is to go through the five questions, one at a time.

1. Why Are We Here?

In order to perform well, an organization must have a shared objective based on values that *all* members of the organization can understand and support with *passion*. In Porsche racing, one such value was: We will never participate in any race without the objective of winning.

Stated generically, it could be: We will never participate in any commercial activity without the objective of being the best at what we do. This is a way of enlisting people in the pursuit of excellence, which is frequently more effective than striving only for success.

There is a wonderful old story about the importance of knowing "why we are here."

Three men were working on a construction site. All three were performing exactly the same task. A passerby asked the first one, "What are you doing here?"

The answer was, "I am busting rocks."

The passerby asked the second man the same question. (Remember, he was doing the same thing as the first man.)

This time the answer was, "I am earning my living."

These are two possible views of work. They differ slightly in their perspective, but neither is a good answer to the question, *why are we here?* If the people in the organization believe they are busting rocks in order to earn a living, how might they decide to improve their job? They might ask:

How can I bust fewer rocks for more money?

And what is management thinking?

How can I get people to bust more rocks for less money?

This is unlikely to result in a happy relationship; it is certainly not the key to getting extraordinary results.

I have known many highly educated and experienced managers who view management in that adversarial manner.

When the passerby asked the third man what he was doing, he got a very different answer.

The third man's answer was,

I am helping my colleagues build a temple.

It is not the activity that defines a job, but how someone sees their activity in the context of an organization's culture and style that matters. If people are working together to build a temple, the hammers are not as heavy, the rocks are not as hard, and the days are not as long. It is no longer the same task.

It is not what people are doing, but how they view their collective effort as part of a mission that puts passion into the activity; passion that can lead to extraordinary results.

To create and sustain real driving force, people must build a temple together, not bust rocks for a living.

The definition of the temple is not only a statement of what is to be accomplished, but includes a value statement of what will *not* be done (or tolerated) in the process. There are always rules and values associated with a temple.

"We will never go to any race without the objective of winning" turned out to be such a statement.

It is up to management to define the temple.

If management cannot (or will not) communicate what sort of a temple the organization is building, the work ethic can easily become: How can I bust fewer rocks for more money?

Since managers are committed to get "more work for less money," it is easy to see how a dysfunctional conflict can occur.

2. What Is Expected of Me Around Here?

There are many ways to tackle the question of what is expected. Only when you are clear on the first question, *Why are we here?* will an answer to this second question be possible. When we evaluate the answers to the question of what is expected, it should not be about when I come to work or where I park, but rather, *What is my role in helping the organization build the temple?*

When we went to Le Mans, someone on the team had to change tires. Two or three of the people who had been recruited to help work the race would draw that assignment. In some cases, these people had never been more than 50 kilometers outside of Stuttgart and we had brought them to the incredible spectacle that is Le Mans. There were over 450,000 people—a maelstrom of humanity and an overwhelming experience. If you spent all your time changing tires, it could be a rather underwhelming experience.

Changing tires on the wheels of a racecar is what some might describe as donkey work. It is heavy labor and generates a lot of dust and dirt. We had a separate tent for tire work to keep all that dust and dirt out of the engines.

A number of people had been recruited to help work the race. Now it was time to explain the job.

What if the job is explained as follows: "Every time someone brings a worn tire into this tent, I want you to remove the worn tire from the wheel rim, put it on that stack over there, get a new tire from the other stack, mount it on the wheel rim, and blow it full of air. Now, have you got that?"

Then with the race in full swing and the fur flying, an observer walks into the tent and asks, "Hey! What are you people doing in here?"

Chances are, the answer would be, "We are changing tires." (Just "busting rocks.")

Consider an alternate job structure and explanation:

"Do you see this little scooter? I want you to take this scooter and drive it over to the racing pit area. When our car comes into the pit for a tire change, I want you to put the worn tires on the scooter and bring them back to this tent. Take the worn tires off the wheel rims, put them onto that stack over there, take new tires off the other stack, mount them on the wheel rims, and blow them full of air. Then, put the tires back on the scooter and drive them over to the pit area. When our car comes into the pit for a tire change, I want *you* to make sure that the correct wheel is mounted on the correct corner of the car."

What if the job is structured and explained in that way, and the race is in progress, the fur is flying, and someone walks into the tire tent and asks, "Hey! What are you people doing in here?" Perhaps this time the answer would be:

We are helping to win the race.
(We are helping to build a temple.)

I still remember my first real job. I was 14 years old and worked as a stock boy at a wholesale jobber on East 47th Street on the south side of Chicago. One part of the job consisted of unpacking cases of various drugstore supplies and putting them on the proper shelves. The other part was to pick orders, take items off the shelves, line them up on a long counter, check the order to make sure it was correct, and pack them into a properly labeled box. I spent many Saturdays doing this job.

It was a boring, repetitive task. My bosses, the Sager brothers, Eddy and Melvin, were wise. About every fourth or fifth week, I was allowed to go with the truck to deliver the packed boxes. WOW!!! It made it a different job. No longer were these just boxes with labels; I got to know the people who were waiting for them. I never forgot that.

In later years, I applied that to many situations with considerable success.

At Cummins, we made it possible for engineers to visit truck fleet operators so they could see *their engines* in operation. It gave customers an opportunity to critique the product, but more importantly, it helped the engineers understand the temple: customer satisfaction.

At Porsche, we facilitated visits to the automobile assembly lines so that customers might see how *their car* was built. This was more for the morale of Porsche factory workers than for the entertainment of customers.

There is a story that illustrates my point: Two men were working on an assembly line. One said to the other: "I will retire next month, and *the first thing I am going to do after I retire, is walk down to the end of this assembly line to see what in the Sam Hill I have been building around here for the past 35 years.*"

Henry Ford took the assembly of a complicated machine, an automobile, and chopped it up into a series of sequential operations, each of which could be performed by a relatively unskilled individual. This assembly line concept was so efficient, that Mr. Ford could pay three times the then going rate for factory labor and still build an automobile for a price affordable for working class people.

One would think that with that sort of wage rate, there would have been little turnover at the Highland Park plant of Ford Motor Company. Instead, turnover was about 300 percent. Some of the first truly violent labor unrest took place at Ford assembly plants. It was the highest paid factory workers of the period that formed the core of what was to become the United Automobile Workers Union.

If people are put into what I call an empty job, a job that seems to have no meaning, there is not enough money in the world to keep them motivated. If they are breaking rocks, there will never be enough money to get anywhere near extraordinary results with *any* people, even geniuses.

In today's world of people with more education and higher expectations, it is more difficult than ever to provide meaningful jobs. Managers must re-think job content and structure.

The more opportunity people at all levels of the business have to be in touch with the customer, the more clearly they will understand their role and the better the chances that extraordinary results will be achieved.

People who will not "bust rocks" might help you build a temple.

3. How Am I Doing?

If someone has been given a job and there is no way to measure the result, it is likely they will conclude, "If there is no way to measure what I am doing, it cannot be very important."

When managers practice management by walking around, a frequent question is, "How are you doing?" A frequent answer is, "Fine."

That can be an opportunity to impact the culture of an organization. The manager can say, *"How do you know?"* If a member of the organization does not know how to deal with that question, it can be the sign of a problem.

If people in the organization are only doing the same old things they have been doing for the past five or ten years, the answer does not matter; people can *feel* they are doing fine. They have extensive experience. However, if the organization is moving into uncharted waters, doing new and innovative things that have not been done before, and moving to the next level, there is no experience by which they can gauge performance. Performance must be measured and communicated.

In the absence of such feedback, people cannot take initiative or action to achieve extraordinary results.

4. What's In It for Me?

This book is dedicated to my wife, Sheila. I have courted this lady from the first time I laid eyes on her, and I love doing it.

The longer I have worked as a manager, the more I have come to believe that perhaps that is one of the most important concepts I have learned about management:

Courtship.

As managers, we can:

- court our customers;
- court our suppliers;
- court our employees;
- court our peers;
- court the owners of the business (if we are a "hired hand");
- and, yes, in some circumstances, even court our competitors.

If we can learn to do that well and enjoy doing it, we can achieve outstanding results as managers.

If you do not enjoy courtship, it may be advisable to look for another profession. (If you have not already gotten married, and you do not enjoy courtship, perhaps it would be wise to avoid marriage—everything about marriage can, and usually does, get old, but courtship can endure and be a joy forever.)

Today, Sheila is the manager of our little business, Harris & Schutz, Inc. She does the selling, marketing, scheduling, pricing, etc. All I have to do is go out and do my lecturing and management coaching.

A few years ago, while out doing what I do, I received a message to call Sheila. When I did, she said, "Today I was driving along Tamiami Trail here in Naples and saw a used 1994 Audi convertible on the Porsche dealer's lot. It is a metallic purplish red, a really beautiful little car. I stopped in to see Reggie Smith, the manager. He said, 'If you like that car, Sheila, take it and drive it for a few days.' I have been driving this car, and Peter, I must have this car. This car is me!"

When I returned home, the car was sitting in the driveway. I changed into my work clothes and washed Sheila's car, waxed it, polished the wheels, and cleaned the interior. It was shining like a jewel.

I then went into the house and announced, "Sheila, I have cleaned your new car."

I wanted Sheila to come out to the driveway and be blown

away. "WOW!—and you cleaned the wheels; and will you look at that interior!" This need only take a minute or so, but it is an important minute for the person who cleaned the car.

This was not about a clean car. It is not the car I care about. Instead, *it is about a reaction. For me, cleaning the car is a form of courtship.* As long as I continue to get the proper reaction, I will keep the car clean.

Courting Employees

Most managers have people in their organization who hold what might be viewed as a menial job. To the job holder, it is the most important job in the world; it is the only job they have.

Perhaps someone in the organization is responsible for keeping the entryway to the business clean as a part of their job. Every so often, the boss must take a few moments of valuable time and take this person to the job site and say something like: "As you probably know, we are _____ (building a temple). An important part of that is an image of quality and caring. When this entryway looks the way it does when you take care of it and customers or suppliers come to call on us, we have taken the first steps to our objective. If this place looks like a pigpen instead, then with all the wonderful things we are doing in the back, we would still have an uphill battle. Thank you. What you do around here matters."

Only the top manager can do this effectively. There are many tasks in the organization that can be delegated; this is not one of them.

Yet many managers conclude, *I do not have time for that sort of thing.*

Is it important? It *is* important, if the objective is to get extraordinary results with ordinary people.

It can be one of the most important functions of a manager. Delegate something else and spend some time courting the most important asset in the business—the people. They need to know how they are doing, and when they do well, they need to know their efforts are noted and appreciated.

Courting the Customer

In 1984, Don Johnson was starring in a television series called *Miami Vice*. Sheila received a telephone call from Gahl Burt, the wife of the U.S. ambassador to Germany, asking if she could be a tour guide for Johnson and show him around Germany. Of course, she accepted.

Sheila met Don at the Frankfurt airport and they immediately hit it off. After a quick ride to Stuttgart, Don went to dinner with Sheila and me. He explained he was planning to pick his new Porsche 911 Turbo cabriolet up at the factory the following morning. He disclosed a plan to have a mechanic in Miami modify the car, because he believed what he really wanted was not available in a factory car. I listened to this horror story. After a short while, I had had enough and announced, "I will not deliver the car you ordered, consider your order cancelled. Instead, Don, I invite you to come to my office tomorrow morning at nine o'clock. We will develop your specification for the exact Porsche you desire, and then build exactly the car you want!"

Don Johnson and Sheila arrived at my office at nine o'clock. What I had not disclosed was that I had invited Professor Porsche to meet with us. He and Don got along very well. Professor Porsche announced, "Come, let us go over to the factory together and design your Porsche just the way you want it."

We had a great day. It was a tremendous morale boost for people at the plant. Don Johnson specified the Porsche of his dreams, something special for a special customer and a vehicle that was much more profitable for the company.

Recognizing the Winning Team

The morning after Porsche won a race at Le Mans, a picture of the winning car, with all the race mechanics lined up behind it, would appear in the Stuttgart newspaper.

How did that picture get into the newspaper? Since neither Porsche nor the newspaper could know which car was going to win, how did they get a picture in time to publish it in the morning newspaper? This was in the 1980s, before the days of the Internet and satellite picture transmissions.

A week or more before the race, I had Manfred Jantke, my public relations chief, photograph each of our four racecars—three cars and the back-up car. Each was photographed with the full complement of mechanics standing behind it. We cultivated positive relationships with elements of the automotive press, including the Stuttgart daily newspaper. As soon as we knew which car (if any) had won the big race, we dispatched the appropriate picture to the press for publication.

That concludes the nonfiction part of this story. I would like to illustrate the possible impact of this example with a fantasy.

Imagine ten-year-old Hans, a fifth grader in a Stuttgart school. His dad works at Porsche and is assigned to be a mechanic at the Le Mans race. Porsche wins the race. The next morning, the Stuttgart newspaper carries a big headline on the front page: "Porsche wins Le Mans!" A picture of the winning car with all the mechanics lined up in back of the car accompanies the headline.

Hans takes the newspaper to school and explains proudly, "That's my Daddy; he won Le Mans."

Next to Hans sits little Fritz. Fritz's Dad is the chairman of Daimler-Benz. That evening, Fritz looks at his dad with a long face and says, "Dad, sometimes I wish you had an important job like my friend Hans' dad."

The activities necessary to get extraordinary results with ordinary people require purposeful effort and preparation. It is not about size. It is about how we see ourselves and the temple we are building. Most people want to take pride in the organization to which they belong. Give people an opportunity to shine and take a bow. Not just the top people, not just the salesperson who closed the deal, but also those who worked behind the scenes to make it possible.

If you are failing in this, you can anticipate how people will answer the "How am I doing?" question. Their answer to this question might be, "I don't really know, so I might as well try to get away with doing less work for more money." If people do not feel they are helping to build a temple, if they do not feel involved, they may conclude that what is in it for them is, breaking fewer rocks for more money.

What's in it for me? Pride and passion. Courtship is a key element in building the pride and passion that can give rise to extraordinary performance.

5. If I Fail to Perform, Where Do I Go for Help?

If the organization is only doing the same old things it has done for years and people fail to perform, it is a different sort of problem. If the organization is embarked on a mission to do new and different things in a changing and challenging environment, then there will be times when even our most capable and experienced people will find themselves in circumstances where they will be faced with acquiring a new skill. They become vulnerable to failure.

This must be a learning experience, not a basis for punishment. Withholding a reward is a punishment. If people are punished for failure to perform in such circumstances and do not feel they can get help without being judged, they will cover up failures. (The CYA rule, Cover Your A__, will apply.) Instead of seeking solutions as a team, they will instead try to avoid blame for failure. If this begins to characterize an organization, the operation can become sterile and nonproductive. As I often point out, every manager has the organization they deserve.

If we punish failure in periods of change, we might end up with:

- An organization that does not like change. Change is not what many people actually dislike; some dislike being punished for failure when they are learning a new skill. Remember, some people learn faster than others, and the fast learners will not necessarily become the best performers.
- An organization in which people become more proficient at covering up mistakes than they are at solving problems.

261

If the leader is the one who must avoid even an appearance of failure, the organization can be severely handicapped in times when new skills are a key to better performance.

The best managers are not those who are perfect. Perfection is not necessary for good leadership. It's OK to be Tony.

A place to go for help is essential if people are to perform at extraordinary levels.

In the military, this role is often filled by a chaplain. In a peacetime military, a chaplain often feels superfluous, but it is said there are no atheists in foxholes. When the pressure of combat is felt, the role of the chaplain becomes important.

In today's business, people are typically under intense pressure to perform. It is important to provide a mechanism to help people when the pressure to perform becomes too great. The nature of the pressure can range from coping with challenges in personal life to the need to acquire new skills dealing with modern technology.

When an organization strives for excellence, the pressure to perform builds and the chaplain role becomes important. There must be someone to whom people can go for help. Make sure you know who that person is, encourage them to play that role well, and provide the resources they need to be truly helpful to those who need it. It is rarely a person's immediate supervisor.

I found that Larry Wilson's insights about performance were effective in most organizations I have encountered. They make for a simple, but powerful, perspective on leadership. To make sure I have passed them on clearly, I am going to repeat them.

The five questions that most frequently correlate with extraordinary performance:

1. Why are we here?
2. What is expected of me around here?
3. How am I doing?
4. What's in it for me?
5. If I fail to perform, where do I go for help?

In organizations that know the answers to these five questions at all levels, extraordinary performance is often the result.

Lew Haskell

VICE PRESIDENT—FIELD OPERATIONS,
TEC INTERNATIONAL, INC.

I have known Peter for over 12 years and consider him to be a significant resource both personally and professionally. From a business perspective, I find myself quoting his advice and referencing his insights in many situations. He has the unique ability to communicate complex ideas in a simple and memorable fashion.

At a personal level, my contacts with Peter have helped me recognize my strengths and areas for development. His style, which can be both blunt and encouraging in equal measure, has been a catalyst for my growth as an executive. I don't believe I would be where I am today had it not been for his encouragement and confidence in me "as simply an ordinary person trying to produce extraordinary results."

Ozzie Gontang

TEC CHAIRMAN

*P*eter W. Schutz has presented to my TEC group four times in the past eight years. Peter has also presented to the Frances Parker School's leadership forum. In this event Peter reached 80 student leaders from 15 San Diego schools and 20 local CEOs.

Peter has the knack and ability to relate true experiences that make his message come alive and remain as "hooks" in the minds of business leaders. Peter's collection of "generic corporate values" has guided many executives in managing their businesses.

Peter has set his mind and spirit to improve the mind, soul, and spirit of business leaders. Besides a powerful model and teacher of leadership, I value his kindness, generosity, and friendship. He truly lives his values and leadership principles.

19

Values and Leadership

My challenge at Porsche was to take the business to the next level. Not just a higher profit level, but a higher level of performance throughout the business. The concept of a high-performing group that can achieve extraordinary results is captured in the phrase *driving force*.

Taking Business to the Next Level

Since leaving Porsche and returning to the United States, I have been on the speaking circuit, addressing business leaders and students. The objective is to help managers operating in a competitive business climate achieve success and have a bit of fun in the process.

The rate of change has continued to accelerate. My objective has been to focus on things that do *not* change. Among these things are business ethics and the challenge of getting extraordinary results with ordinary people.

In this chapter, I will share some of my experiences and observations from that work. I will also focus in particular on a critical element of driving force leadership: value-based management. The values which define ethical conduct have become increasingly important. That they are important to me may have been evident in earlier chapters, especially those concerning my views on culture and my belief that an open-handed approach yields the most in the long run. I learned these values from my father and personal experiences and have found them beneficial in business. If you open the business section of the newspaper, you may find examples of managers and businesses who apparently do not put a high value on ethical behavior and get into trouble as a result. How does it happen? What can we do to avoid such debacles in our own organizations?

There are more opportunities for people to take *initiative* when changes are needed to awaken driving force. That is a good thing, but it can lead to trouble. People may take the initiative to do good things, or on occasion, *bad* things. The headlines are often full of shocking stories of corporate misconduct and it will continue to be so for some time to come. It is not enough to change the structure of the business or the job descriptions if you want people to make sound, ethical decisions. You must provide a level of personal leadership that ensures a strong orientation toward ethical values. I will explore some links between leadership and ethical misbehavior in this chapter. First, let me digress a little to set the stage for my recommendations.

My Work with The Executive Committee (TEC)

The accelerating rate of change manifests itself in some interesting developments.

One of these is the emergence of organizations that have come into being to support managers in their efforts to deal with the growing challenges of management.

Such organizations have emerged in a variety of forms. Foremost among these is an organization known as "The

Executive Committee" or TEC. TEC has grown into a world-wide organization of chief executive officers. At this writing, it is a growing organization that exceeds 9,000 member CEOs located around the world.

CEOs who are members of TEC are organized into chapters of about 16 businesses each. The members in each chapter must be engaged in non-competing activities. They meet monthly and are exposed to experienced managers and speakers who make presentations about three hours in length on a large variety of business subjects. Each TEC chapter has a chairperson who is an experienced manager. They manage the group's business discussions and meet with each member one-on-one monthly.

I have had the privilege of being a part of this activity for a number of years. Since retiring from Porsche, I have made over 800 presentations to members of this organization at their monthly meetings. As a result, I have had numerous opportunities to learn about the challenges and successes experienced by these CEOs.

As recently as the middle 1950s, such groups did not exist in any structured fashion. Bob Norse, a business manager who felt a need to share knowledge and skill with his peers in an informal and strictly confidential setting, started TEC in Milwaukee, Wisconsin, in 1957. As the rate of change accelerated, the need to communicate and learn grew and led to today's worldwide TEC organization of CEOs.

Such organizations address the need for managers to become more professional, but beyond that, I have found that the TEC organization leads the way for managers to grow to the next level.

Factors that Impact Growth and Profit

The History Channel runs a television series entitled *Modern Marvels*. One program in that series is "The History of the Assembly Line." The program depicts how Henry Ford invented the assembly line.

After Mr. Ford got his assembly line working, it was time to improve it. This was done by speeding the line up.

Some people could not keep up with the faster moving assembly line.

When management observed this, additional people were assigned to fill the gaps.

Two things were happening:

1. Management was solving the problem.
2. When the problem was solved, each job on the line became smaller.

When Toyota, the Japanese automobile manufacturer, began to assemble automobiles, they took the same approach as Ford. After the assembly line was operating, instead of speeding the line up to improve performance, Toyota removed 10 percent of the people and told the remaining people: "You figure out how to keep up with the line."

Two *different* things were now happening:

1. The people working on the line were solving the problem.
2. When the problem was solved, each job on the line had become bigger.

Superior efficiency and quality resulted.

Who Has Their Finger on the Button?

A number of factors impact manufacturing quality. Statistical concepts have had a major impact on quality in many industries.

One that struck me as decisive in differentiating the challenges of driving force management was a much simpler one, and profound in its implications for management. A "button" was placed near the assembly line. Anyone who saw something that was not right, could *push the button, and stop the line.* They were not required to tell a manager in the hope that the manager might take corrective action. No. They should push the button and stop the line.

With the simple addition of this control measure to the work environment, *everyone becomes involved in solving problems.*

The "O"-Ring Incident

Most of us remember Challenger, the space shuttle that exploded shortly after lift-off.

Why did Challenger explode?

The O-ring seals in the booster rockets were inadequate at temperatures below 50 degrees Fahrenheit. There was ice on the launching pad in January 1986. I recently watched a History Channel program that explained how a large number of engineers and lower level managers knew that those O-rings would probably fail that morning. Numerous top managers knew; it was a widely discussed subject. Many people at many levels of the operation knew.

But no one had a button to push to stop the decision to proceed with that ill-fated launch.

The information was there, but not the opportunity for people to become engaged in the action.

From the executive perspective, NASA has an immense investment in each launch. A lot more than the lives of astronauts are riding on a launch. Traditional management thinking might run something like this: It could cost us millions each time some fool pushed the panic button. The press could have a field day feasting on us. We'd never get a flight off the ground. Besides, most of our people lack the experience and skill to make an informed go, no-go decision. We simply can't risk opening the operation up to anyone who thinks they know better.

Without direction, good information, and the ability to take action, a team cannot act to improve the business and is therefore limited in effectiveness.

In the absence of good information and a mechanism that enables action, knowledge and skill serve primarily to raise the frustration level of an organization.

I imagine there is quite a bit of training and strategic discussion of teamwork at NASA, as there is in most large organizations. There is also no doubt that a strong emphasis on safety and the organization's values include the conviction that job number one is to get astronauts safely back home from each mission. What went so terribly wrong to allow a known hazard to be bypassed and a space shuttle to explode? Nothing more or less than what goes wrong in many organizations every day, except that at NASA, the risks are often higher and the consequences more dire. It would be easy to say that NASA was an uncaring organization where the value of human life was put behind the economics of keeping to a launch on schedule. I do not believe that is so. There are many caring people at NASA. What may have looked like a heartless decision to launch was more likely just the inability of people to take action when they saw a problem.

Beyond that, it would seem that Tony (see page 225) was making the launch decision.

The motion picture *Apollo 13* depicted a great example of how NASA *can* work. Numerous team members "pushed a button" when something in their area of expertise was lacking and became pivotal in determining the mission outcome.

I recall as the situation began to deteriorate, one of the first moves by the leader, Ed Harris, was to issue instructions: "Everybody get all your people in here!" This leader refused to deal with a serious situation without everyone's participation.

The structure of the organization can and often does determine whether the people within it will do the right thing in any situation. The probability that each person will make the right choice in a tough situation is enhanced if there is a clear, relevant value to guide the decision and authority delegated to act on that value.

It is important that the leader organize the business and define the culture in simple and understandable terms. *Too many priorities can result in no priorities.* There is much at stake here.

The leadership during the Apollo 13 incident set a clear priority: *"Let's work the problem!" Singular—one problem at a time!*

(The problem: Get the astronauts home safely!) Failure was not an option.

A Functional (Traditional) Business Structure

Managers and business owners tend to like functional structures because they are simple and at least *seem* easy to control. The theory that management requires more than authority and that the real power is out there where people are implementing decisions amplifies the shortcoming of such a simple organizational structure.

A functional organization is structured according to *functions*. This structure will typically assign responsibilities for functions like:

- sales and marketing
- engineering
- manufacturing
- finance and accounting

Managers are responsible for a *function*, as opposed to a *business*. In such a structure, only top managers are responsible for *business results*.

A functional business structure is useful when an organization is struggling to survive. This would include start-up and turnaround situations. This structure is also effective if the business is being prepared for sale or merger.

A functional organization can make good numbers in the short term.

The attractions of a functional organization are clear: concentrated control and focus on profits, particularly short-term profits that garner short-term rewards and impact things, such as stock price, favorably.

A functional structure introduces the following limitations:

- *Difficulty in attracting the best people.* In my experience, the best people are rarely attracted to a business that is obsessed with short-term results. They might join in a battle for survival but usually make a major commitment only if there is a longer view of something beyond.

The promise of short-term profits associated with a functional structure may attract some people, but in many instances not what we might classify as the sort of people who are indispensable in taking a business to the next level.

- *Difficulty holding the most desirable people.* Many young capable people today are not looking for a job. They are looking for the opportunity to:

–Run their own show.

–Own a piece of the action.

–Help to win a race instead of busting rocks.

They want to be in a position to run a business as though it were their own. They seek an opportunity to own a business or a piece of a business. Because a functional organization generally offers only the limited opportunity to manage a functional department, it becomes relatively difficult to offer the opportunities that would motivate today's best people. Running a functional department may offer success, but is often limited in opportunities that can lead to fulfillment. The opportunity to run a business exists in only a limited number of top management jobs. If relatively capable young managers occupy such jobs, the organization can stifle the people it needs most and lose them to the competition.

- *Becoming embroiled in a commodity business.* The lack of resources allocated to proactive development of future products and marketing activity can result in a commodity business. This can give rise to a brutal cost competition, a circumstance for which a functional structure is well-suited. A commodity business will be a constant struggle for profitability and possibly even survival.

- *Surviving when real change occurs.* Because there is little or no structural provision for development of new products and concepts, a typical functional structure has great difficulty dealing with significant change. In many cases, only the top people have the opportunity to become aware of such change; others are too busy with day-to-day business challenges. It is possible that this may be the root of the statement, "It's lonely at the top!" Of course it is. Everyone else in the organization is focused on short-term performance.

- *Being driven by the bottom line.* A functional organization tends to be driven by the bottom line to the exclusion of all else. In the crisis of start-up or turnaround, this is as it must be. Over the longer term, this organizational structure has the potential of burning people out. There is the possibility of developing a culture that dictates:

there is never enough.

The first order of any business is to achieve performance that will assure survival. If that is not done, there is no tomorrow. In this era of rapid and accelerating change, however, there is more to an enduring business than survival.

A functional organization can inhibit the ability of a business to advance to excellence and the next level.

Next Level Business Structure

The structure that is most appropriate for an organization striving to go to the next level is quite different from a functional structure. In order to move to the next level, a business must get out and, stay out, of the commodity business. It must attract and hold top people and attain market leadership. A business will do well to abandon a functional structure and transition to a structure that is more suited to proactive and non-commodity business operations.

The important features of an organization that can operate at the next level include:

- The opportunity for people to accept responsibility and be accountable for an activity that is a business unit, not an operational function.

- The opportunity for people to exercise control over functional activities in a defined business unit. This includes control of
  - sales.
  - elements of production. Definition of products and/or services provided to customers; packaging, shipment terms, customer inventory, etc.
  - tracking performance to be accountable for results.
  - staffing.
- The opportunity for people to be accountable for the results of a business unit.
- The opportunity for people to manage and attain ownership in a business they can control.

Business structures that facilitate these provisions require a massive increase in delegation of responsibility and authority. *Strict accountability is indispensable.*

The delegation of business control dictates a major prerequisite. If this cannot be achieved, a business would be well-advised to stay with a simple functional structure that is easier to control.

Striving for excellence at the next level, a high-performance organization has to have a culture of critical values.

There is a subtle, vital role for corporate culture. The first and foundational step a leader must take to assure an organization stays on track is to create a corporate culture that articulates, applies, and enforces clear values.

Creating a Foundation of Values

Why is this subject so important when taking a business to the next level?

Among the elements that can take a business to the next level is the ability to delegate responsibility. This allows the organization to go beyond the capabilities of the founders and managers who will inevitably become Tony. Failing to establish accountability based on an explicit set of values—an integral component of a business's culture and ethic—can result in disaster.

I would like to relate one specific instance in which this happened.

I was privileged to serve as a member of the board of a U.S. corporation in the early 1990s. It was a rapidly growing company that had operated profitably for over a decade.

The advent of major growth opportunities resulted in a significant leveraging of the company's assets, generating a great deal of bank debt. With this, came a number of covenants imposed by lending banks, conditions that required a specific level of profit and revenue over specific time periods.

Managers of all company divisions had revenue and profit objectives to comply with these covenants. The capable young manager of one operating division was meeting his business objectives on a regular basis.

One Saturday, I received a call from the CEO. It was a conference call that involved all board members. It would appear that Walter (not his real name), the manager of this operating division, had overstated revenues over a period of about nine months. Instead of reporting a shortfall, the books were doctored to show operation within specified operating goals. It was done in the firm belief that the shortfall could be made up in succeeding months.

The shortfall became larger with each successive month, until it exceeded $400,000. This put the entire company outside committed bank covenants.

The subject of the board conference call was what to do and when to do it.

Company managers did not have a clear understanding of what to do next. The problem was bumped up to the board in part because company managers lacked a clear idea of what an appropriate response should be. Why? Because *the company's culture, its committed values, did not exist in an explicit form that could guide a management decision.*

Several factors were discussed in the board conference call:

- The exact amount of the revenue shortfall was not known. It *was* known to be large enough to violate bank covenants.

- It was uncertain how the lending bank might respond to this development.
- What should be done about Walter, the manager of the offending division?

I did a lot of listening. The decision was developing as follows:

- First, let's determine the exact size of the shortfall, the exact magnitude of the problem.
- Until the above is complete, don't contact the lending bank. No need to needlessly alarm them until we know more about the details of the problem. Do not rush to judgment.
- Consider relieving Walter immediately for unethical conduct.

All of this sounded rational and like good business. However, the more we discussed it, the more aware the board became that these initial reactions seemed to be lacking some critical elements. When the members of the board became aware of some missing culture and values after the fact and applied them to the situation that confronted us, they gained a different perspective.

The result, after a long and wrenching discussion, was a new perspective on several aspects of the problem. *The new perspective resulted from a realization that values and elements of culture, which were needed as a basis for decision, were missing.* Without these missing elements, a good business decision was not likely to occur.

a. The exact magnitude of the shortfall is not the major issue. The fact that there is such a shortfall is the issue.

The missing value: We will never go into denial over details and delay action on a business issue.

b. The lending bank is a member of our family. We are in this together. Contact the bank president immediately following this call; not tonight, not tomorrow, but immediately after this call, and tell the bank president that: "We have a problem. We do not know the exact extent of the problem, but it involves a revenue shortfall that is large enough to put us outside our committed covenants. We will know a great deal more in the next few days and inform you promptly as additional information becomes available."

The missing value: We will never delay or withhold the sharing of a problem with members of our family. We are in this together.

c. Do nothing about Walter at this time. *Walter is not the problem.* It is likely that members of Walter's management team are involved in this unfortunate development. They were not doing what they did for personal gain. They thought they were acting to protect the company's covenants, they were trying to protect the company from problems with the banks. *The problem is a revenue shortfall. The shortfall must be made up as quickly as possible and that can be done more readily with Walter and his team than without them.*

The missing value: If anyone acts in the company's interest, and does not violate the company culture as expressed in a clear value statement, they are not in line for punishment. Instead, it will be a learning experience.

Upon being contacted while golfing, the bank president appreciated the promptness of the information. By the time Monday rolled around, he had instructed his people to work with our company to resolve our problems. The people at the bank told our people, "Contacting the president on a Saturday was the smartest thing you could have done." Without the president's blessing, it would have been impossible for them to await information on the exact magnitude of the problem without reacting. A quick reaction, once set in motion, could have triggered irreversible negative consequences.

The shortfall turned out to be significantly larger, by about 50 percent, than the original estimate.

The bank was complimentary about the decision to retain Walter and his management team. They let us know that had we fired Walter, it would have been more difficult to formulate and implement a solution.

Walter and his team did a great job in rectifying the shortfall problem. The situation was cleared up within one year.

Walter then quit his position and went on to other pursuits; firing him became a non-issue.

I was sorry to see Walter leave. I did not feel satisfied. Somehow, there was unfinished business. I could not get comfortable with the conclusion that Walter and his team were unethical people. It seemed like a scapegoat explanation for what had happened. I was convinced this incident had resulted from a management failure. Somehow, responsibility was delegated without an adequate definition of corporate values and culture.

I remember raising the question at a subsequent board meeting: "What really went wrong here? I cannot believe Walter is an unethical person."

The board members decided, after discussion, that Walter had the wrong priorities. He believed that making revenue objectives was more important than inflating revenue entries and planning to catch up later.

In the course of this discussion, the senior manager of the largest business unit disclosed the following:

> *There have been times in my 15 years with this company that my division has shipped defective product in order to fulfill an operating period shipping objective.*

Wow! Did I hear that correctly?

Who did more damage to the company, Walter, who inflated revenue, or the senior manager who shipped defective merchandise?

I felt that shipping defective merchandise did more real harm to the company. A revenue shortfall can be caught up, but how do you rectify the shipment of defective product, even occasionally, over a period of 15 years?

Both occurred because good people had no clear statement of culture and values about what is most important in the company. There was a "button" to push; people had the authority

to push it, but no explicit culture to guide action. It was not clear what we *do not do* in this organization.

Every Business Is a Family Business

I believe that if a company is to become all that it can be, one of the most important elements is an *explicit* culture. Culture is a significant component of what is called leadership. One way to look at culture is that a business must operate as though it were a family.

A family is getting ready to leave on a vacation and is packing the SUV or minivan. The six-year-old son is sitting in the passenger seat, and the father asks, "Why are you sitting there?" The youngster might reply, "My things are all loaded, I am finished." The father replies, "You get your butt out of that seat and help your mother and sister. No one is finished until everyone is finished. We are a family; *we are in this together!*"

When there is a problem in a family, no one individual ever has a problem. The family has the problem and will deal with it together. It is a core value of a family. It is also an essential part of corporate culture.

What makes a family a *family?*

Perhaps it is useful to first address the question: What is a family?

For the purpose of explaining corporate culture, a useful definition might be:

A family consists of a group of people who have made a commitment to each other and to a set of shared values.

The shared values that define a family are not procedures. Procedures most often explain what to do or how to do it. By necessity, such procedures must change in order to accommodate changes in industry and society.

Values are different. They are timeless. They endure, even in times of change, *particularly* in times of change. Procedures tell us what to do. Many, about 80%, of the values that define a culture tell us what _not_ to do.

279

Thinking about a rational explanation for this, I was brought to the perception that one of the foundations for what can be described as our western culture are the Ten Commandments in the Bible. These are not the Ten Suggestions, but they are not the Ten Commandments either. Only two of the ten command us to do anything: "Honor thy mother and father," and "Keep the Sabbath holy." The other eight all start, "Thou shalt *not* ____." They are not commandments; they are prohibitions.

In like manner, I have come to believe that the documented culture of a business is most effective if it is about 80 percent prohibitions *Thou shalt nots.*

Setting Limits

During my tenure in Europe, I was exposed to an interesting perception by some German friends:

- America is a wonderful country. In America, everything is allowed, except that which is specifically forbidden.
- In Germany, everything is forbidden, except that which is specifically allowed.
- In Italy, everything is allowed, especially that which is specifically forbidden.

In a highly oversimplified and stereotypical manner, this articulates three distinct cultures:

- In the first one, people are allowed to take initiative, to think freely, as long as they do not cross the line to that which is forbidden.
- In the second, people wait until they are told what to do before they take action.
- In the third, people do whatever they darn well please, with no limits or restraints.

The question is: What sort of culture are we striving for in business? If we are striving for excellence, I would submit that the first of the three would be most effective. It means that significant effort must not go into telling people what to do; rather it must go into defining, as clearly as possible, the things that they must *not* do.

Prohibitions, not commandments, are the basis (about 80 percent) of most effective free cultures.

The implications for leaders are clear: We must stop telling people what to do. Instead make sure that they know what not to do and then allow them to proceed on that basis to apply their ingenuity and formulate solutions. It is the most effective way I have found to get people to use their ingenuity.

Perhaps the key is freedom. History has repeatedly confirmed:

A free society will outperform other social models.

There can be no freedom in a society or business without rules that arise out of values and apply to all people involved.

We must acknowledge that values are more important than people.

I believe this is confirmed in the preamble of the U.S. Constitution with the phrase: "All men are created equal." It does not mean that all men and women are equally strong, or intelligent.

It means they are *all equal under the law.*

The laws under which free men and women are equal must be drafted within a framework of values.

It is nearly impossible to define what we *are* going to do within a business. In today's world, there is rapid change, change that can spell opportunity if acted upon and disaster if ignored.

A business culture is defined, in large measure, by what we do <u>not</u> do. *Culture and values are the most important elements that make a business unique and make it different from others competing for the same customer and market. No one can give it to us and no one can take it away.*

Procedures are dictated by changes inside or outside the business. With the rapid change that characterizes today's business climate, it is essential that procedures are reviewed and reconfirmed from time to time. Values and culture are different. They are of an enduring nature.

It is not by accident that it is difficult to amend the U.S. Constitution. Elected representatives of the people can make new laws and change old ones, but an amendment to the Constitution is a very different matter. A change in the Constitution must be ratified by two-thirds of the states, an intentionally difficult task. *Values must endure.*

The ability to delegate responsibility, allowing the organization to go beyond the capabilities of the founders and top managers, is a key element in taking a business to the next level. In the absence of a defined culture and values, indispensable delegation can and will result in serious difficulties or disaster.

Being Accountable to Our Values

We can destroy our culture if we allow violations to occur without prompt and decisive consequences.

Earlier, I told the story of a company whose eager young manager falsified his revenues to make operating targets, and board-level discussions ensued.

Responsibility was delegated and people were encouraged to be innovative and creative in the absence of a clear culture and values.

The first remedy was to articulate and communicate a set of values that would, if followed, ensure no further lapses of a similar nature. That was just the beginning of the remedy. It is not enough to have a culture and explicit values. Management must be ever vigilant to assure that the culture is not violated. A willful violation of the culture must be dealt with promptly and firmly. Failure to do this can destroy the culture.

Management accountability must aim to control the fundamental human propensity for corruption. This requires a set of values combined with an appropriate business structure.

Without rules of conduct that are more important than any one person, there can be no effective civilization. Without rules, man reverts to an uncivilized animal; civilization and business are not possible.

Consider the following:

> *At the dawn of human civilization, as man evolved from animal behavior, accountability was established by*

the emergence of a "higher power." This was the beginning of religion(s). Religion established a set of rules of conduct. An incentive program was defined as a system of reward and punishment. The reward was "heaven" and the punishment was "hell." These accountability concepts made provision for atonement in varied forms. People were held accountable for their behavior. There was little provision for passing blame on to other people or circumstances.

This is a *moral structure* to govern behavior.

As civilization progressed, an increasing number of people ignored the moral system of accountability. Laws formulated and enforced by governments assumed an increasing role.

This is a *legal structure* to govern behavior.

Like the moral structure, the legal structure made provision for an incentive plan. "Heaven" is defined by material gain. "Hell" is defined by confinement (jail), deportment from the society, or in some cases, execution.

A fundamental shortcoming in both systems is the human inclination to "beat the system." People frequently focus on the reward and punishment provisions rather than the fundamental strategy. People cram before an exam, ignoring the objective of learning (the strategy) and focusing instead on getting a good grade (the reward) or avoiding punishment (failing a course).

In business and social behavior, people often structure their actions to avoid getting caught, rather than to "do what is right."

For those committed to abide by the ancient framework of moral rules and values, even if driven by the reward and punishment framework, moral accountability is frequently adequate. Moral accountability is not burdened by the need to protect the innocent; it is an internal process administered by the harshest judge that exists for such moral people. They become their own judge and jury.

In contrast, I have come to believe that it is not possible to establish adequate accountability in business management with a framework of legal rules or laws. Many people have become too clever at manipulating and interpreting a legal structure. For those determined to circumvent the legal framework, accountability based on a legal structure can be inadequate. The provisions necessary to avoid punishing the innocent provide a maze of avenues with which those committed to beating the legal system can do so successfully.

Some recent developments in U.S. business are signaling a major management problem. At this writing, activities such as insider trading of stock, using investor money to cover operating losses, management compensation, and "creative accounting practices" (also called "aggressive accounting practices") to finance complicated "pyramid schemes" are becoming all too common business practice.

I do not believe that this trend can be controlled adequately by legislation at the federal, or any legal, level.

It is likely that the root cause of these problems is a lack of accountability on the part of business managers. This disturbing and destructive trend must be controlled and reversed. Effective accountability rooted in business structure may be part of a solution.

Rethinking Accountability

To whom is the management of a company accountable?

- The shareholders who have invested their money.
- The employees who have invested careers and lives.
- Society that has provided the framework that makes modern business possible.

How can this accountability be accomplished? How does it break down?

Of all the systems in which I have been privileged to work and manage, the German system has proved most effective for me. That system of *"Mitbestimmung,"* described in Chapter 7, provides the following major elements of accountability for a CEO and top management.

- A "supervisory board" appoints and dismisses company top managers. The supervisory board, not company managers, has responsibility for financial audit.
- Half of the supervisory board members are elected by owners (shareholders), the other half by employees. *Employee interests are represented.*
- No member of company top management can serve on the supervisory board.
- Mandated companywide meetings are orchestrated by employees, not management. Employees, not employers, decide the agenda. Any employee can ask any question of any top manager. There is no time limit allowed and the meetings take place on company time with full pay.

Management accountability to owners and employees is clear in such a system.

It is up to the supervisory board members to represent the interests of society as part of their board duties.

It is not uncommon for the CEO of a public U.S. corporation to be a member of the board of directors. Not only that, the CEO is sometimes also the *chairman of the board.* Employees are rarely represented with a seat on the board of directors or given the opportunity to ask questions that represent the employee agenda or concerns in a forum where management is obligated to respond promptly.

In these circumstances, it would seem naïve to conclude that power would not be abused.

Several actions could be taken voluntarily by publicly held U.S. corporations to stem the rising tide of impropriety and abuse without waiting for legislation.

- Company officers could resign from membership on their company's board of directors.
- Employees could be represented on company boards of directors.
- Employees could be given an opportunity to address *their* issues with management in an open forum. This does not

have to mean big employee meetings. It can be accomplished effectively by structured meetings of management and employee-elected representatives.

I feel strongly that such action must be initiated and implemented voluntarily by the companies involved, not through legal action by the government. As the necessity to go beyond functional organization spreads authority and encourages initiative in businesses that strive for the next level, we will see more opportunities to cut corners and deceive auditors, customers, investors, and even one's own managers. We need to rethink ways in which we structure the values of our companies and hold people accountable to them. Leaders of next-level organizations that go beyond functional structure must exercise greater moral responsibility and ethical care.

Jim Liautaud

FOUNDER AND CHAIRMAN OF
NINE SUCCESSFUL COMPANIES

*A*s a chairman having nine company presidents reporting to me, and a long-term CEO involved in the education of other CEOs through my affiliation with the World Presidents Association, I have never met a CEO with more global experience and accomplishments than Peter W. Schutz. He is committed to helping educate others and has been a huge help to me.

Quite simply: "Peter is the best!"

20

The Next-Level Business

W hen I was named vice president of sales and service at Cummins, I operated in a functional business structure. I was responsible for sales *volume*. My performance was measured in engines shipped (to truck manufacturers) and market share, that is, Cummins' share of new truck registrations. My annual bonus was a function of those volume derived measurements.

At the beginning of a 12-month planning period, I would be asked to make an engine sales forecast. My bonus was a function of engine volume shipped. The more engines shipped, the bigger my bonus check. Since no engine could be shipped before it was built and I was striving to earn a big bonus, my forecasts would be ambitious and high.

When Leo Brewer, then head of manufacturing, received my forecast for review, he cut it back considerably. Why? Because he did not want to build engines that I might not sell.

Unsold and unshipped engines became *his* finished inventory headache, not mine.

When John Hackett, our chief financial officer, received this revised forecast, he promptly cut it back further. "Unsold engine inventory is our most expensive capital," was his viewpoint.

By the time our CEO, Henry Schacht, got this re-reworked forecast, he could not be sure just what he had received. He knew us well, could calibrate our varied motives and fears, conduct some brief interviews, and come up with a 12-month sales forecast. His forecast had to be a best guess of what he could push us to do, given his insight into our conflicting perspectives. None of us looked at that forecast in the same way our CEO did. None of us could approach the task of forecasting sales with complete objectivity and the company's broader interests in mind because of the business structure within which we worked.

Only the CEO has a real commitment to these numbers. In a functional organization there is a tendency for only the CEOs to concern themselves with the entire mission of the business. Others take care of *their departmental function*, instead of *the business*.

To maximize driving force in an organization, as many people as possible need to think like business managers, not just the CEO.

Leader to Salesperson: "What's Your Home Address?"

The transition to market niche operation at Cummins began for me in a forecast meeting. I had submitted my usual ambitious sales forecast. I recall my boss, Marion Dietrich, looking me in the eye and saying, "Peter, this is a very ambitious forecast." I recall responding, "Marion, this sales organization can achieve those results, I am sure of that." Marion replied, "OK, I believe you, Peter. We will build all of the engines in your forecast, but any engine that you do not sell and ship will be shipped to your home address."

WOW! I finally got the message.

I was being asked to think like a business manager, not like the head of a functional sales department.

The Pricing Problem

A similar situation exists in some aspects of pricing. What sort of pricing pressure might one expect from a typical sales manager? Up or down? In most cases, sales managers will exert downward pressure on prices.

This is true and understandable in a commodity business and can also occur when a differentiated offering is involved. Why? *Because most sales managers are volume (not profit) driven, and volume is more easily achieved with lower prices.*

With few exceptions, business is about making money, not just generating volume. High volume might require new investment in capacity, raise the break-even volume, or worse, result in diminished margins or losses. A typical sales manager in a typical functional organization might not feel responsible for such developments.

In a next level organization, managers must think like managers of a business. This is indispensable if accountability for business management is to be delegated.

Market Niches: The YPO Story

During my time at Porsche, we achieved differentiation by assigning responsibility for Porsche activities in a number of market niches.

The first niche identified during my Porsche tenure was the Young Presidents Organization (YPO). YPO is a worldwide organization of outstanding men and women who have become company CEOs or presidents of qualified companies prior to turning 40. When they become 50 years old, they are transitioned out of YPO.

I had just taken the job of CEO and was visiting with one of my mentors, Larry Wilson. He is the genius whose insights about people performance are in Chapter 18. It was Wilson who came up with the suggestion that YPO would be a market niche of people perfectly suited to become Porsche customers.

YPO holds "universities," first-class educational conferences, several times a year at locations all over the globe. A bit of research revealed an upcoming YPO University was scheduled for Munich, Germany, in August 1981.

I contacted the education chairman of the YPO Munich University and offered to host any YPO members who came to Germany on the weekend preceding the week-long university. If they came to Stuttgart, I would be honored to host them at the Porsche Weissach technical center.

About 12 YPO members came to Stuttgart with their spouses. It was a sensational day. There were rides in Porsche racecars around the Weissach proving grounds track and the opportunity to drive Porsche production cars. We sold 12 new Porsche automobiles that day and made many new personal friends. Among these are Jesse and Marcie Jones, two of our most cherished friends to this day. Jesse is a prototype YPO/Porsche customer; a successful Indiana building contractor, automobile racer, and owner of a number of significant collector cars.

Getting to *Wow!*

Several YPO members drove their new Porsche cars to the university the following day. Shortly thereafter, I received a phone call from Munich. One of the new Porsche cars had been stolen from the Munich Sheraton Hotel garage during the night.

I dispatched my assistant to the factory with orders to find a Porsche *exactly* like the one that had disappeared, drive it to Munich, and deliver it personally to the couple whose Porsche had been stolen. I instructed him to tell the owners that Porsche would handle all the paper work with insurance, title, etc.

By the time I got to Munich the following Thursday to make a presentation to the university attendees, everyone—all 400

YPO members present—had heard about the sensational time at Weissach and the story of the stolen Porsche replacement.

For years after that, Porsche hosted YPO members at races. We also offered many unique experiences that money cannot buy to this outstanding group of people. This was a market niche that offered Porsche an opportunity to differentiate an offering. We sold many cars to YPO members in the years that followed.

In similar fashion, Porsche served professional women tennis players all around the world, women of all professions in Germany, and members of the U.S. Porsche Club. By assigning qualified people to manage such business opportunities, granting authority to staff the activities, and develop appropriate supporting programs, a significant number of Porsches were sold. These were frequently special colors and accessories, the sort of items that lifted the product out of the commodity business and enhanced profits.

Tilman Brodbeck, my assistant during some of my time at Porsche, learned this game so well that today he is in charge of a business unit at Porsche—the "Porsche Exclusive" organization. This business supplies differentiating accessories that enhance value and differentiate Porsche automobiles.

To be most effective, a differentiated business is organized around customers and market niches, not around products and services. It is nurtured by excellent customer service, because every opportunity to interact with a customer individually is an opportunity to further differentiate the product. A problem, such as the YPO member's stolen car, is an opportunity for an organization to solidify its non-commodity status.

The Business Units

Business units with accountability for their success and failure are important to the differentiated business as it applies the principles of next-level structure. For every customer market niche that can be identified with potential to achieve a differentiated posture, the organization needs a unit structured to make money in that market niche.

It is essential to put a competent business manager in charge of a business unit. This manager has responsibility for the following:

Sales

They are responsible to see that selling is accomplished. It can be done personally, or salespeople can be hired. The objective is to *make money in a business unit.*

Production

This means to define the value-added for customers in the market niche for which the manager is responsible. Included are: specification, packaging, delivery terms, etc. In most instances, this will not include building and managing a production facility, but rather defining differentiating aspects of a product or service to be supplied by the manufacturing or purchasing part of the business.

Managing Capital

Effective employment of capital investment and management of operating capital. This has a great deal to do with pricing and production volume. The objective is to minimize investment and maximize return with product and service differentiation tailored to the market niche.

Staffing

The business unit manager has control over who and how many people are employed in the operating business unit.

Each business unit is a "company."

The business unit is sustained as long as it manages to stay out of a commodity business. Once the business fails to remain differentiated and becomes a commodity business, it can be dissolved and the product or service integrated into a commodity-operating unit with entirely different cost-minimizing operating criteria.

Failing to make this transition promptly can result in a cash hemorrhage.

The organization can establish as many business units as there are market niches. In many instances, this will be limited by availability of people capable of handling such responsibility.

Can this advice apply to a smaller business too? Sure! Take the case of a successful owner-operated store with one highly profitable location. The owner recognizes the opportunity to expand the business by opening other locations.

Often, the owner will recall a long history of difficulties in hiring good management staff for the store and conclude that whatever the growth plans, they must be predicated on the owner continuing to micromanage each store. This might mean instead of spending most days at the current store, the owner would plan to shuttle between the existing and new store.

But even if the owner puts in long hours, it will prove harder to manage two stores than one. Margins will inevitably slip. The owner will feel chronically tired and begin to fantasize about selling out and retiring. This is not a good growth plan.

What if, instead, the owner recognized that competent business-unit managers were the key to expansion? Then, they would start by hiring and training a new sort of person, someone with perhaps more potential (if less initial skill or experience) who could practice their store management skills under the owner's watchful eye for a year or so and then take over the old store while the owner opens the new one.

Repeating this pattern, the owner might open a new store each year as financing could be arranged, always training a manager for the next store.

That is what a franchising concept like McDonald's does on a large scale. It recruits people who are willing to bring in their own capital as well as their management abilities. These people get plenty of support and advice from headquarters, but they own their franchises and always think and act like CEOs. No wonder franchises have spread so successfully across the business landscape. An independent franchise owner will outcompete a salaried store manager mired in administrative red tape if all else about their businesses is equal. It is a better way to organize a competitive enterprise. There are of course other ways to ensure that each unit manager feels and thinks like a CEO, but the franchise, or business unit, is more likely to make this happen than most other business structures.

CEO Role in the Next-Level Organization

The role of the CEO in a functional organization is somewhat like that of a general leading the charge. The CEO, like the general, is the only person with a comprehensive overview of the entire business. It thus falls to the CEO to be central to all important business decisions. This degree of authority concentration is desirable, if not essential, to the operation of a typical commodity business, as well as to a start-up or turnaround.

The role of the CEO in a next-level organization (as opposed to functional structure) is quite different. Much of the decision-making is delegated to the business unit managers. The primary responsibilities of the CEO will now include:

- *Custodian of the company culture.* The culture must be nurtured and enforced.
- *Identification and explanation of the "temple."* Why are we here?
- *Public relations.* Custodian of the company image to the public and industry.
- *Development of human resources.* Recruiting and nurturing company managers, present and future. Making provision for orderly succession at all levels of the business.

I believe the responsibility for human resource development belongs with the chief executive officer. In most instances, the CEO will have a small group to assist in this task.

During my tenure at Cummins, the development of future managers was controlled directly by the CEO, Henry Schacht.

A number of top company recruits were assigned to various operating officers. I, as vice president of sales and service, was one of the company officers to whom such people were assigned. Company officers were not allowed to change the assignment of such people without clearing it with Schacht. This assured a varied and comprehensive operating experience to prepare people adequately for future management assignments.

I replicated this activity as CEO of Porsche AG. A number of people who were managed in this manner are now doing an outstanding job leading Porsche.

The only other task I never delegated during my time at Porsche was the management of relations with the press and public. A small group under Manfred Jantke, a close associate reporting directly to me, was responsible for this activity.

The Missing Link

After I completed a management presentation to a group of CEOs, the young founder of a successful west coast software company approached me and asked if I would be willing to spend a day with the management team of his company?

I replied, "Of course, that is my business. Why do you feel that such a meeting is necessary? What is the problem?"

The problem was explained, "The business has been successful in recruiting a number of top people. The problem is that they leave the company after a relatively short tenure."

I agreed to take the job, and asked, "Could we spend some personal time the evening before the management meeting?" The reply was, "That would be fine. We'll have dinner." At dinner I asked, "May I ask you a few questions?" Upon receiving a positive reply, I asked, "What is the most valuable asset in your company?"

The answer was "My people." (Most CEOs will respond in that manner.)

"Who occupies the office next to yours?" I continued. The answer was, "My chief financial officer." Count on it, this will be the case in many young growing companies with a strong capable CEO.

"Where does the person responsible for the development and growth of your most important asset, your people, have their office?" I asked. The very hesitant and tentative answer was, "I am not sure, probably somewhere on the next floor."

I replied, "I believe I understand the problem."

I have come to believe that only the CEO can effectively deal with the challenge of attracting and holding the best management people. It is a challenge of leadership, culture, and definition of the "temple." The top leader must assure that qualified people are given the opportunity to grow into key jobs.

This became clearer to me when I thought about the transition I had to undergo when my three children became adults. When they were young, probably before age eight or nine, I had to be a father. I had to make decisions for them; they were young children.

I had to formulate a framework of values and indoctrinate them into a family culture.

This is much like the role of a CEO in a functional business organization.

At some point after that, they grew up and became young adults. Instead of a father, who was nurturing and, to a degree, controlling, I had to make the transition to become a parent. I had to learn to delegate and let go.

I now had to enforce family values, the family culture. I had to enforce a framework of values within which they made their own decisions.

This is much like the role of a CEO in a next-level organization.

This proved painful at times. My daughter, Lori, in particular, seemed to be out of control, during a phase when she was "finding herself." In the end, it was the culture, the basic values with which these children were raised, that was decisive. They are now adults that any parent would be proud of.

If they are to grow and develop to their full potential, managers must have authority delegated to them so that they can run a business, even when it hurts.

The CEO has the responsibility to create and/or nurture a business culture in which this can take place.

An Example

Imagine that a company owns and operates a soap factory. Management has identified three distinct market niches:

Hotels and Motels

How do they want their soap packaged?
- Small cakes of soap with colorful customized wrappers.
- In packages of a few dozen cakes.

How do they want the soap delivered?
- Very quickly and responsively; they are not good at soap inventory control.

Grocery Chain Stores

How do they want their soap packaged?
- Several larger cake sizes.
- Wrapped in private branding wrappers, or the supplier brand if it is recognized.
- Packed in larger boxes, but not so large that a young or slight employee cannot lift it.

How do they want the soap delivered?
- As efficiently as possible. In full truck loads if that will save delivery cost.

The Military Services

How do they want their soap packaged?
- So that it can be stored easily, for extended periods, and shipped overseas.

How do they want the soap delivered?
- In large blocks; when they need it, they will cut it up to suit their needs.

It is the same soap, but there may be opportunities to serve various customer niches with specialized support.

Suppose there are three managers, each responsible for one of these businesses.

A fourth member of the company has been traveling to South America for the past two years attempting to get the company into the South American soap business. They have finally received an initial order, with 20 percent to be delivered in February, another 30 percent by the end of May, and the balance of the order before the end of August. The problem is, business is good and there is not sufficient capacity available to fill this unanticipated demand.

Who should get the scarce soap? Which of the four business managers should get the soap to satisfy their market niche?

One option might be to give the soap to whomever can get the best profit. Since South America is not established as a profitable customer, they will not get the scarce soap. Here is where culture steps in.

Suppose an element of the corporate culture is: We will never walk away from a commitment. If any member of this family (company) makes a commitment, we are all committed. We cannot ignore the business commitment to South America.

So how might managers deal with this dilemma?

They cannot go to the CEO. They would be told, "This not a problem for the CEO; either you solve this problem, or I will get someone who can."

If the CEO solves the problem, it will undermine the next-level organization concept.

The company will slide back to a functional operation. It can lose much of its driving force.

The operating managers will have to find a solution. Perhaps the South American customer can be persuaded to accept a slower delivery schedule. In any event, operating managers must find a solution *together* that is within the framework of the company culture.

The Essentials

- A comprehensive administrative system is absolutely critical to the operation of a next-level operation. Without it, management of differentiated offerings for customer market niches and the degree of authority delegation and accountability required cannot be achieved. Administration of each business unit should include responsibility for all the essentials, such as bookkeeping, legal support, a management information system, and a central archive for unit operating data. *The activities can be farmed out, but accountability cannot.*

- Managers who understand customer market niches, democratic decision-making, and dictatorial implementation are also paramount. Managers must work together as a business family. Without these skills and commitments, performance in this mode becomes limited.

- The chief executive officer must assume responsibility for human resource development, public relations, and be custodian of the company culture. Centralized accounting, marketing, and new product development is the responsibility of the CEO.

- Finally and very importantly, *the CEO must define the "temple" for the entire organization.*

Anthony Sarandes

FOUNDER OF EQUIFLOR CORPORATION

*A*s I have said many times to many people, we at Equiflor were truly blessed to have you share your time and be a mentor to me personally and the Equiflor management team as a group. We clearly are where we are today largely because of your teachings.

Peter has an uncanny ability to get you and your organization to think "outside of the box."

Peter's concept of setting up weekly meetings outside of the business was invaluable in getting Equiflor to function as a team.

When we are not talking business, I always keep a yellow pad handy so as not to miss anything.

Robert F. Snodgrass Jr.

GENERAL MANAGER OF
BRUMOS MOTOR CARS, INC.

*P*eter W. Schutz is a friend, a teacher, a role model, and my *hero. Never in my 30-plus years in the automobile industry have I witnessed the combination of mind, understanding, and passion that Peter possesses and shares willingly with those around him.*

Guiding Porsche to record sales and profit years is an achievement worthy of any MBA student's investigation. Beyond that, his personal ethics and understanding of core business strategies are staggering.

Peter's input to my business has materially strengthened my operation to the point of national recognition; his input into my life has made me a better thinker and fairer employer.

21

Excellence: Beyond Success

W hat rewards can a business earn from moving to the next level, beyond just making more money? What sort of excellence lies beyond material success and perhaps becoming rich?

I have experienced the pride and fulfillment of being part of an organization that moved to the next level. In every instance, the organization must become successful first. It is not possible to move to the next level without first becoming profitable.

If you ask a doctor or physical trainer, "How can I get into good physical condition?" the reply might be, "Run for 20 minutes at your optimum heart rate every day, but be advised, only the last two minutes will really do you any good." Many people would like to run the last two minutes without running the first 18.

A great deal of effort is required to move a business to the next level, to advance it to the last two minutes where good things begin to happen.

In many instances, a business will become more profitable as it moves to the next level, even though making money may no longer be the singular focus.

My Last Le Mans Race

The 1987 Le Mans race was shaping up as a major event for Porsche. In 1985 and 1986, Jaguar had mounted major challenges that fell short of victory. A new car for the 1987 race carried victory hopes for Jaguar. Five brand new cars, powered by large V-12 engines constituted an awesome challenge. Porsche was to be represented by Porsche 962s, improved versions of the venerable 956, powered by renovated six-cylinder turbocharged engines.

Two weeks before the race, Hans Stuck wrecked one of the new Porsche 962 cars at the Weissach proving ground during a test drive. The winning car from the 1986 race was quickly reconditioned and went to Le Mans as our number 17 car.

Qualification went uneventfully, but the race did not. Within the first hour and a half, five of the six Porsche 962s, three customer cars, and two factory cars retired from competition with burned pistons—race-ending failures. The number 17 car, the "used car" from the previous year's race, was the only Porsche 962 still running. It was immediately ordered to slow down to save the engine, pending investigation of the general problem.

Several members of the European automotive press sought me out. They wanted to arrange a press conference with me after the conclusion of the race, anticipating a huge Jaguar triumph.

It was quickly determined there was a problem with the racing fuel. The rule at Le Mans was that racing must take place with the same fuel used for qualification. Something was clearly out of order. Porsche engines had failed as a result of violent pre-ignition. Fuel octane was clearly below that used during qualification and not adequate for the turbocharged Porsche racing engines.

In 1987, Porsche equipped the Porsche 944 Turbo production car with an electronic knock-sensor. If the engine suffered pre-ignition due to inadequate fuel octane rating, the knock-sensor mechanism would retard the engine ignition timing until pre-ignition was eased.

Helmut Bott quickly commandeered a 944 Turbo car, filled it with racing fuel, and drove it with an instrumented knock-sensor. A series of lights indicated the status of engine ignition timing. The suspected reduced octane rating of the racing fuel was quickly confirmed and calibrated.

A young female fuel system engineer generated a modified computer chip for the car system to compensate for the reduced octane rating. The lone Porsche 962 was recalled to the pit and fitted with the revised fuel chip. It was then possible to resume racing and go on the hunt to catch the leading Jaguars.

The mood in the Porsche racing pit was somber. We were facing five new Jaguar cars. The naturally aspirated V-12 Jaguar engines were not affected by the reduced fuel octane rating in the manner the turbocharged Porsche six-cylinder engines had been.

I addressed the gathering in the Porsche racing pit. I asked, "How many cars can win this race?" The answer was, "Only one car can win. Well then, we have enough cars left in the race," I said. "Beyond that, we have something Jaguar does not have. We have a car running that won the race last year. It may be an old car, but we know it is a winner!"

One by one, the Jaguars dropped out of the race with a variety of technical problems. By 11:00 A.M. Sunday, Derek Bell, in our number 17 car, was following the last remaining Jaguar down the Mulsanne-straight when the Jaguar's gearbox disintegrated in a huge cloud of oil and smoke. Suddenly, number 17 was all alone, several laps in the lead, covered with oil from the failed Jaguar gear box, but still one of the most beautiful race-cars I have ever seen.

Our car won easily after that—a difficult but sweet victory. I was incredibly proud of the Porsche team that persevered in true Porsche tradition just when everything seemed lost.

Although I looked for press representatives after our victory, the requested press conference never took place.

Time to Move On

After six World Sports Car Championships, three Formula I World Championships, and seven profitable years, it was time to move on to other things. Many of the technical features that differentiated Porsche production sports cars were becoming high production items in the automobile industry. Porsche was gradually sinking into a commodity business, facing increasing competition from well-financed and competent manufacturers using technical components that were once rather exclusive but had now become high production hardware available to most car builders.

There were opportunities to move Porsche into other fields where there was a realistic chance of redefining an industry. The possibilities included engines for light aircraft, small helicopters, and top-of-the-line speedboats. Initial efforts in these fields showed some promise, but Porsche was destined to stay in the automobile business.

It was time to bite the bullet and get serious about reinventing the Porsche sports car and the entire manufacturing concept to achieve a competitive posture in the fiercely competitive industry that was emerging in the late 1980s.

I retired from Porsche at the end of 1987.

Professor Porsche, the man who gave me an incredible opportunity and always supported me, passed away in 1996. Franz Blank retired in 1988; Helmut Bott, my chief engineer and outstanding manager, left this world in 1992. The Porsche team and I had stood on their capable shoulders to achieve the notable successes of the 1980s.

Porsche is in good hands today. Dr. Wendelin Wiedeking, Porsche CEO at this writing, is the right man at the right time.

Under his competent leadership, Porsche has achieved things that looked impossible to my team and me in the 1980s. A fresh new product line, produced in a thoroughly modern manner, is competitive and profitable (See Chapter 22). I think this illustrates another important leadership lesson. No leader should ever consider themselves indispensable, or try to manage as if that were so.

Every business founder, owner, and CEO, would like to leave a business that is successful and profitable for heirs and successors. I have seen true fulfillment in which people beyond heirs and successors became beneficiaries. People, all of the people, that actually built the business became beneficiaries and achieved fulfillment.

Equiflor Corporation

I first met my friend Tony Sarandes after my return to the United States from Germany in 1988. He asked me to join the board of directors of Equiflor shortly thereafter. He is the founder of Equiflor, a company that imports fresh flowers from South and Central America and distributes them over most of the United States.

From the beginning, Sarandes did a number of things that would position Equiflor to move to the next level. A major effort resulted in defining a set of Equiflor values and principles. As described in this book, most of these were prohibitions, not commandments. The entire organization was engaged in the project and it did not take place quickly. Equiflor created an invaluable foundation for delegating authority and democratic decision-making. Equiflor had established an explicit, documented culture.

The workload at Equiflor had a distinct weekly cycle. Monday and Tuesday were very busy, Wednesday was usually slack, and Thursday and Friday were once again very busy. The slack time in the middle of the week had a tendency to cause a letdown, from which it was difficult to get up to speed again. The organization addressed this issue, and a democratic approach to solving the problem resulted. Wednesday was established as a day in which everyone participated in marketing and proactive planning.

One of the developments that grew out of these meetings was a plan to take a part of Equiflor's business out of the commodity mode. A flower is a flower is a flower, unless it is a *Rio Rose*. A Rio Rose has become a differentiated product among flowers. There is, in fact, a difference. Rio Roses are genetically superior to other roses. They are bigger, last longer, and have a better fragrance than ordinary roses.

Equiflor has established a brand for a differentiated product.

Fresh flowers are packed and shipped in specially designed "boxes." Rio Roses command a higher revenue per box than others.

Beyond the obvious advantages of potentially greater profit, this program has added to passion and employee engagement. Equiflor has established a *process* to lift its operation out of a commodity business.

Equiflor addressed the issue of administration and performance measurement to let people know how they are doing. This is essential if the important issues of feedback and engagement are to be effective at all levels of the organization.

The concept of *break-even volume* turned out to be a useful tool to this end.

Suppose a business is successful and earns a 10 percent profit. If the normal work week is 40 hours, it means that the first 36 hours are necessary to cover the cost of operation. Only the last four hours, 10 percent, earn a profit. *It takes 36 hours a week to just break even.*

If the organization slacks off and calls it quits for the week at noon on Friday, there is no profit.

On the other hand, if we find a way to work four additional hours in any week, we double our profit.

How can we let the entire organization know when break even is reached? That would signal the time to really turn it on.

I have found it most effective if the break-even point is defined by performance other than money. Break even is better defined by accomplishment. At Equiflor, performance is measured by the number of boxes of flowers shipped. By tracking and posting the number of boxes shipped, the entire organization receives feedback on how they are doing.

*Employee bonuses are based on box shipments **beyond** the daily break-even point.*

This is not just about money. It is not just about breaking more rocks. It is also about impacting cost of operation. People learn quickly that various fringe benefits impact the break-even point. Employees at all levels of the organization can impact the break-even point. A new coffee machine, or free lunches, suddenly have a noticeable negative impact on break-even. This enhances the ability of people to become engaged and improve performance.

Equiflor has established feedback and engagement on the cost side of the business.

Equiflor has become a partner with the organizations that grow flowers in South and Central America. The decision to invest in its suppliers required a thorough study to identify growers who would fit into the Equiflor culture. This has been an important element in Equiflor's push for quality and reliable delivery.

Equiflor has chosen its supplier-partners effectively.

A great deal of effort goes into finding and hiring people who are prepared to become a part of the Equiflor family. If a candidate does not share the values and principles that define the Equiflor culture, they are not right for Equiflor and are not hired. They may be great people with many skills, but if they are not prepared to join the family, Equiflor will take a pass. Equiflor has had minimal employee turnover.

Hiring at Equiflor is a structured and patient process controlled by the CEO.

Having achieved a differentiated product and brand, Equiflor undertook the task of implementing a plan to integrate

Rio Rose wholesalers and retailers into the Equiflor family. Equiflor is adding value to these independent businesses with a series of activities including advertising support and an institution called "Rio Rose University."

The curriculum includes courses in the proper handling of Rio Roses to optimize life and value for the customer as well as constructive general management council.

Equiflor is implementing Rio Rose distribution with a concept that acknowledges "the wildcat in the hole" and an "Equiflor temple."

Equiflor is creating a family with growers and distributors in a spirit of **"we are in this together."**

A few years ago, Sarandes felt the time had come for him to step aside and smell the roses (yes, a pun). A process was developed by which the people who had built the company could purchase it from Sarandes and his partner. Today, Equiflor people are majority owners of the company and are highly qualified to lead the company into the future.

Brumos Porsche, *"Kein Vergleich"* (No Comparison)

In 1983, as mentioned, I had a trial by fire with the botched Porsche dealer concept in the United States. One of the Porsche dealers who stood by me in that difficult period was Bob Snodgrass, the general manager of Brumos Porsche. Today, Brumos represents Mercedes-Benz, Lexus, and Porsche in Jacksonville, Florida.

Brumos Porsche is steeped in racing success and history. It is the legacy of two men, men of vision and courage, who turned a dream into reality by their personal strength and firm commitment to a set of values. Hubert L. Brundage founded the organization in 1954. Larger than any one man's dream, Brumos has become a legend, a mark that others aim for.

Brundage became one of the first Volkswagen dealers in the United States at a time when post-war America wanted big, fast, Detroit automobiles. Brundage had a vision. Within two years, he was serving Florida, Georgia, and South Carolina. The "Beetle" was catching on.

Then, Brundage stumbled upon another equally obscure German automobile which, with his efforts, changed both amateur and professional automobile racing forever. The car was the 356 Porsche, dubbed "the bathtub" by sports writers due to its tubby rounded appearance.

Brundage raced those early Porsches, both by driving and sponsoring others to victory in Sports Car Club of America (SCCA) events throughout the southeastern U.S. It was largely through these efforts that the Porsche racing legend was born in the United States.

By the late 1950s, Brundage had become the Porsche distributor for Florida, South Carolina, North Carolina, Alabama, Louisiana, and Mississippi. His management skills were as sharp as his driving.

In February 1962, Brundage opened his own Porsche dealership in Jacksonville, Florida. In addition to two Volkswagen stores, this Porsche venture was a major gamble at the time.

The selection of a name was easy: BRUMOS, a contraction of the international cable address, BRUndage MOtorS.

In the next few years, Brumos Racing Porsches, and those sponsored by Brumos, made Southeastern SCCA racing a contest for fourth or fifth place. Brumos cars always captured the top three places.

For H.L. Brundage however, seeing the dream take shape was all that he was allowed. Brundage was killed in an automobile accident on a lonely country road in Jacksonville in November 1964.

Peter Gregg was a customer and friend of both Brumos and Brundage. A young naval officer with a burning desire to become a top racing driver, he was suddenly presented with an opportunity to keep the Brumos legend alive. With navy service behind him, Peter Gregg purchased Brumos Porsche in August 1965. In the following 15 years, Peter Gregg made the white Porsches with red and blue stripes the cars to beat in any race they entered. Through his courage and skill, Gregg earned a reputation for excellence that will be linked with Porsche racing forever.

For Gregg, Brumos was always more than racing. From the day he purchased Brumos, he built and nurtured a culture of excellence with his heart and soul. He was committed to provide the best product and the best service, with a driving force of people that would rise to perform extraordinary deeds. In 1979, Gregg extended that commitment to include a second Porsche franchise, Brumos in Atlanta, Georgia.

Gregg died an untimely death in December 1980.

Today, the Brumos legend lives and prospers under the leadership of Bob Snodgrass, part owner and general manager and a 30-year Brumos veteran.

Brumos racing continues to be successful in motorsport. A vice president in the Brumos organization, Hurley Haywood, drove factory Porsche cars every year I was at Porsche. He has won more 24-hour races than any other driver at LeMans and Daytona, as well as the 12 hours of Sebring.

Brumos features one of the finest automotive museums in the world, displaying historic Porsches and other notable cars. It is an integral part of the Brumos culture, a true "temple" for all to see.

Today, Brumos employs over 200 people in Jacksonville. Due in large part to Bob Snodgrass's leadership skill and commitment to "the driving force," the extraordinary performance of his Brumos team in the everyday car dealership business is awesome. A committment to excellence pervades the entire organization.

A significant number of Brumos employees are people Snodgrass has reclaimed from potentially shattered lives. Recovering drug addicts and alcoholics as well as youngsters from broken families comprise a significant portion of the Brumos people. These folks are among the most committed, loyal, and outstanding performers in this incredible organization.

How do Brumos people at all levels of the organization know how to make decisions? One of Snodgrass's value statements that guides such decisions is:

When in Doubt, Always Choose the More Expensive Way

This has nothing to do with over-repairing cars, or overcharging customers.

It means:

- Do it right, really right, the best we know how. The Brumos reputation for excellence is "the temple."
- Doing it the best way we know how retains and builds the customer base. The Brumos market niche consists of people who appreciate excellence.
- Doing it the best way we know how is the most profitable choice in the long run. We may lose money on an occasional job, but nothing is more costly than doing a job more than once and risking losing a customer in the process. *Doing it best is good business.*
- Not cutting corners; we do not compete on price and are not in the commodity business. We strive for the lowest total cost for the customer.

I do not buy cheap shoes. They cost too much.

This is a clear, concise commitment to excellence, but a concept that would be unthinkable in the absence of a commitment to "the temple," a strong culture, and a strong feeling of family. Brumos has mobilized the driving force in an outstanding manner to achieve excellence.

These are not just successful companies. They are families and legacies. In my view, Tony Sarandes with Equiflor and Bob Snodgrass with Brumos have mobilized the driving force and moved their businesses to the next level of excellence.

Richard Matheis

FOUNDER AND RETIRED CEO OF SEVERAL
TRANE AIR CONDITIONING COMPANIES
IN ST. LOUIS, MISSOURI

*I*first met Peter and Sheila after Peter retired as CEO of Porsche
and we became neighbors in Naples, Florida. Upon learning of
his extensive management background, it was obvious his views
could be invaluable in developing the business philosophies of my two
companies in St. Louis, Missouri. This assessment proved to be very
much on the mark.

One of my sons, Todd, now owns and operates a business in St.
Louis started by me in 1980. He is a member of TEC, an organization that has engaged Peter's services on a regular basis. Todd has been
pleased to tell me how much Peter has influenced him in developing successful leadership policies within his firm. The growth of that company
has been phenomenal due in part, I am certain, to concepts learned
from Peter Schutz.

Several years ago, I had the opportunity to travel in Europe with
Peter. A main purpose of the trip was to visit Porsche. While there, I
experienced the esteem in which Peter is held by his former employees.

In light of my experiences referenced above, there is no doubt in my
mind that Peter's book is powerful and can be a benchmark for the
success of future and present business leaders.

22

Porsche Leipzig

The Porsche Leipzig facility
In October 2004, I was invited to the new Porsche facility in Leipzig, Germany. For many years following World War II, Leipzig was in the DDR, East Germany, under communist rule.

It was good to see so many things about which I have written brought to fruition. The open information, the empowerment of people at all levels, as well as imaginative product and market concepts, confirm conclusions drawn from personal experience.

During the course of the 1990s, the Porsche facility in Stuttgart Zuffenhausen reached 100% capacity, building the 911 and Boxter automobiles. In order to produce the new Carrera GT and Cayenne models, Porsche built a new assembly plant and office complex in the Leipzig area. The new facility includes a museum and an on-road track and an off-road track. The entire complex is very modern in both structure and concept.

The approximately 400-acre Leipzig complex is located within a 4,000-acre protected nature preserve. This underscores respect for ecology and conservation as an integral part of Porsche culture.

The Road Courses

An on-road course replicates curves that are classics on a number of famous race tracks all over the world, including:

The Loews-Kurve from the Monaco Formula 1 course

The Parabolica from Imola

The S-Curve from Laguna Seca

The Bus Stop from Spa

And several others.

An off-road course is built within a portion of the protected wildlife refuge (with support from various environmental organizations) and is home to ten wild horses, and 23 Auroxen, a European breed of cattle with a lineage that dates back over 800 years.

The courses are integrated into a system that includes a conference center. Business organizations from all over the world may hold management meetings in the Porsche Leipzig facility. After completing business, the attendees have an opportunity to drive Porsche sports cars on both driving courses. Like much of what Porsche does, the road courses do not cost money, they earn money.

The Business Structure

Beyond the physical facility is an underlying business and cultural concept. In addition to adding capacity for new products, Porsche made the move to Leipzig in order to implement an advanced business concept unburdened by previous physical and organizational structure. The organization of work process implementation, as well as the manner in which people are organized and empowered, required significant changes in the layout of the entire facility.

The resulting business is setting new standards of focused teamwork resulting in outstanding levels of productivity.

A number of concepts described in The Driving Force *have been implemented by Porsche in Leipzig.*

Play with your own nickel!

Alexander Rankin has been a friend of mine since the mid-1950s when we were both stationed at Ft. Belvoir, Virginia during our service in the U.S. Army. Sandy (his nickname) built a very successful and profitable business called Vulcan Spring Company, which is now run by his son Scott since Sandy's retirement.

In building and growing Vulcan Spring Company, Sandy has adhered to a concept of operating without debt. To a large extent, the freedom of action facilitated by the lack of pressure for short-term results that can be imposed by debt repayment pressures and public ownership has been a major factor in Vulcan's profitability and success.

In the entryway of Sandy and Joanne's magnificent home near Philadelphia, is an old slot machine that Sandy (who is an expert toolmaker) has rebuilt. This is a mechanical slot machine, as opposed to modern computer-controlled electronic units. Next to the slot machine is a bowl of nickels.

On one of my visits, Sandy pointed to the slot machine and suggested: "You ought to try playing this machine, it is really fun. If you like, you can play with the nickels in the bowl next to the slot machine, but let me clarify something. **If you play with my nickels and win, I get to keep the winnings. If you play with your own nickel, you may keep what you win.**"

Whether a slot machine or a business, *a lack of dependency facilitates success if* you *play with your own nickel.*

If you play with other people's money in business, you cannot expect to reap the full benefit of earned profits. If things go against the business, the entire business can end up working for the bank, rather than the founder, managers, and those working in the enterprise.

From the time that I served at Porsche, the company has operated without debt. To this day, Porsche continues to operate without debt or subsidies, *because debt and subsidies create dependencies*. The independence from outside special interests is considered a pillar of the company.

Much of what is being accomplished by Porsche today can be credited to the freedom of action that results from operating without debt or dependency.

Extraordinary Results

The outstanding results that characterize Porsche today are the consequence of implementing a number of basic concepts in a most competent manner.

Credibility

Operational elements in the Leipzig operation impact on the credibility management has with its people.

The Porsche Leipzig operation is *paperless*. All operational information is in cyberspace. Through computer monitors installed throughout the facility, *operational information is available to everyone at all levels*. There are no operational secrets or mysteries.

Meetings with management are held at the initiative of the technicians (they are technicians, not workers) in the facility.

The resulting culture is one of people being *led*, not *pushed*.

Accountability

People working in the Leipzig plant are organized into teams reminiscent of racing pit crews. People are organized into teams of 10 to 15. Each team selects a team leader, a rotating position. As many people as possible are given an opportunity to function in a leadership capacity.

Most of the people at the facility grew up within 100 kilometers of Leipzig. This promotes a common culture and work ethic.

Teams are accountable to carry a mission that must be coordinated with other teams and implemented to achieve targeted results. Beyond that, each team is free to structure its activity and divide the work among its members. The paperless system tracks performance in detail so that each team can evaluate its effectiveness in context of total plant performance. This constitutes accountability and is a foundation for constant improvement.

Make decisions like a democracy.

In large measure, the operating teams in the Porsche Leipzig plant design the team activity in a participative, democratic manner. The primary objective is to build commitment and understanding within the team in order to implement like a racing pit crew, like a dictatorship.

Implement like a dictatorship.

The democratic participation of every team member sets the stage for efficient, timely, coordinated implementation. The activity is reminiscent of a winning pit crew at an automobile race.

A consistent business concept

Porsche continues to do what it does best: build exciting automobiles.

In keeping with the philosophy of its founder, Professor Porsche, the company is committed to only build the automobiles that customers dream of. This was once articulated to me by Professor Porsche and is a fundamental business concept to this day.

Two activities implemented in the 1980s continue to be fundamental to Porsche:

1. The Porsche 911 product concept.

    Saving of the 911 from demise in 1981. There is very little in today's 911 and other Porsche products that is technically interchangeable with the 911 that was rescued in 1981, and yet it represents an unmistakable continuity in the Porsche product line. It is faithful to the quality, performance, and sounds that are unmistakably Porsche. It is what Porsche customers have come to expect. The company strives to be true to this legacy.

2. The proprietary Porsche Car North America distribution concept is replicated worldwide to present and deliver the company's products and services.

The next level

A great deal of what is happening at Porsche today goes far beyond anything that was imagined back in the 1980s.

In manufacturing, Porsche has moved beyond the automated warehouse concept, which characterized much of the operations in Stuttgart. Such activities are replaced by a modern, paperless just-in time inventory management system without peer.

Marketing and product innovations, like the Cayenne and Carrera GT, are developments that "no one asked for." They are outstanding results of pro-active marketing.

It was exciting to see how far Porsche has come and think about where the organization is headed in the future.

Back in the 1980s the Porsche world consisted in large part of Western Europe and North America. Addressing a global opportunity by setting up operations in new markets, such as China, Russia, and Eastern Europe, is taking Porsche to new levels of success.

Perhaps the real secret is an unwavering culture of excellence.

The Driving Force **at Porsche has not been, and is not, just money, but a passion for excellence that is shared by the entire company at all levels.**

23

Epilogue

I would like to express my sincere gratitude to the readers of my book for sticking with it to this point.

Yogi Berra, the great catcher for the New York Yankees, once said, "You can observe a lot, if you just watch."

The material in this book has been accumulated by my watching and trying to be aware of what has happened *to me* and *around me*.

I have watched the driving force (motivated people) accomplish great deeds in both business and family situations.

In the past decade, statistics disclose that the most vigorous and growing segment of the U.S., and, I believe, the world economy, has consisted of companies that employ fewer than 100 people. Organizations that once employed more than 10,000 people have, in fact, become smaller. An exception would be growth resulting from mergers, most of which end up smaller than the sum of the organizations that entered into the merger.

Most of my time as a top manager, lecturer, and business advisor has been spent with small organizations. This includes companies that are part of the worldwide TEC organization mentioned in the body of this book, as well as member organizations of trade associations to whose conventions I have been privileged to speak.

This book is directed primarily at those relatively small organizations rather than large businesses that employ over 10,000 people. I believe it is difficult to accomplish major changes in the basic culture of such large organizations.

An alarming number of large organizations have been involved in corrupt and unlawful activities as well as mismanagement.

Perhaps the task of addressing this challenge is comparable to changing the values and life habits of a grown adult. Knowledgeable experts have taught me that the basic value system and culture of an adult is largely in place at an early age; some researchers say as early as three to five years.

What a person is likely to become as an adult is set early in life.

What a business organization will be after it has grown into a large organization may be determined early in its corporate life, perhaps in the first few years of its existence. I believe that if large organizations of the future are to avoid the pitfalls of corruption and premature decay that characterize some companies today, small organizations with the potential for major growth must establish sound management activities early in their corporate life and make such activities a major commitment.

Let me restate some basic leadership steps addressed in this book:

- *Become credible.* Take steps to be accountable by putting yourself on the line, face to face, with those whom you want to lead to great deeds.
- *Do not take before you give.* It's give and take, never the reverse.

- *Do not put people in the position of busting rocks for a living, or any other reason.* Instead, define a common objective. Describe the temple and win the race together.
- Do not exclude people from the decision-making process. *Decide democratically.*
- Do not allow people to be above the rules. In a free society, *rules are more important than people.* All people are equal under the rules.
- *Do not get in a hurry.* Managing a free society takes patience and understanding, but a free society will outperform most others.
- Do not underestimate the skill required to lead people to great achievements. Learning any skill, including leadership, will include failure. *Make provision for a learning experience.*
- *Implement dictatorially.* Implementation is a time to do, not talk.
- *Do not come across as perfect.* People will love you for your imperfections. If you are perfect as a leader, what will they have to contribute? People will be reluctant to approach you and contribute if you are perceived as (too) perfect.
- *Do not compromise your values and principles for material gains.* The short-term success that is realized in this manner can lead to disaster, frequently in the not-so-long term. *Success can be fleeting and fickle. Excellence will endure.*

My personal failures have occurred when I have deviated from one or more of the foregoing.

My greatest successes have been the result of being true to these concepts to the best of my ability.

My hope is that this book may, in some small part, help the leaders of today's companies lay a foundation of excellence that will become the standard for companies of tomorrow.

Index

For More of
The Driving Force:

If you have found *The Driving Force* inspirational and educational, you may wish to share Peter's message with others in your organization.

Peter Schutz offers his services as a mentor and keynote speaker on a wide variety of topics, at conferences and conventions as well as company meetings of all sizes.

For information, CDs, videos, or to book a speaking engagement, contact us at:

Harris & Schutz, Inc.
455 Palm Circle East
Naples, FL 34102
Telephone: 239-434-8186
Fax: 239-434-2030
E-mail: XQOP@AOL.com
Website: www.harrisandschutzinc.com